3/22c

E.
?ore
N.

rao

F

THE SMALLER GARDEN

GARDEN

PLANNING & PLANTING

THE SMALLER GARDEN
PLANNING & PLANTING

Penelope Hobhouse

COLLINS
St James's Place, London
1981

ACKNOWLEDGEMENTS

I would like to thank the following owners for allowing their gardens to be photographed for this book: Mr Addey, Lady Burney, Miss Carter, Mr Conn, Mrs Crocker, Countess Charles de Salis, Miss Fowler, Mrs Gardner, Mr Hopper, Mrs Le Fanu, Mrs Le Rougetel, the Hon. Mrs Mark Lennox-Boyd, Mrs Leslie, Mrs Maclachan, Mrs Melluish, Mrs Millward, Mrs Reid, the Countess of Rothes, Mr Peter Silsby (and jacket front), Mr & Mrs Sinfield, Miss Lila Smith, Miss Pamela Street, Mrs Talbot, Mrs Targett, Mr David Tierney, Mrs Wardroper, Mrs Westover, Mrs Wilson, Mrs Daniel Worsley, Mrs Wolff, and Mrs David Wolton.

The photographs were taken by: The Harry Smith Library (HS), Pat Brindley (PB), Steve Bicknell, Pat Hunt, Tania Midgley, Hazel Le Rougetel, Charles de Salis, Pamela Street, Arabella Lennox-Boyd and John Malins.

I am specially grateful to the owners who have allowed photographs to be used for the garden plans: Countess Charles de Salis (pp.16-17); Mr Budwin Conn (pp.34-5); Mr & Mrs Daniel Worsley (pp. 46-7); Lady Burney (pp.58-9, 144-5 these were used in imaginary gardens to illustrate special points); Mrs David Wolton (pp.62-3); Mr Addey (pp.86-7 – to illustrate an imaginary garden); Mrs Millward (pp.112-13); Mrs Maclachan (pp.118-19 – to illustrate an imaginary garden).

William Collins Sons and Co Ltd
London . Glasgow . Sydney . Auckland
Toronto . Johannesburg

First published in Great Britain 1981
© 1981 John Calmann and Cooper Ltd
This book was designed and produced by
John Calmann and Cooper Ltd, London

Hobhouse, Penelope
  The smaller garden
  1. Gardening
  2. Gardens - Design
  I. Title
  712'.6   SB453

ISBN 0-00-216644-5

Filmset in England by S. G. Mason (Chester) Ltd.
Printed in Hong Kong by Mandarin Offset Ltd.

CONTENTS

INTRODUCTION

Smaller gardens come in all shapes and sizes, from the pocket handkerchief front garden and the tiny basement area of the town flat to the long thin rectangle we meet so often in back gardens. Many people have said to me that they have an impossible site – too narrow or too irregular, too shady or too dark, with poor soil, an unpromising aspect, in short, every possible fault. Some ask for practical advice, while others lament that they would like to develop a garden, but are afraid that its upkeep would absorb all their spare time. It is in an attempt to meet this need that I have written this book and I hope that readers will find that a garden can give pleasure all year round without taking up too much of their time.

The smaller the garden, the more important it is to get all the proportions right, and to plan ahead so that plants and architectural detail work together to make a coherent attractive picture. It is also important to take into account the changing relationships of plants as they grow and mature. The ideal design will take advantage of the changes of growing plant material and consider it against the background of the firm unchanging masonry as both contribute to the outlines of the garden scheme. Success depends on a subtle blending of straight formal repetitive patterns overlaid with the informality of billowing and sprawling plant shapes which give an impression of naturalness. Planning and planting can all take place in one season, but the real atmosphere of a garden depends on plants and architectural style maturing happily together.

I am very grateful to the publishers for allowing me to express my ideas. I would also like to thank the many owners who have allowed me to visit their gardens in search of inspiration. So often a new planting combination or some clever use of limited space has set off a train of thought which has helped me to see more clearly what is the ideal. Nancy Pattenden gave much thought and time to introducing me and a photographer to gardens hitherto unknown to me many of which are illustrated in the book. Elisabeth Ingles and Diana Davies have given painstaking editorial help and Nick Rowlatt has shown great skill in interpreting my rough design sketches. I would like to express my gratitude to them. Above all, I am grateful to John Calmann for suggesting that this book should be written and I would like to dedicate it to his memory.

1   Attractive planting frames a winding path leading to the garden shed. Paving stones set in the grass guide the feet. On the left tobacco plants *(Nicotiana affinis)* scent the evening air and the striped grass *(Miscanthus sinensis* 'Zebrinus') gives height and elegance. (PB).

Chapter One

THE IMPORTANCE OF PLANNING

Small gardens can be made in shady backyards, can be conjured up from unpromising and awkwardly shaped situations where builders' rubble and excavated sub-soil must first be removed, and can be carved from an exposed corner of a country field. The piece of ground to be used may be a slice of an old garden which has been split into modern building sites and may contain old fruit trees, a fine specimen tree and the remains of well-dug flowerbeds. As building land in town and country becomes proportionately more expensive so the garden will be restricted, as in a city terrace, to the width of the house frontage both back and front, and access and space for a motor car will further diminish gardening possibilities.

2 *left* In this late-flowering border grey-leaved anaphilis and pale pink sedum contrast with the vivid yellow of *Rudbeckia speciosa* beyond.
3 A raised bed in the corner of a small town garden. Creeping plants look attractive scrambling over the stone edges.

The problem of the town gardener has always been to create privacy and quiet while reconciling planting and general utility areas. This now applies to most country and suburban situations. Few new gardens are made in open and attractive countryside where the whole landscape becomes part of the view. Of course, a clever design will make use of discreet vistas to distant features such as hills, woods, a church tower or a glimpse of water, but essentially the garden is intended to be remote and private – a haven from the outside world.

It is the task of the professional designer to marry the capabilities of any site to the requirements of the owner, but most amateurs will prefer to learn and themselves apply the simple language of design as it relates to basic structural items as well as to planting material. Walls, paths, and pavements (and the house itself) remain unchanging, but plants live and grow and their effect depends both on time and on future management and care. The more restricted the area the greater is the importance of a firm initial concept and the greater the need to arrange the permanent features so that building materials, a tree (or group of trees or large shrubs), hedges for boundaries or compartments and flowerbeds all enhance each other, and please the eye of the onlooker as well as satisfying the requirements of the owner.

Plants must harmonize and balance in form and texture as do the solid features of brick, stone or cement which form their background. To plant appropriately you must have some knowledge of plant behaviour and requirements as well as a good visual sense. Trees,

shrubs and plants must be suitable to the aspect, the soil and the climate, and the owner needs to consider their future increase in size and provide for this by thinning and pruning as it becomes necessary. Basic planting to create a skeleton framework is as important as the permanent masonry features. The skilful and effective management of a garden not only entails changes every year, but changes in every season throughout each year as the garden matures. The choice of suitable plants at the outset will simplify and reduce effort and expense later.

A good garden with properly arranged structural framework and elegant planting should make an excellent black and white photograph. Colour, and particularly colour schemes in beds or borders, will be thought of in the second stage of planning, and will vary accord-

4 A ribbon of grey-leaved *Stachys lanata* defines the curving line of a lawn.
5 A Mermaid rose entwined in iron fencing shows simple and effective planting for a shady narrow border fronting on the street. Glossy green leaves frame pale yellow single flowers which are produced all summer. (HS).
6 *opposite* A garden seat attracts the eye and invites one to rest a moment. (PB).

ing to personal taste and the amount of sun or shade available in planting areas. As a general rule if a piece of ground to be laid out as a garden is small and bounded by straight lines, a scheme based on a form of geometric style is preferable, especially when the surface is flat. You can then make curving borders and beds full of thick planting along the outer edges which will distract the eye from rigid boundary lines. Similarly, the rigidity of walls and fences can be broken and softened by planting bulky climbers which offer pockets of shade and concealment.

The untrained eye can admire the beauty of a skilfully planned and planted garden, but is seldom capable of analysing the quite simple principles behind it.

The ideal small garden may well be one with a very definite formal pattern of masonry, paths, hedges and inner compartments, which is then deliberately disguised by the outlines of plants themselves which break and soften straight edges and introduce varying patterns of light, shade and colour.

If the ground slopes very steeply terracing, steps and raised beds may be necessary. You may want to make a flat platform outside the house with space for sitting, or build a retaining wall, above or below which plants can tumble over or clamber up. If the ground slopes unevenly or has an irregular surface, curving beds adjusted to contours and banks of low-growing plants or grass look more appropriate than a formal repetitive pattern.

The traditional cottage garden evolved over several centuries – a mixture of fruit trees, vegetables, herbs and hardy plants all disposed in what seems a slightly

haphazard fashion but essentially arranged for convenience. Paths, sheds and beds were in sensible, accessible places. Plants which needed extra care were near the door, as were the herbs in constant daily use.

Vegetables grew in and among ornamental perennials and roses; honeysuckle and jasmine clambered over simple frameworks and above doorways. Plants were freely exchanged between neighbours, cuttings rooted and seed saved and sown. The occasional exotic came as a 'slip' from a grand garden nearby where plants from abroad were often in trial planting schemes or in greenhouses. Local stone or brick was used for paths and walls. Hedges were simple extensions of those in local fields, often of quickthorn or holly, primarily intended for keeping farm animals out, but also clearly expressing a need for the security and snugness of a home with barriers against an outer world. The success and character of this kind of garden derived largely from its being adapted to a way of living combining use with beauty and a feeling of timelessness.

Today modern buildings call for clear simple garden designs and for broad sweeps of ornamental pavement and flowerbed. The increase of gardening knowledge and new techniques, the use of weedkillers, artificial fertilizers and insecticides offer exciting gardening poss-

7 Here trees from neighbouring gardens give shade and privacy to a narrow town garden. At the far end, a raised pavement in sunlight reduces the feeling of length and a small formal pond adds interest. Stone paving overhung with bold foliage plants lines the lawn edge and gives dry access to the water garden.

8 right In small gardens grasses give a feathery lightness of touch to planting schemes. Soft pendulous leaves and flower heads contrast with dense dark bushes and with the rigid outline of perimeter walls and fences. (PB).

ibilities. A gardener can maintain quite an elaborate piece of ground with much less sheer manual effort than was needed in a traditional cottage garden.

Small gardens need to have a character of their own connected with the life style of the owner and should never become a jumble of differing themes. Do not try to combine in miniature the diverse design features possible in larger areas. Even if a small garden is cleverly planned to give the illusion of greater space, the atmosphere it evokes should be restful rather than stimulating. Too much is now available to us and only self-restraint will prevent the garden from becoming just a collection of interesting plants. The use of too many different ideas and schemes will make it difficult to create an integrated whole. Planning a garden also means having the patience to let it emerge slowly, each part and plant carefully chosen and allowed to settle and mature.

Chapter Two

TYPE OF GARDEN

Before getting out the drawing paper it is helpful to look at the different categories of garden.

The town garden

The city or town garden is practically and visually an extension of the house and its style must reflect this. Neighbouring and boundary walls, raised beds or natural changes in level, as well as plants themselves, will be used to hide unsightly objects and adjacent buildings. The feeling of privacy will be enhanced by green exotic foliage used cleverly to give an illusion of greater space. The garden should be a remote world, removed as far as possible from noise and interference and as private as a sitting room. It can be designed round a paved area with a seat, or a lawn, or focused on a feature such as a statue or pool.

Even the smallest garden site will be looked at from inside the house and this view into the outer space needs as careful designing as any interior decoration. The temperature in small sheltered town gardens is normally a few degrees higher throughout the year than that in exposed sites so the difficulties of shade (see below) and aspect are in part compensated for by a warmer growing atmosphere, and tender evergreens will flourish. A neighbour's tree, which perhaps casts deep shade in his garden, may just strike the correct balance which is desirable in your adjacent plot without adversely affecting the growing conditions there. Suburban gardens can make clever use of neighbouring planting schemes and the theme of a garden can embrace these extra features, while still maintaining essential privacy.

The natural wish for seclusion and privacy in the garden must be weighed against the difficulties of growing living plants in the shadows cast by boundary walls and adjoining houses. Eliminating the outside world means making high screens of trees, climbing plants or trellis which in their turn throw extra shadows onto both the available ground and onto the inner walls and fences. Roots are often strong and vigorous in cool shady positions, but plants need light and heat to make healthy growth and produce flowers. Before deciding on which plants to grow and how to arrange the other uses of the garden you need to determine how far the sun's rays

9 *left* A front area is cleverly planned and planted to hide the dustbin stand below. Grey-leaved plants thrive in full sunlight and the raised beds provide excellent drainage.

10 Thick planting of mixed shrubs screens a road and a curving bed disguises the rectangular garden shape. The May-flowering *Olearia phlogopappa* has trusses of white daisy flowers and pale grey leaves. (PB).

PLAN, RIGHT:

NORTH

SCALE IN FEET

A FORMAL COUNTRY GARDEN

Statues, an arbour, strong repetitive planting and a colour scheme of pink and white give this sunken garden a formal flavour. Over-sophistication has been prevented by allowing cottage-type plants to spill over on to York paving, and plants such as Alchemilla mollis *and* Viola labradorica *(already just outside the prescribed colour scheme) seed haphazardly in beds and paving. Size is 88 × 62ft (27 × 19m).*

Small clipped domes of Phillyrea angustifolia *line the central walk, which leads to a metal-framed arbour, over which a musk rambler rose and a fragrant summer-flowering jasmine intertwine. Planting against the back wall is mostly of evergreens, which give striking foliage interest in winter. The glossy leaves of* Magnolia grandiflora *contrast with the matt holly-like leaves of* Olearia macrodonta *and the leathery corrugations of* Viburnum davidii. *A pair of variegated phormiums frame the descending steps, their sword-shaped leaves contrasting with the mounded shapes of neighbouring plants. Tall pyramid shrubs give vertical emphasis at the opposite corners, while the central beds are filled with horizontal growing perennials and low shrubs. All the beds are then linked by the copious planting of grey-leaved groups which create a restful atmosphere. The statues are symmetrically placed in the centre of the flat beds, and* Rosa 'Max Graf' *has been trained to make dense groundcover, its branches of glossy dark leaves pegged to the soil. Clumps of cistus, lavender, germander* (Teucrium chaemaedrys), *the grey-leaved prostrate hebe,* H. pinguefolia 'Pagei' *and* Ballota pseudodictamnus *continue the theme of grey-foliaged pink and white flowers. The garden has been designed for mid and late summer use with plenty of flowers and scent, but its planting bones are good enough to make it an attractive winter foliage garden as well, seen at its best when viewed from a distance. (See Plate 11, right).*

1 *Rosa* 'Frances Lester'
2 *Jasminum officinale*
3 *Clematis spooneri*
4 *Olearia macrodonta*
5 *Viburnum davidii*
6 *Magnolia grandiflora*
7 *Escallonia iveyii*
8 *Hoheria sexstylosa*
9 *Raphiolepsis umbellata*
10 *Salix lanata*
11 *Pittosporum tenuifolium* 'Purpureum'
12 *Itea ilicifolium*
13 *Philadelphus* 'Manteau d'Hermine'
14 *Deutzia setchuensis*
15 *Pittosporum tenuifolium* 'Garnettii'
16 *Cotinus coggygria* 'Foliis Purpureis'
17 *Hemerocallis* 'Pink Damask'
18 *Anemone hupehensis*, pink and white clumps
19 *Clematis* 'Nelly Moser'
20 *Rosa* 'Penelope'
21 *Phlox paniculata*, in pink and white clumps
22 *Astrantia maxima*
23 *Escallonia* 'Donard Seedling'
24 *Rosa* 'Iceberg'
25 *Viburnum henryi*
26 *Paeonia lactiflora*
27 *Phormium cookianum* 'Variegatum'
28 *Anaphalis triplinervis*
29 *Rosa mutabilis*
30 *Lilium regale*

31 *Rosa alba* 'Celestial'
32 *Abelia* × *grandiflora*
33 *Hebe* 'Autumn Glory'
34 *Alstromeria ligtu* hybrids
35 *Buddleia crispa*
36 *Phlomis italica*
37 *Hebe albicans* (3)
38 *Escallonia* 'Apple Blossom'
39 *Rosa* 'New Dawn'
40 *Phillyrea angustifolia* (4 on each side)
41 *Rosa* 'Max Graf' (2 and 2)
42 *Lavandula angustifolia* 'Nana Alba' (5 and 5)
43 *Teucrium chaemaedrys* (5 and 5)
44 *Ophiopogon planiscarpa* 'Nigrescens' (15)
45 *Bergenia stracheyi* 'Rosea' (15)
46 *Lavandula angustifolia* 'Loddon Pink' (5 and 5)
47 *Hebe pinguefolia* 'Pagei' (5 and 5)
48 *Geranium endressii* 'Wargrave Pink' (5)
49 *Cistus* 'Peggy Sannons' (3)
50 *Chrysanthemum parthenium* 'White Bonnet' (9)
51 *Cistus lusitanicus* 'Decumbens' (5)
52 *Liriope muscari* (15)
53 *Ballota pseudodictamnus* (3)
54 *Malva moschata* 'Rosea'
In the back beds *Alchemilla mollis* seeds freely and *Viola labradorica* has been allowed to colonize throughout.

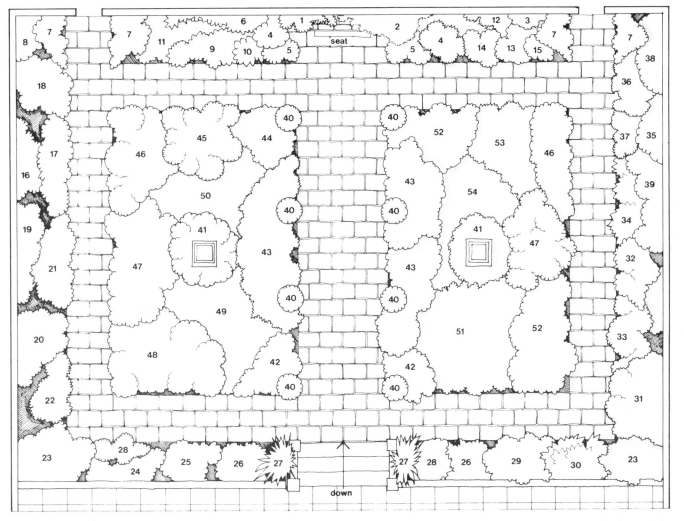

penetrate. Obviously this varies greatly between winter and summer. In winter the sun is low in the sky and rises in the east and sets in the west. In summer the sun rises to the north-east and sets in the north-west and is high in the sky reaching to areas of the garden which receive no sun at all through several winter months.

A very keen gardener placed in the position of acquiring a new house or ground-floor or basement flat with a garden might do well to consider the advantages and disadvantages of the street alignment. If the houses are a connected row or even semi-detached with a narrow but open space at either side, the front garden is usually very small (sometimes non-existent) and the back and principal garden runs to greater depth. Exposure to the sun is severely limited. If the street runs from east to west, the front gardens of the houses on the south side, and the back gardens of the houses on the north side will be in

12 *opposite* In a narrow north-facing bed the bronze-grey leaves of *Macleaya cordata* give summer interest and height, while the golden-leaved ivy, *Hedera* 'Angularis Aurea', glows even in winter. Ideal restrained planting for a garden with poor soil and shade.

13 *right* Lawn, paving and thick planting make an attractive corner. A mixture of evergreen and deciduous plants gives all year round colour; small creeping mint and thyme grow in the paving.

14 *below* Plants in containers clamber up the railings of a sunken front area. Honeysuckle and acacia scent the air for passers-by.

shade much, if not all, of the winter (depending on depth). The shadows cast by the boundary fences, which may be ten feet (3m) in a garden only twenty feet (6m) in width (the width of the house), will be at their greatest on this orientation. On a north-south street the situation is better, as at midday throughout the year there will be no shadow except that cast by the southern wall or fence of each garden. This applies, too, to the back gardens of the houses to the south of the road which are in full sun every day of the year but where the fences will cast maximum shade. The northern side of a semi-detached house will be in shade for most of the winter. On a street on a south-west and north-east axis the sun will shine throughout the year on front and back gardens and on both sides of a semi-detached house, and all plants will get some sun. All this is common-sense reasoning but often overlooked. A further point to bear in mind is that not only does soil get very dry at the base of the walls, but walls and buildings create 'rain shadows' and in a small walled backyard many areas are quite dry even after hard and prolonged showers.

A smaller garden still may be a balcony or roof garden which can be designed with trellis and plants to form a backdrop to the room inside and to frame a distant view of trees and buildings or a city square. This kind of

15 Water bamboos, cobblestones and a cleverly designed trellis give an oriental flavour to this town garden. A mature apple tree shades a simple seat built round its trunk.

garden presents special problems of drying winds and sun; containers need frequent watering (see page 137).

The country garden

The true country garden (however small in area) will use the surrounding landscape as a feature in the overall design; distant hills, a group of trees, a spire or even one tree may be framed by planting. If the boundary merges into countryside, trees planted in the immediate foreground or the middle distance not only give more instant framing or screening effects, but also tend to increase the feeling of space and distance in the whole garden. Planting should be natural as native trees and shrubs will help the garden to merge gently into fields and woods. The more exotic plants should be near the house where growing conditions can be specially created for them, or hidden from immediate view so that they do not seem out of place and artificial. If there is sufficient scope on a site, formal areas near the house can gradually blend into wild or natural gardening at the far end, with a path or vista on to a separate area which helps to lead the garden into fields beyond. Behind an inner hedge, longer grass, spring bulbs and perhaps a fruit tree help to change the atmosphere and give the feeling of orchard and countryside, however small the garden. A modern stream-

16 The spring-flowering *Magnolia* × *soulangiana* is underplanted with the blue *Brunnera macrophylla* and gives a country feeling to this town garden.

lined country house can have a garden of curves and hard masonry lines in abstract shapes, mixed with sweeps of massed low groundcover, which would be entirely inappropriate for an old country cottage where brick or local stone should be used for walls, paths and paving, or if this is now too expensive, the nearest and least garish man-made equivalent.

The front garden

The front garden in a row of houses – or even in a detached country house or cottage – poses all sorts of design problems. In a sense the garden belongs visually to the whole street and the passers-by, so that the best overall results may be achieved by some kind of open-plan gardening without rigid dividing fences, but privacy may still be important, particularly if this is the sunny side of the house. Access must be provided, not only for the owner and family but also for dustmen, postmen and milkmen, and dogs and children may need to be kept in or out. Today, sadly, much garden has to be given up to adequate space for the motorcar, arriving, turning and standing. A suitable hard surface for this is important but gravel on hard core is infinitely preferable to plain tarmac or cement which never weathers, remaining stark and ugly. Some clever ideas for combining good paving with central cement panels for car wheels need to be thought out.

17   A front garden is thickly planted with flowering shrubs. A newly planted weeping pear, *Pyrus salicifolia* 'Pendula', will eventually give height and privacy.

18 *below right*   The emergent fronds of the royal fern, *Osmunda regalis*, are exotic. It thrives in moist acid soil and in woodland gardens. The developed leaves look lovely with the sword-shaped foliage of irises and phormiums. (HS).

When a small front garden is very exposed to the public it may be helpful as well as attractive to make a raised bed or beds. Suitable soil can be provided for low-growing plants which will not obscure views from the window and will also trail downwards to the pavement. People and animals will not walk across the beds and further fencing is unnecessary. A straight path to the front or side access can be combined with horizontal groundcover plants of a permanent evergreen type which give a smooth uncluttered look. If the garden is in deep shade a good selection of evergreen shade-tolerant shrubs can be closely planted and the earth beneath covered with ivy, with pockets of scented plants such as lily of the valley and Solomon's seal. If in full sun a border of cottage-garden plants at each side or edging the path may be appropriate, but remember that the garden must harmonize with its neighbours, all equally open to view. It is best to stress simplicity and not to incorporate a plethora of design features. Intricately shaped beds, elaborate and fussy stonework and planting are not advisable where all gardens are visible to the casual glance. Where privacy is essential a simple hedge of some well-chosen shrub or groups of shrubs arranged along the boundary with the pavement and along the access path or driveway may be chosen and can be placed quite close to the windows as long as all light is not obscured.

I know one successful front garden with a central path to the front door where the rectangular panels on either side are simple box hedges enclosing mown grass. The lawn is kept tidily clipped but a less energetic owner could well use a total evergreen cover such as the variegated dead nettle (*Lamium galeobdolon*), rampant in shade, or a good form of periwinkle (*Vinca minor*), which will thrive in any conditions. The same scheme in full sun could be repeated in santolina or lavender, as well as box, with a mixture of low-growing grey foliage plants intermingling in the bed giving a light textured effect, while repressing weed seedlings. Beds of annuals will be set off by the rigid framework which provides a simple foil to massed colour. I would use just one vivid shade, but someone with an excellent and developed colour sense could interweave and blend.

19 *below* Wide windows frame the planting in a front courtyard. The garden has become an extra room of the house. The golden leaves of the *Robinia pseudoacacia* 'Frisia' match the decorations of the dining room and give a feeling of sunlight.

20　Raised beds in a south-facing London street make attractive front gardens. Planting schemes are appreciated by passers-by, and children and dogs do little damage.

21　At the top of steps plants sprawl between stone and grass. A low-growing cotoneaster, striped grass and a bushy hydrangea make a pleasant grouping in this back garden area.

22　The soil in a sloping front area is thickly covered with sprawling ivies and lamium. Grey-leaved shrubs and roses make a solid planting mass which is attractive to the passer-by and easy to maintain.

Chapter Three

WHAT YOU NEED

Each owner wants to create the most attractive garden possible while also leaving adequate and appropriate space for other activities. You must make your own list of requirements and these need to be incorporated into the design at the outset. For example, a family needs a place for sitting at leisure as well as an open flat area for recreation, and perhaps a climbing frame or sandpit. (As children grow up the sandpit can be turned into a flowerbed and space for the washing-line restricted.) The warm sitting area will necessarily compete with space for ornamental plants, and provision of beds for vegetables and fruit further encroaches on the best or better sites for other planting. Somehow a compromise is reached and positions chosen for the dustbin stand, the fuel tank, the compost heap, a garden shed, frame or greenhouse. The relative importance of all these different uses for the

existing space must be weighed up so that the house and garden can be lived in comfortably and conveniently. In a very small town backyard it may be tempting to plant lavishly to give a sense of visual pleasure from the windows, forgetting how necessary it is to allow space for a table and chairs in the summer. An enthusiastic gardener tends to grab space at the expense of family comfort, but above all, the garden should combine beauty with suitability to the owner and his way of life.

Having decided on the essential utility features and found suitable sites for each one, it is a good idea to link them up by dry paths. These must also connect with the kitchen door or with a dry paved area next to the house.

23 An enclosed yard softened by lavish planting. Here roses and foliage plants provide an attractive mixture. The paving joints are set at an angle to the boundary walls and distract from their rigidity.

Before any constructional work begins, careful consideration should be given to existing manholes, drains and downpipes. If the soil is heavy clay it may be necessary to make adequate tile drains under any new hard surfaces; but plans must be made for run-off of heavy rain into existing water drains rather than into flowerbeds or on to lawns. Clay soils, which expand and contract with damp and drought, make an unstable base to masonry so foundations need to be firm and deep. Sand and gravel, which can eventually be enriched with nutrients and moisture-holding humus for planting purposes (see Chapter 5), are much easier as a base.

Smaller gardens, and especially those surrounded by walls, are often hot and dry from April to October and plants need frequent watering. An average growing perennial needs one inch (2.5 cm) of water every ten days which is equivalent to four and a half gallons (16.5 litres) per square yard (m) of soil and these figures can be doubled for plants against walls. Outside watering points for cans or hose attachments can therefore become a priority. Perforated hoses giving a permanent filtering water system can be concealed in flowerbeds so that the earth can be slowly saturated by turning a tap. For extra convenience it is possible to connect this with a time-switch device, but the vagaries of the British weather and

its swift changes from wet showery conditions to those of drought make it difficult to regulate for long periods. Some such device, however, is ideal for holidays and for weekend houses. In a heavily polluted city atmosphere, where much dirt accumulates on foliage, overhead spraying may be a great advantage and this too can be made automatic.

If flowerbeds are going to be constructed against a house wall it is vital to make sure that proper waterproof plastering is used to a height well above the proposed level of the soil and above any existing damp-proof course that has been installed. This is especially important if a neighbour's wall is involved. If the damp course is still under guarantee it may well be advisable to discuss your proposed beds with the firm involved. Water not only penetrates from the damp soil but inevitably gets heavily splashed on to higher areas during watering.

Some features will already be in the garden and these may be usefully maintained and incorporated into future planning. The existing boundary wall, fence or hedge establishes the limit of the property as well as giving

24 In a warm town garden a seat in shade is essential. On a raised terrace a magnolia gives light shade and *Pittosporum tobira* has strong sweet scent in spring.

25 *above* Simply constructed walls adjust levels and provide ideal growing conditions for many plants. A knotweed, *Polygonum affine*, rapidly makes a sprawling mat and softens the hard line of masonry. (HS).

26 *right* A door is partly hidden by thick climbers. Variegated ivy and *Hydrangea petiolaris* intertwine and campanulas seed in the paving. A steep drop to the left is concealed by the prostrate *Cotoneaster horizontalis*.

27 *below* Foliage plants disguise old London brick. Variegated elaeagnus, hostas, bergenias and *Euphorbia characais* make a good mixture.

privacy. A fine specimen tree may give desired height and balance and an atmosphere of age and maturity to a new garden. Old fruit trees, besides being objects of beauty in their own right, can become hosts to climbing roses or clematis. The fortunate owner of an old mulberry tree (which is impervious to town pollution) has already got an important design asset and this could become the focal point around which all other plans revolve. In an old neglected garden an area of rough grass may well hide a splendid collection of spring bulbs. Plants or sheds may screen from prevailing winds and blanket sound; if old and ungainly they can be obscured by vigorous rambling and twining plants. Quite often a previous owner has discovered over a period of years some of the advantages and problems inherent in the site and it may be worth considering why something was maintained that you now think serves no purpose.

28 Trees in adjacent gardens can make an ideal background to informal planting. Here cascading pink roses intermingle with contrasting foliage and plant shapes carefully planned to look natural.

29 *opposite top* Mown lawn makes paths between borders of roses and herbaceous plants. The delphiniums and phlox need rich manuring and the neat grass edges require meticulous maintenance.

30 *opposite bottom* A garden roller is surrounded by rich planting of variegated ivy and leathery-leaved bergenias. This gives purpose to an untidy corner which might otherwise have looked neglected.

Before planting too ambitiously, consider how many hours will be available weekly for upkeep after the garden is completed. It is pointless to spoil the pleasure of a garden by allowing it to become a burden, and a high cost in initial outlay may well be justified by the saving in future maintenance costs and effort. A very small shady garden may look well if it consists entirely of paving, gravel or cobbles with perhaps one small tree, but a scheme of this sort depends on the most meticulous tidiness and upkeep. Fallen leaves or accumulated pieces of rubbish, particularly when near to containers with growing plants, can immediately spoil the whole effect. The smaller the garden and the more like a room of the house it becomes, the more important it is to keep things tidy, the paving brushed and clean, and plants healthy. In a large garden, small areas of tightly mown lawn and formal weeded beds can be enhanced by longer grass and more relaxed foliage and intertwined shrub groups beyond.

If the structural work is to be carried out on a do-it-yourself basis be realistic about the manhours involved and the time-scale to which you are working, as well as about the costs of building materials and the expense of buying the plants. A long-term programme will allow time for growing plants from seeds and cuttings, while herbaceous perennials can multiply in a nursery bed. Even if the trees and shrubs which are to be the main framework have to be purchased for quick effect, the next stage of infilling can be done in a more leisurely and economical way. If you want to erect trellis on boundary walls or cover them with rampant climbers, or plant a tree which may cast shade into a neighbour's garden, it is wise to discuss mutual needs in advance. No one likes an argument and recourse to the law is disagreeable and expensive.

31 A spring-flowering *Ceanothus thyrsiflorus* looks lovely with the white *Choisya ternata* and the latter's glossy leaves are emphasized by the elegant foliage of the acanthus in a pot.

32 A bed in shade near the house could be planted with the very fragrant winter-flowering Christmas box, *Sarcococca hookerana digyna*, which grows more upright than others in the genus, leaving room for underplanting. Here it is shown with variegated ivy. (HS).

Chapter Four

MAKING THE MOST OF YOUR SITE

A gardener can take certain steps to control the immediate environment in which he is growing his plants, but it is, of course, not possible to alter the prevailing climate, which includes temperature, sunshine, rainfall and frost drainage. Its effects on the garden will depend on the alignment of the plot, the shelter available and prevailing winds, not only in the immediate garden but as influenced by neighbouring buildings, trees and hills. A garden can be specially favoured and have a microclimate inside the prevailing climatic conditions of the area. A

33 The smallest and most unpromising space can be filled with foliage plants which grow happily in containers. In these conditions soil needs frequent renewing and enrichment.

good example of this would be a small walled garden near the river in London where because of high population density, shelter from cold winds, humidity of the atmosphere and nearness to sea level, there will be virtually no frost.

The counties south and west of London and those on the west coast of the British Isles are more favourable to plant growth than those to the north and east where the winds are colder and the temperatures lower. Inside this broad area it should be recognized that for every 250 feet (75m) above sea level the temperature drops at least one degree. Plants only continue to grow at ground temperatures above 42°F (6°C) – optimum growing temperatures vary between 75° and 85°F (24° and 29°C) – and growth stops altogether when the roots reach a temperature of 90°F (32°C) – quite possible when containers of plants are exposed on a roof or balcony and suffer from the combined effects of drying winds and strong sunlight.

Nature has endowed plants with special characteristics to help them to thrive in their own habitat. Many seem to adapt readily to our generally mild climate, but those which come from areas of hot summers and consistently cold winters find our lack of hot sun to harden and ripen wood and the recurrent warm and cool spells throughout the winter difficult to accommodate. A false warmth in early spring often leads to premature growth and the new young shoots will succumb to searing winds and low temperatures in April and May. Grey-leaved

plants are adapted to withstand hot sun but cannot endure long periods of cold and wet. Smooth large leaves allow plants to shed excessive moisture and the oils in aromatic leaves provide an armour against alien climates and disease. Evergreens are particularly unhappy in low temperatures combined with freezing winds which prevent them replacing the considerable amount of moisture they transpire through their leaves.

Wind lowers air and ground temperatures rapidly so that the first consideration for an exposed garden is to provide wind-screens and shelters. Solid walls or masonry, which are now impossibly expensive, are not in any case particularly effective against violent winds. When wind meets a solid barrier turbulence is created on the inner lee side of a wall, while a screen such as a hedge or fence filters and reduces the wind speed (see page 111). Town gardens with high walls often have wind funnels, too, and care should be taken not to choose a sitting-out area or a bed for tender plants in just such a position. Individual plants can be protected against cold damaging winds by other tougher plants or by artificial screens of hessian, hurdles, wire netting, bamboos woven into rabbit netting and fronds of pine branches. Plastic or polythene acts like glass, absorbing heat by

34 Gentle pale flower and leaf colour make a harmonious and restful border. Variegated iris, anaphilis, eryngium and *Alchemilla mollis* are planted in solid blocks and need little attention except for cutting down and tidying after flowering is over. The alchemilla will flower twice if cut down immediately after its first blooming.

day, but does not prevent heat loss at night, and needs removing on warm winter days to prevent build-up of excessive temperature.

Frost is most likely after a winter sunny day with a clear sky (as clouds prevent rapid heat loss into the atmosphere at night). Overhead canopies of growing plants at any level protect other smaller plants below, and in a small garden it is easy to give quick temporary protection with sacking or newspaper when frosts are threatened. It is not, of course, wise to garden only with tender material that may be lost at periods of low temperatures, but many plants are most vulnerable when young and would need artificial shelter only for the first season. Trees protect shrubs below, shrubs protect herbaceous plants and the latter protect emerging spring bulbs. A brick or stone wall collects and stores heat giving frost protection to nearby planting (heated vents in brick walls used to give protection to fruit blossom). Frost also drains down a slope, but unless there is free outlet at the bottom will gradually build up again towards the top. In fact, the final deciding factor in whether a plant will survive or not in a given garden is the lowest temperature it may have to endure. Up to a point the gardener can improve on his local and prevailing climate, but by how much will

35 Rainwater can be collected from adjacent roofs in a barrel and is especially useful where the soil has a high pH. All container-grown plants can be watered with a watering-can.

36 In the plantsman's garden (see details on next page) the very rich planting is designed to spill over steps and the edges of raised beds. A strong sense of colour and the use of fine plants makes this an exciting and beautiful garden.

1 *Clematis armandii*
2 *Lonicera japonica* 'Halliana'
3 *Clematis montana*
4 *Eucalyptus glaucescens*
5 *Lonicera serotina*
6 *Phlomis chrysophylla*
7 *Azara microphylla*
8 *Rosa longicuspis*
9 *Acacia pravissima*
10 *Leptospermum grandiflorum*
11 *Escallonia iveyii*
12 *Vestia lycioides*
13 *Hoheria sexstylosa*
14 *Clematis × jouiniana*
15 *Clematis alpina*
16 *Rosa rugosa* 'Blanc Double de Courbet'
17 *Ruta graveolens*
18 *Passiflora caerulea*
19 *Clematis orientalis* 'Bill Mackenzie'
20 *Anemone hupehensis*, white form
21 *Ceanothus × burkwoodii*
22 *Abutilon × suntense*
23 *Clematis viticella*
24 *Magnolia × soulangiana*
25 *Magnolia stellata*

26 *Eucryphia nymansensis* 'Nymansay'
27 *Pittosporum tobira*
28 *Ceratostigma willmottianum*
29 *Salvia officinalis* 'Purpurea'
30 *Raphiolepsis umbellata*
31 *Eucalyptus nicholsii*
32 *Convolvulus mauritanicus*
33 *Hedera helix* 'Green Feather'
34 *Lavandula angustifolia* 'Hidcote'
35 *Helichrysum angustifolium*
36 *Anemone hupehensis*, pink form
37 *Rosmarinus officinalis*
38 *Sambucus racemosa* 'Plumosa Aurea'
39 *Ceanothus thyrsiflorus* 'Repens'
40 *Cornus kousa* 'Chinensis'
41 White tree paeony
42 *Viburnum plicatum* 'Mariessii'
43 *Euphorbia cyparissias*
44 *Eucryphia intermedia* 'Rostrevor'
45 *Phygelius aequalis*

46 *Itea ilicifolia*
47 *Hydrangea quercifolia*
48 *Lamium maculatum* 'Beacon Silver'
49 *Camellia williamsii* hybrid
50 *Camellia williamsii* 'Cornish Snow'
51 *Camellia williamsii* 'Cornish Snow'
52 *Rhododendron yakushimanum*
53 *Astrantia maxima*
54 *Epimedium rubra*
55 *Bergenia Ballawley* hybrids
56 Ferns
57 *Begonia evansiana*
58 *Hedera helix* 'Glacier'
59 *Rodgersia podophylla*
60 *Dicentra formosa* 'Alba'
61 *Dicentra formosa* 'Boothman's'
62 *Rhododendron* 'Lady Chamberlain'
63 *Lamium maculatum* and creeping *Campanula poscharskyana*
64 *Rosa* 'Madame Gregoire Staechelin'

65 *Alchemilla mollis*
66 *Saxifraga fortunei* 'Rubra'
67 *Ajuga reptans* 'Burgundy Glow'
68 *Acer palmatum* 'Senkaki'
69 Parsley
70 *Pelargonium* 'Royal Oak'
71 *Pelargonium crispum* 'Variegatum'
72 *Fuchsia* 'Sharpitor'
73 *Euphorbia mellifera*
74 *Lavatera bicolor*
75 *Rosa* 'Ballerina'
76 *Rosa* 'Escapade'
77 *Fuchsia magellanica* 'Versicolor'
78 *Daphne × burkwoodii*
79 *Phlomis italica*
80 *Iberis sempervirens*
81 *Dictamnus fraxinella*
82 *Teucrium chaemaedrys*
83 *Cestrum parquii*
84 *Eucryphia glutinosa*
85 *Hydrangea villosa*
86 *Clematis flammula*
87 Creeping mints and *Lysimachia nummularia*

A PLANTSMAN'S TOWN GARDEN

In this rectangular garden skilful use has been made of steeply ascending ground to the east of the house. Raised beds and terraces in a formal layout with central steps have been softened by a profusion of excellent planting. The impression is one of hanging gardens with the thickly planted back boundary wall as the final backdrop to a theatrical setting. Strong architectural plants draw the eye and give depth and height, and small trees such as magnolias, eucryphias, eucalyptus and maple break the rigid horizontal lines of the perimeter and balance with the house and adjacent buildings. It is the garden of a true plantsman, who has not only chosen fine specimens which give horticultural interest, but has also so arranged them as to enhance each other and blend into the design. Foliage with contrasting colours and textures emphasize light and shadow, and flowering shrubs and perennials are mixed with annuals to prolong the seasons. A very favourable microclimate makes it possible to grow tender plants, and the arrangement of steeply ascending beds gives excellent drainage.

A few years ago the site was barren with crumbling ugly loose stone terraces of poor masonry. These were roughly tidied and rapidly disguised by tumbling plants. Simple aubretias and candytuft (Iberis sempervirens) were mixed with good forms of sedum, heuchera, achilleas, acaena and small phlox to fill in cracks and act as coping stones. Larger climbers now hide the vertical surfaces and twine among the flowering shrubs. The soil has been enriched and is continually fed, so plants are disease resistant and grow quickly, necessitating continual cutting back and shaping. High-density planting of this sort needs constant supervision to prevent blurring of outlines by jungle growth, but the sense of distance and change is remarkable in such a small area.

A wide path along the back wall at the top of the steps is hidden from immediate view and small plants arranged cleverly in the shady beds on either side are revealed as one walks past and give a feeling of surprise and secrecy. Behind the house an ugly area is concealed by a metal pergola where Rosa 'Madame Gregoire Staechelin' hangs her scented blooms, which are appreciated from the lower kitchen steps, and clematis scrambles through the rose to extend the flowering season. (Size is about 57 × 43ft : 17.5 × 13m).

depend on the special characteristics of the site. A maximum and minimum thermometer will help in finding favoured spots.

If the garden slopes towards the south, even to fifteen degrees, it can absorb more than double the heat from the sun than if on the level, and consequently periods of growth are much increased. On any site the incidence of sun varies a great deal throughout the seasons, and a north-facing bed which receives no direct sunlight in the winter may, in summer, have sun from the north-east in the early morning and from the north-west in the evening, and make a pleasant sitting-out area at dusk. Where sunlight is very intense a light canopy of leaves overhead makes an admirable filter. In the smaller garden trees and shrubs which have a tracery of delicate foliage are more suitable than those which can cast dense shade. Most plants are tolerant of what we call 'dappled shade' but all plants need some light. In the town garden surrounded

37 *opposite top*　A back-sloping brick wall has been designed to let in extra light to a dark kitchen. Variegated ivy makes a balustrade for the steep steps and gives a feeling of security.

38 *opposite bottom*　Ferns, grasses and ivy grow happily in a damp shady corner. In the joints of the paving in this London garden the creeping *Helxine soleirolii* is taking over and making a pleasant rich green carpet.

39 *right*　Neighbouring trees give a country feeling to this town garden and the very thick planting hides secret corners with different planting schemes.

40 *below*　A grassy path leads enticingly into a hidden corner in shade where woodland plants will thrive. The contrast of sunlight and shade increases the illusion of size.

by high walls a large part will be in shade for most of the day, but there are many plants which thrive in these conditions and appreciate the extra warmth and comfort which comes from wind protection. Some indeed need to be placed in a west-facing bed where rays from the early morning sun cannot thaw out the frozen petals too quickly. Among these are spring-flowering camellias, magnolias and tree paeonies.

Moisture is vital for plant survival but all plants vary in their water requirements, and inside any garden there

41 *left* Planting in deep shade is difficult but not impossible. Ivies will flourish in poor soil and need little attention. The large-leaved *Hedera colchica* and the small-leaved common ivy, *Hedera helix*, both have excellent variegated forms which cheer up a dark corner.

42 *below* The harsh outline of plants such as the New Zealand flax helps to break up the flat surface of formal paving. Like irises varieg-ated phormiums make ideal foils to masonry or to rounded plant shapes and soft foliage. (PB).

43 *opposite* Brick walls give reflected heat and protection from wind. The evergreen bergenia contrasts with the spikey leaves of flowering irises. The blue potato plant, *Solanum crispum* 'Glasnevin', is a vigorous climber.

44   The best effects are often achieved by simple planting schemes. London pride, *Saxifraga umbrosa*, mixed with a white sedum makes a quiet edging for a dark path.

45 *opposite*   Under an old pear tree a long narrow strip of a garden is broken up by central paving with urns and a statue. Steps at the far end make a further division and the garden appears broader.

will be areas where rain does not penetrate (especially in town gardens where walls form rain shadows). The soil at the base of a wall or hedge dries out very easily and must be watered regularly in a dry spell. In a hot enclosed garden with heat-reflecting walls and pavement it is ideal to plan sunk beds which receive all rainwater run-off as it falls. Equally, many plants cannot tolerate their roots in water, especially during prolonged cold spells, and for them it is necessary to construct raised beds with well-drained compost adapted to their requirements.

Different types of plant have widely different needs and you must select the ones most suited to the situation in your garden (see the Select List, page 146). Mulches applied in spring conserve moisture, but ideally should not be given until the soil has had a chance to warm, as temperatures rise. Mulches in the autumn keep the heat in and excessive moisture out.

46 *opposite left*   The exciting architectural *Melianthus major* benefits from the warmth of an enclosed garden. Its silver-grey pinnate leaves are a delight all summer, and after a mild winter it produces bronze-brown flowers in spring. (PB).
47 *opposite right*   The house wall gives shelter to tender plants. *Olearia phlogopappa* flowers freely in a protected site and grey and variegated leaved plants mingle below. (PB).
48 *opposite bottom*   Tree paeonies have beautiful foliage and flowers. *Paeonia suffruticosa* 'Rock's Variety' is one of the best. (PB).
49 *right*   For a sunny position *Nerine bowdenii* is a good choice. (PB).
50 *bottom*   *Olearia macrodonta* with its fragrant June flowers is an attractive bush to have near a window. (HS).

Chapter Five

THE SOIL

Plants vary widely in their reaction to soil and it is worth considering the different soil types and their texture and workability. In a small garden it is relatively easy and inexpensive to alter and improve the balance of the components present in the soil, so making it possible to grow successfully a wide range of plants.

First there is the fundamental question of measuring the relative acidity or alkalinity (or what is often referred to as the 'sourness' or 'sweetness' of soil). For this we use a formula of measurement known as the pH factor, which is a symbol for relative acidity or alkalinity rather than a straightforward arithmetic scale. A pH of 7.0 indicates what we call a neutral soil, and acidity increases as the numbers decrease. In this country the range is from about 8.5 to 4 (in the world at large there is a range from 10 in desert areas of arid alkalinity to 3.5 in peaty swamps). For most plants the best pH is around 6 to 7 but experience has shown that there are certain plants which will only flourish in a soil registering a pH of 4.5 to 5.5. Among these are most of the *ericaceae*, including rhododendrons, azaleas and heaths (although some come from limestone areas and have different requirements), camellias, many magnolias, most eucryphias and a lot of good woodland trees and shrubs. Basically, what has happened in this kind of soil is that over the course of thousands of years the alkaline chemical elements have been washed away leaving peat or sand. The pH can be raised by adding lime, making it possible to

51 *opposite* Thick planting necessitates rich feeding. In this scheme pale roses and the yellow flowering biennial, *Angelica archangelica*, are underplanted with grey foliage plants and the mixed bed is backed by an old pear tree.

52 *above* Damp acid soil loam makes ideal growing conditions for camellias, variegated astrantias, epimedium and ferns. In small gardens it is essential to have healthy plants.

53 *below* Hostas, periwinkle and London pride grow happily together under camellias in a garden in deep shade. In restricted space pavement is often preferable to lawn.

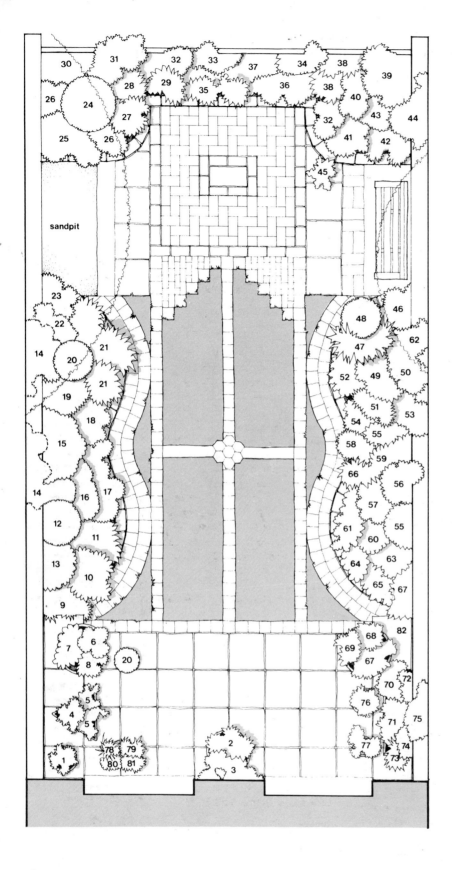

1 *Campanula carpatica*
2 *Euonymus japonicus*
   'Ovatus Aureus'
3 *Jasminum stephanense*
4 *Lonicera japonica*
   'Aureorecticulata'
5 *Hedera helix* 'Bodil'
6 *Ceratostigma plumbaginoides*
7 *Hydrangea paniculata*
   'Grandiflora'
8 *Galanthus nivalis* (3)
9 *Galanthus nivalis* (6)
10 *Hosta fortunei* 'Aurea' (3)
11 *Hosta crispula*
12 *Hebe salicifolia* 'Spender's
   Seedling'
13 *Hydrangea* 'Tricolor'
14 *Jasminum nudiflorum*
15 *Hydrangea quercifolia*
16 *Danae racemosa*
17 *Lysimachia nummularia* (5)

NORTH   SCALE IN FEET

46

18 *Sarcococca ruscifolia*
19 *Astrantia maxima*
20 *Hebe salicifolia* 'C.P. Raffil'
21 *Hosta sieboldiana*
22 *Clematis montana* 'Rubens'
23 *Abelia grandiflora*
24 *Prunus subhirtella* 'Autumnalis'
25 *Pittosporum tenuifolium* 'Garnettii'
26 *Euphorbia robbiae*
27 *Rosa* 'Nozomi'
28 *Helleborus orientalis* (3)
29 *Helleborus angustifolius* (3)
30 *Ceanothus* 'Cascade'
31 *Vitis vinifera* 'Purpurea'
32 *Sedum spectabile* 'Autumn Joy'
33 *Chaenomeles speciosa* 'Nivalis'
34 *Chaenomeles speciosa*

'Moerloosii'
35 *Euphorbia polychroma*
36 *Alchemilla mollis*
37 *Daphne mezereum* 'Album'
38 *Euphorbia polychroma*
39 *Ceanothus thyrsiflorus*
40 *Choisya ternata*
41 *Euonymus fortunei radicans* 'Silver Queen'
42 *Rosmarinus officinalis*
43 *Berberis thunbergii* 'Aurea'
44 *Hedera helix* 'Buttercup'
45 *Acanthus mollis*
46 *Ajuga reptans* 'Atropurpurea'
47 *Iris pallida* 'Variegata' (5)
48 *Euphorbia myrsinites*
49 *Coronilla glauca*
50 *Hedera helix* 'Buttercup'
51 *Daphne odora* 'Aureomarginata'

52 *Bergenia cordifolia* (3)
53 *Clematis flammula*
54 *Kerria japonica*
55 *Mahonia aquifolium*
56 *Rosa* 'Climbing Cecile Brunner'
57 *Lilium regale*
58 *Lamium maculatum* 'Beacon Silver'
59 *Stachys lanata* 'Silver Carpet'
60 *Anemone hupehensis* white hybrids (5)
61 *Acanthus spinosissima*
62 *Mahonia aquifolium*
63 *Geranium* 'Johnson's Blue'
64 *Daphne* × *burkwoodii*
65 *Bergenia cordifolia* (3)
66 *Mahonia trifoliata* 'Glauca'
67 *Coronilla glauca* 'Variegata'
68 *Pieris forrestii* 'Wakehurst'

69 *Geranium endressii* 'Wargrave Pink'
70 *Hedera helix* 'Green Feather'
71 *Helianthemum* 'Wisley Yellow'
72 *Geranium cinereum* 'Ballerina' (3)
73 *Crocus tomasinianus*
74 *Hedera helix* 'Bodil'
75 *Clematis macropetala*
76 *Fragaria vesca*
77 *Cyclamen neapolitanum*
78 Chives
79 Tarragon
80 Lovage
81 Mint
82 *Saxifraga umbrosa* and *Saxifraga umbrosa* 'Variegata'

A SMALL GARDEN IN ISLINGTON

A thirty by fifteen ft (9m × 4.5m) area of solid concrete, enclosed by tumbledown brick walls which supported eight-foot cat-netting, has been transformed by Mr and Mrs Worsley into an oasis of calm planting with strong formal shaped horizontal beds which draw the eye. The one desirable feature in the view, a magnificent Victorian church spire, has been framed by careful planting, but the character of the garden remains strongly secret and inward-looking with solid windproof perimeter walls and trellis covered with good scrambling and flowering plants. Plants support each other, filling this small space with colour and fragrance through much of the year.

The owners had two main aims: to create a feeling of spaciousness by using curves and thick planting to distract the eye from the rectangular pattern, and to keep the view to the church spire uncluttered. At the same time the garden has been divided into three distinct sections where the varying heights of raised beds and changes in horizontal surface material add to the illusion of space. It is also very much a family garden for small children and therefore an extra room for relaxation as well as a collection of fine plants. The main planting emphasis has been on evergreen shrubs and perennials with variegated leaves, and the skeleton framework is thus quite a strong structure. Flowers for colour and scent have been added in great profusion, and plants in pots (both permanent and annuals) are continually rearranged and sorted to increase interest and beauty. Rigid colour schemes are undesirable in such a small space but pale pink, soft yellow, and blue and white flowers for evening give a misty air; garish orange or scarlet would have clashed with the strong mass of variegated foliage.

The central compartment is partly lawn, with curving horizontal lines of tiles leading to the raised beds at the sides, and experiments are being made with camomile (Anthemis nobilis) where grass is unsatisfactory. Perhaps in a small garden partly overhung with trees the idea of a cool green lawn should be abandoned altogether.

47

grow roses, viburnums, and other lime-lovers. It is much more difficult to convert an alkaline soil into an acid condition. In a small space raised beds can be constructed and a peat-based compost used, which makes it possible to grow shallow-rooted lime haters, but those with deep roots will never really succeed and thrive.

It is quite easy to measure your pH by use of a kit, but in rural areas a glance at the surrounding countryside and undergrowth and identification of indigenous plants will act as a sure indication to soil. In towns, neighbouring gardens will give a fair idea of types of garden-plant which thrive locally. Dictionaries of plants and most nurserymen's catalogues indicate the individual plant's degree of tolerance to low or high pH rates. Specialists can grow many plants not normally suitable for the local soil in a prepared compost in containers which, if arranged in groups or architecturally beside gateways or doorways, can add richness and profusion to the whole garden scene. Given a basically acid clay, such as is

54 *right* *Phormium tenax* 'Variegatum' contrasts well with the creeping tanacetum and variegated hosta and makes a strong architectural feature in any garden. (HS).

55 *below* A pretty view of this small garden, showing how the church tower has been framed by plants (see details on previous page).

56 *opposite* A general view down a well-planted garden. Weeping pears, *Pyrus salicifolia* 'Pendula', frame a pathway into a rose and lavender garden and an ornamental beehive in the distance leads the eye forward. Few small gardens have such rich variety of planting and quiet flower colours.

found in London, it may be possible to construct terraces on different levels (often necessary in a garden on a steep slope) with different soil mixes, but generally speaking I prefer to see plants which would thrive together in their natural habitat adjacent to each other, and not to introduce a note of artificiality.

The soil is the living quarters for the roots of all plants, and its texture or workability, as well as the actual composition, need to be considered. The texture itself does not supply the nutrients essential for plant survival but it provides the conditions whereby plants can best take advantage of all the minerals and the air and water which are necessary. Soil itself is composed of mineral elements, vegetable and organic matter, which are turned into humus by the action of teeming hordes of earthworms and insects, bacteria and fungi, as well as of air and water.

The roots of many plants do not penetrate beyond the layer of topsoil and it is that layer of soil which we can most easily improve and alter. The subsoil, which is often compacted, is made up of small fine particles and almost impenetrable to roots, so that it will benefit from breaking up to allow free drainage. Topsoil is most likely to be acid in content as rainwater runs through it, washing away lime and other nutrients. The steeper the slope the more likely it is that the topsoil has, over a long period, been eroded. In a new garden site the essential topsoil may well have been buried under the inhospitable sub-

strata during building work. If soil is shallow over almost impermeable rock the roots of plants may rest permanently in water, and it is not enough to import generous rations of new well-balanced topsoil, you must also make certain that there is some form of free drainage below the roots.

In an old garden the soil has probably been constantly worked and humus-forming organic manure added so that it has become friable and is easily prepared for planting, whether originally composed of particles of sand, clay or grit. Microbes work on materials such as leaves, grass mowings, straw, peat, sawdust, spent hops, pine needles, and well-rotted animal manure to form humus which holds the soil particles together. In a light soil the texture itself can be very coarse. Mainly composed of sand and loam, it is easy to work after rain, draining quickly, and warms up easily in spring. On the other hand, nutrients can be washed away, it dries out in drought, and needs heavy mulching to prevent evaporation of moisture and to provide the essential humus.

At the other extreme is the cold clay-soil which is

57 Viburnums like rich feeding but can adapt to most soil conditions. *Viburnum plicatum* 'Mariesii' grows in regular tabulated layers and carries flowers all along its branches. The leaves turn bronze-red in autumn.

58 *opposite* Warm sun and well-drained soil suit the cotton lavender, *Santolina incana*. Sculptured lovage leaves make a splendid background for its grey feathery leaves.

formed by many small particles which compact when wet and make working difficult. Clay if wet becomes sticky like plasticine and when dry can become as solid as concrete; it is slow to drain and very slow to warm up in the spring (but retains warmth well in autumn). Organic matter is essential for workability and in low-lying areas some sort of drainage should be provided. In between these extremes exist wide ranges of soil composition, but the ideal texture from the gardener's point of view is a natural mixture of sand, silt and clay, in well-balanced proportions. This provides the conditions where plants can best absorb food through their roots; it requires the minimum of mulching to preserve moisture, and yet gives reasonably free drainage.

Oxygen in topsoil is essential for the roots of most plants as well as for the microbes which inhabit it. Pockets of air occupy almost as much space as the soil volume

and water flows easily through these spaces, which are formed between the crumbs of soil particles. Obviously fine clay particles attract and hold water, make drainage difficult and the soil tends to be airless. On the other hand the nutrients also are trapped and the soil is very fertile, providing it can be improved in texture to allow the roots to take up the stored food. Roots should be encouraged to go down deeply and the plant will be stable in high winds. Surface watering can be as damaging as a water-logged site as this encourages roots to stay near the surface in search of moisture, so an occasional thorough soaking is preferable to a daily sprinkle.

Spring and autumn are good times to feed the soil with mulches. The mulch applied in the spring on wet ground can be anything from one to six inches (2.5–15cm). It prevents evaporation, suppresses weed seed germination and, with the aid of earthworms and bac-

teria, helps to build up humus in the soil. A mulch of granite chips or limestone grit allows moisture to run through, while thick organic mulches can prevent rain reaching the soil below. If plants are grown in containers they must be given adequate drainage through good potting soil and large crocks placed over the drainage holes to keep them from being blocked by fine particles of soil (see Chapter 14). (Plants in a water-controlled area standing on capillary matting, or on moist gravel or special granules, need a form of water-conducting medium to act as a wick to draw moisture upwards.) If the ground lies low and is very water-logged it may be necessary to lay drains.

In a small garden the whole question of workability should be considered before determining the actual nutrients which have to be added. If the original topsoil is compacted it is probably as economical to buy new soil as to spend effort and expense on moving the existing layers. You can buy the topsoil in bags which can be

59 *opposite* Plants should harmonize and contrast and the skill of the gardener lies in striking the correct balance and making the best use of the soil conditions. Here the little white *Viola septentrionalis* grows happily around the base of irises, and dark yew makes a sombre background which enhances the whole planting effect.

60 *top Othonnopsis cheiriifolia* has strange spoon-shaped grey leaves and yellow daisy flowers. A raised bed in full sun with light soil is necessary. (HS).

61 *right* Some plants can survive with surprisingly little soil. Rosemary, rock roses and mint mix with cotoneasters which clothe the walls.

carried in through the house, in the case of a terraced row with no side access, and old sour and heavy soil can be removed at least down to fifteen inches (38cm). The substrata and subsoil can be broken up with a pick to provide drainage. Nowadays garden centres provide, at a price, ready-mixed loams and lime-reduced composts for immediate use, and in country districts it is often possible to acquire topsoil from the local council or from a merchant who will mix as required, varying the quantities of loam, sand and peat.

Soil contains mineral elements which are necessary for plant survival and health. The principal three are nitrogen, which stimulates vegetative growth, phosphorus, which encourages root development and formation of flowers and fruit, and potassium, which balances the other two and helps to combat disease. Other nutrients are also essential but are needed in very small quantities and can usually be given in a balanced fertilizer which contains the basic elements of Nitrogen – N, Phosphate – P, and Potassium – K in different ratios. It is much better to obtain these fertilizers ready mixed and blended. They can be entirely of chemical composition or made from organic sources such as dried blood, fish-meal, seaweed and animal and poultry manures. They can be added to the soil in granular, pellet or crystalline form, or sprayed on and absorbed by the plant through its leaves. Manure and home-made compost feed the soil as well as helping to improve its structure. Well-made cow manure contains a nutrient ratio of approximately 5:1:5 in the NPK scale, but if left uncovered while rotting down will lose much of its food value. Peat consisting of decayed vegetable matter is very useful, both for its moisture-retention quality and for helping to lighten and condition a heavy clay soil. Although it contains no nutrients, it can be mixed with any general fertilizer. Leaf mould also conserves and holds moisture and will contain the nutrients of the original leaves.

When using mulches such as peat, leaf-mould, straw, sawdust and pulverized bark to retain moisture and to prevent erosion on steep slopes, you should remember that during their rotting-down period they take nitrogen from the soil so it will be beneficial to scatter a handful of sulphate of ammonia to each square yard of mulch. (Forest Bark from ICI has already had nitrogen added.)

Compost making has become almost a fetish and there are as many different methods as there are artificial activators on the market. Basically the compost heap is made up of animal and vegetable waste in the process of decay. An activator is sometimes used to hasten decomposition. Organic kitchen waste can be used for compost and most soft vegetable matter from the garden (leaving aside woody prunings), including lawn mowings and animal manure as available. The idea is to generate heat in a confined space, and some air and moisture are necessary, but exposure to the elements – sun, wind and rain – should be limited. The simplest cover is black polythene, which is easy to remove and can be securely fastened. The heap needs constant turning (or most people think so). Ideally you need three heaps: one just starting, one almost ready and one in use. The material is right when black-brown in colour, friable and loose to handle, slightly moist and when none of the original wastes are identifiable.

62 Untidy walls and fences can be disguised by planting profusion. Here ivy above a flower border makes a secluded area for sitting.

Chapter Six

SIMPLE PRINCIPLES OF DESIGN

The smaller garden should not be a miniature reproduction of a large one, nor indeed a small-scale landscape. Trying to reproduce the features and interest of a larger site leads to an atmosphere of restless confusion. As the scale of a garden decreases it is advisable to aim at simplicity of design and planting so that the garden has a definite and coherent theme and purpose. It is in essence an outdoor room, to be used for a life style similar to that of the house. We must therefore consider both the visual effect, from inside and outside, and its practical use.

It is best to keep the central space uncluttered and to create mystery and depth by changing levels near the outer edge or by drawing the eye towards further compartments partly screened from view by hedges, trellis or

inner walls. Clear and deliberate boundaries give a real sense of purposeful decision which increases the feeling of space. If the ground slopes steeply it is a good idea to have raised beds or descending steps and small terraces. Walls and steps for adjusting levels play an architectural role and provide ideal background and shelter for tender plants. Hard lines can be softened by billowing and creeping foliage.

Many small gardens are long and thin, often rectangular, and are ideally divided into three squares or a square and a rectangle. Lines across a long thin garden increase the feeling of width. If the site is on the north side of a house the first area can be full of structural plants with glossy heavy leaves, leading into a second com-

partment of sunlight, bright flowers and grey foliage. A third section, perhaps overhung with trees from a neighbour's garden, could be made into a miniature woodland suitable for a winding path, rough grass, bulbs and groundcover - a mysterious area inviting exploration.

If the garden lies to the south of the house the sun will reach all parts of it, although the boundary fences will inevitably cast some shadow (see page 15). The warm sitting area may be a pavement directly outside the windows, with tender wall shrubs or even peach trees benefiting from full sun and heat from the house wall. A shade area can be created by planting a tree in the middle foreground and finally to the south you could have a light open area for fruit and vegetables. Espalier apples and pears can act as a formal screen for the last compartment and look very attractive with their spring blossom and autumn fruit. Although needing quite firm initial supports, with stout posts and taut wires, they take up very

63 *opposite* In a basement courtyard a mirror has been cleverly used to increase the feeling of space. This elegant garden has been planted with care and restraint, reflecting the owners' sure sense of colour.

64 Undulating curves of borders and water distract the eye from the rectangular shape of the garden.

little space in the garden. They are a useful hedging device, somewhere between the strictly formal clipped linear outline of yew, holly or box and the looser lines of informal hedge material such as roses and shrub groups.

Another way to create an illusion of space is to align on the diagonal rather than on the boundary lines parallel to the walls of the house. Any diagonal across a rectangle must be the longest straight line and the design can be arranged to take advantage of this. You could have a lawn in the open space across the middle with separate compartments for which there is appropriate space arranged round it. Thick planting obscures the original boundary lines and the garden appears to assume a new shape. To accentuate the new alignment a building, covered arbour or seat at the end of the diagonal axis can act as a focal point, further distracting the eye from the limiting shape of the garden site.

Gardens with irregular shapes need a firm visual direction away from the boundary and a square, rectangular or circular lawn can make a focal point. This will then decide the shapes of paving and flowerbeds. If the garden is very small or in shade, well-designed pavement could become this central focus and again thick planting of shrubs will help to obscure the real shape of the boundary.

1 *Pyrus salicifolia* 'Pendula'
2 *Viburnum davidii*
3 *Rosa* 'Fruhlingsgold'
4 *Cornus alba* 'Elegantissima'
5 *Euphorbia characais*
   seedlings
6 *Elaeagnus × ebbingei*
7 Old apple tree, *Rosa filipes*
   'Kiftsgata'
8 *Hedera colchica* 'Paddy's
   Pride'
9 *Hedera colchica*
10 *Cyclamen neapolitanum*
11 *Symphoricarpus orbiculatus*
   'Variegatus'
12 *Brunnera macrophylla*
   'Variegata' (15)
13 *Hosta sieboldiana* (3)
14 *Salix lanata*

NORTH

SCALE IN FEET

58

15 *Rheum palmatum*
16 Astilbe, pink colours massed together (15)
17 *Primula florindae*
18 *Populus lasiocarpa*
19 *Rodgersia podophylla*
20 *Arundinaria nitida* (3)
21 *Hosta* 'Thomas Hogg'
22 *Ligustrum ovalifolium* 'Aureum' (3)
23 *Euphorbia robbiae*
24 *Magnolia kobus*
25 *Euphorbia griffithii* 'Fireglow'
26 *Philadelphus coronarius* 'Aureus'
27 *Epimedium perraldianum*
28 *Choisya ternata*
29 *Phillyrea latifolia*

30 *Prunus lusitanicus* 'Variegatus' (2)
31 *Koelreutaria paniculata*
32 *Senecio monroi* (9)
33 *Mahonia* 'Buckland'
34 *Rhamnus alaterna* 'Argenteovariegata'
35 *Sarcococca humilis*
36 *Lamium maculatum* 'Beacon Silver'
37 *Punica granata*
38 *Cobaea scandens*
39 *Laurus nobilis*
40 *Cytisus battandieri*
41 *Teucrium fruticosum*
42 *Ficus carica*
43 *Caryopteris clandonensis* 'Ferndown' (3)
44 *Bupleurum fruticosum*

45 *Campsis grandiflora*
46 *Carpentaria californica*
47 *Bergenia cordifolia* (5)
48 *Fuchsia magellanica* 'Versicolor'
49 *Rosa rubrifolia*
50 *Ruta graveolens*
51 *Drimys winteri*
52 *Clematis spooneri*
53 *Indigofera gerardiana*
54 *Bergenia cordifolia*
55 *Viola labradorica*
56 *Buddleia crispa*
57 *Abutilon vitifolium* 'Album'
58 *Osmanthus delavayii*
59 *Hemerocallis flava* (5)
60 *Rosa* 'The New Dawn'
61 *Rosa* hybrid musk 'Cornelia'

62 *Bergenia* 'Abendglut' (5)
63 *Kolkwitzia amabilis*
64 *Geranium renardii* (5)
65 *Viola cornuta* (5)
66 *Geranium endressii* 'Wargrave Pink' (5)
67 *Clerodendron trichotomum*
68 *Rosa* 'Penelope'
69 *Cotoneaster horizontalis* 'Variegatus'
70 *Rosa rugosa* 'Frau Dagmar Hastrup'
71 *Bergenia* 'Abendglut' (5)
72 *Fragaria vesca* 'Variegata'
73 *Fragaria vesca* 'Variegata'
74 *Fragaria vesca* 'Variegata'
75 *Ilex aquifolium* 'Pyramidalis'
76 *Lilium speciosum*

AN INFORMAL COUNTRY GARDEN

This rectangular garden (56 × 40 feet : 15 × 13m) is broader in relation to its length than is usual, which gives it a distinctive country feeling. A wide central lawn is dominated at the far end by a weeping pear, Pyrus salicifolia 'Pendula', *framed in a curving bed by good evergreen shrubs.* Elaeagnus × ebbingei *and* Viburnum davidii *give body and density in the winter. The lower end of the garden is overhung by trees in adjacent gardens and the fence is covered with shade-tolerant ivies. A natural stream runs through the south-west corner giving an opportunity for informal planting of moisture-loving shrubs and perennials.*

A path leads enticingly to the right of the central curved bed and winds into a secret damp dark area where hostas, rheums and astilbes line the edge and give summer foliage interest and colour. The path emerges to the left in full sunlight between the 'pear bed' and a border of roses in front of the sheltered west-facing warm wall. This wall is rich with good planting, an evergreen Osmanthus delavayii *screening the compost at one end and a* Carpentaria californica *flowering freely in sun at the other. The scented shrub* Clerodendron trichotomum *gives height to the rose bed while the variegated strawberry carpets the ground underneath.*

Near the house a raised pavement is edged by a hedge of Senecio monroi *and pots of* Ilex aquifolium 'Pyramidalis' *frame the descending steps. A cobaea scrambles up the house wall in full sun and a pomegranate flowers and fruits beside the drawing-room window. Good foliage shrubs have been planted against the west fence with the evergreen tree* Phillyrea latifolia, *which has small shining leaves, and the yellow-flowered* Koelreutaria paniculata *giving height and helping to lightly screen the house next door.*

The garden with a firm structure (parallel boundary lines provide this) needs some gentle and curving lines to soften it. Plants themselves can do this with billowing and irregular outlines and in a very small garden, such as a paved yard, I prefer to stick to straight masonry lines and allow the plants to introduce informality. In a larger garden and particularly where there is a lawn, flower borders can assume gentle curving shapes without destroying the sense of an overall design. The best way to make a curve is to lay a hose on the ground to mark the edge, carefully altering its line until the desired effect is produced. It is a job for two people, one to move and adjust, the other to observe, and the results should be viewed from different angles and from inside the house. String and bamboos will do as well. Let your curves always be of the same radius so that the design has uniformity. Perhaps a counsel of perfection but worth thinking about; at all costs avoid too many purposeless meandering lines.

Broken shadows and sunlight seen through the leaves of trees or tall shrubs or through trellis work (clothed with decorative foliage and flowering plants) add to the feeling of space and even in the smallest area a light breeze can stir the leaves to give a gentle movement. Often the garden will be seen only from the house so that its design must relate to the inner rooms as well as to the architecture of the building. In winter months the garden will be a static picture, while in the summer the onlooker moves from point to point, however restricted the scale, and hidden features should emerge as surprises rather than initial eye-catchers or exclamation marks. The focal point of the garden may well be a sitting-out area, so choose its position carefully to ensure maximum sunlight and shelter. If the garden is surrounded by houses and

65 A paved path set in grass invites exploration and leads into a shady area of thick planting. The leathery leaves of *Viburnum davidii* contrast well with the silver-grey of the weeping pear. (See details on previous page.)

high walls the sun may hardly penetrate, but by evening the temperature in the still air will be high and an easily accessible place can be chosen for drinks and food. In a small garden with a northern aspect the sitting area might be at the far end of the garden and can attract the eye with a frame or arbour of climbing plants. A dry path, but not across the centre of the garden, should connect it with the area of paving or gravel near the house.

The smaller the garden the more important it is to think about the proportion of empty sky visible and to adjust your planting to this as well as to hedges, walls and horizontal features such as paths, paving and grass. If the site is a very open one the area of sky needs breaking up and framing in much the same way as an artist paints a landscape. Trees and shrubs as silhouettes against the skyline can be of many different shapes with dense or open structure (see page 108) and all have their growing requirements. Their use as architectural balance to buildings is discussed in a later chapter. In the very enclosed garden with an outline of rigid high walls this effect can be achieved by hedge plants and by trellis which will give a feeling of depth (Chapters 11, 12).

Attractive trellis can make compartments in a garden as well as providing a frame for climbers. It adds architectural interest and instantaneous height is given, without having to wait for plants to grow upwards. Neighbours' windows or washing are effectively screened from view

66 *left* A wisteria is trained to frame a seat. In a small garden every plant should play a role in the scheme of a design. (HS).

67 Foliage can be arranged to give interest and colour and is sometimes more important than flower. This is a very carefully planned yard with deceptively simple planting. (See details on next page.)

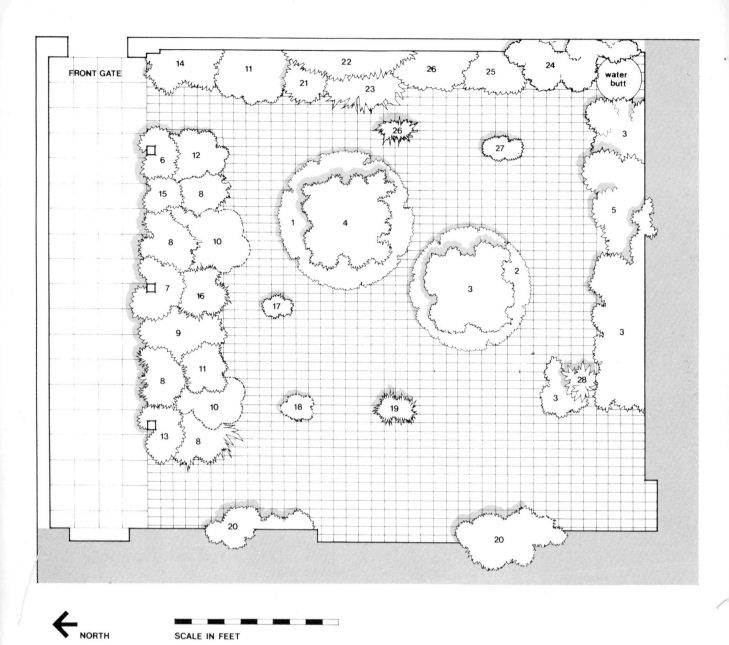

FRONT GATE

water butt

NORTH
SCALE IN FEET

A SIMPLE FRONT GARDEN

Mrs Wolton writes:
This front courtyard garden was designed in 1975 as a space between the formality of the public street and the intimacy of a family interior. A glazed covered way was extended from the house as an inviting gesture and as protection from the elements. The supporting columns form a leafy screen through which to glimpse the peaceful paved court. This idea of the tranquil courtyard entered from a noisy street is typical of Mediterranean and Middle East countries, and to my mind is most attractive; it was certainly the inspiration behind the composition.

Thus we see the various elements which express the intention: first formality, created by the geometric layout of paving and plants; secondly tranquillity, created by high walls, a space screened but accessible to visitors, and a grey-green peaceful colour range; thirdly there is the illusion of sun and heat, reinforced by using Mediterranean plants and

1 *Robinia pseudoacacia* 'Frisia'
2 *Robinia pseudoacacia* 'Frisia'
3 *Hedera anquilaris* 'Aurea' (4)
4 *Hebe pinguefolia* 'Pagei' (5)
5 *Macleaya cordata* (7)
6 *Actinidia chinensis*
7 *Abutilon × suntense*
8 *Rosmarinus officinalis* 'Fastigiatus'
9 *Rosa mutabilis*
10 *Santolina neapolitana*
11 *Atriplex halimus*
12 Lovage (herb for salads)
13 *Vitis vinifera*
14 *Rudbeckia deamii* (5)

15 *Cytisus praecox*
16 *Artemisia arbrotanum*
17 *Origanum vulgare* 'Aureum'
18 *Helichrysum angustifolium*
19 *Viola labradorica*
20 *Jasminum officinale*
21 *Iris pallida* 'Variegata'
22 *Solanum crispum* 'Glasnevin'
23 Blue German iris
24 *Clematis montana* 'Rubens'
25 *Bergenia Ballawley* hybrids
26 *Armeria maritima*
27 Pinks
28 *Fatsia japonica*

golden leaved ivy and Robinia pseudoacacia 'Frisia', which
suggest sunlight even on grey days. By shutting out the wind,
growth has been so prodigious as to suggest the kind of lush
foliage associated with hotter climates. This rate of growth was
accelerated by adding manure and bone meal to the imported
soil at the time of planting. Lastly, the visual preparation is
made for entry into the private realm by views from the
courtyard into a conservatory and through to a garden beyond,
and also into the dining space, the heart of the home.

  The materials used in construction were second-hand red
stock-bricks and indigo-painted steel for the house and covered
way. As a contrast to this and to the silver and grey-green
Mediterranean plants, a bluish semi-engineering brick was
laid on a sand and lime bed. The joints in the paving were
filled with sand and lime and have since grown green with
moss and self-sown alyssum and of course the odd unwanted
intruder. The grey-greens softly blend with the paving, the
yellows provide a complement, only touches of red-orange of
the Rosa mutabilis are in complete contrast and this allows a
mood of tranquil excitement to pervade.

  Over the years plants can be added or subtracted but each
introduction must be considered from the standpoint of the
original conception, so that while elements may alter the
atmosphere will remain the same.
  Size is approximately 41 × 33 ft (12.6 × 10m).

and wind is filtered and its force reduced. Trellis, too, can be used as a decorative feature. Covered in plants, it can separate different areas of the garden, creating inner rooms and divisions. It can be constructed of soft wood treated with a preservative such as Cuprinol (do not plant immediately after using this as fumes are given off by fresh preservatives when the sun is hot), or primed and painted with a durable gloss paint, which can be attractive but is sometimes glaring in a small space. Hard woods are durable but expensive. If the walls are already whitewashed then any trellis work may well be left plain and unpainted and, of course, a good design can enhance any basic scheme. The cheapest and simplest designs are panels of square and diamond mesh which are available at any garden centre.

Some comparatively simple devices create an illusion of depth and distance as well as altering visually the proportions of one part of the garden to another. If a long path is narrowed as it proceeds (as much as from five feet (1.5m) at the near end to one and a half feet (45cm) at the far end of a thirty-five foot (10.5m) length) it appears much longer. A white seat foreshortens distance; a door

68 Bricks can be used as a feature of the design. Here straight masonry lines contrast with the curving pattern of a brick pavement. The warm pink makes an ideal background to the alchemillas and sages which tumble over the edges.

69 *opposite* Repetition of planting themes unifies the garden, which can be made restless by too much variety of plant material. The pale golden leaves of *Robinia pseudoacacia* 'Frisia' give the impression of sunlight and this feeling is increased by rich underplanting of golden ivy, a theme repeated against the wall behind.

in a wall painted white does the same at the end of a walk or view, but also suggests deceptively that there is a further garden beyond. In reality it leads out of the garden, or is even a false door stuck and painted on to a wall, and perhaps realistically framed by climbing ornamental plants. Large trees or shrubs changing to lower-growing plants as the garden recedes increases the feeling of distance, and planting at the side of a narrowing path should also get lower. Different kinds of plants can be used to achieve this effect, or if there is a continuous hedge it can be cut to a lower level. When the garden is already overdominated by its proportion of length to breadth, put higher plants in the distance and bring it

70 *left above*   A weeping pear, *Pyrus salicifolia* 'Pendula', is the focal point of this informal garden. Curving peninsular beds and thick perimeter planting make the garden seem much larger than it is.

71 *left below*   Hybrid musk roses, yuccas and a low-growing hebe line a path of paving leading off a lawn.

72 *below*   Climbing roses make a background to an attractive arrangement of pots and plants. In the urn the grey hairy-leaved *Dorycnium hirsutum* is set off by trailing ivy. Auratum lilies and the hardy white *Geranium sylvaticum* grow in the narrow border.

nearer, and use all these visual tricks across the breadth of the garden. Paved walks (see page 74) can be designed so that the joints increase the feeling of depth and/or distance.

Where the space is too restricted to allow for inner hedges and where trellis divisions might be too dominant you can create the feeling of a compartment by joining simple piers with garlands of rope; plants can twine on the swags without altogether obscuring the view to other parts of the garden. In a larger garden pleached trees have a similar effect.

Sometimes mirrors can be successfully used to enhance confined spaces. Try to reflect a part of the garden or yard which you cannot see until later, and then from a different angle. Use a mirror where you look down steps, and arrange your planting to get beds or pots freely reflected. Steps or a path can lead up to a mirror and plants can frame its shape as if the path continued through this false gateway.

Seats and statues placed at the end of a vista invite a glance and lead one to them. From the seat the view back is often as important as the further outlook to whatever lies beyond. Classical urns and statues are appropriate and restful if surrounded and framed by plain dark colours such as a solid yew hedge, but can be equally successful in a bed or border surrounded by a profusion of cottage-garden planting. Those of less good design and poor reproductions have to be garlanded with trailing ivies and leaves, and should never be given too important a position. Modern sculpture looks best near rather exotic leaves. Attractive containers with appropriate planting can accentuate design features, but handsome stone urns of good proportion need no plants at all.

73 White walls stand out in the foreground and the rich planting recedes into the distance. Ground levels have been adjusted to give a long view up the garden.

Chapter Seven

MAKING YOUR FRAMEWORK: HARD MATERIALS

It is well worth drawing a plan to scale showing the boundaries of the garden and the desirable existing features. Mark in the points of the compass, access doors to and from the house, the height of adjacent buildings – noting whether they allow in sunlight or create shade – and all the possible utility areas. As we have seen in Chapter 2 conflicting demands on the most favoured and sheltered sites must be reconciled and priorities established between family use and ornamental plants. Herb beds are most useful near the kitchen; the compost heap must be easily reached but hidden from view. The oil tank and dustbins have to be accessible from house and road. Although paths to join points are essential for convenience and become important in the main

74 *below*　The curry plant, *Helichrysum angustifolium*, sits alone in brick paving. The leaves of this plant give off a strong aroma of curry when stirred in the wind, hence its name.

75 *right above*　A very small backyard has four changes of level which are accentuated by the use of different materials. The use of bold greens creates an exciting jungle effect.

76 *right below*　Tiles, brick and paving stones make elaborate patterns and the bold leaves of hostas associate well with *Hebe salicifolia* and variegated lamium. Camomile, *Anthemis nobilis*, is used instead of grass between the inner tiles.

framework of the garden design, a small garden can quickly become cluttered if paths cross the main open space or if there are too many. It is better to travel a longer distance between points and keep the design clear and uncomplicated.

As well as making a drawing it is helpful to take photographs of the house and garden from many different angles and mark on them the proposed new features. Tracing paper can be superimposed on the photographs so that alternative plans can be compared. If the garden is on a slope, consider changes of level and the need for steps, retaining walls and banks. Straight lines are more economical of space than bulges and curves so it is easiest to start with a firm geometric design and then later introduce curves to beds and borders. A formal garden, by which we usually mean a firm repetition of certain definite planting shapes and schemes, calls for a flat area or a series of flat areas and it may be necessary to shift soil and to dig down into lower levels. Great care should be taken to conserve the precious topsoil and not to allow it to be covered by poor subsoil (see page 50). However, if builders have excavated on a new site leaving a mound of stones and clay it is easier to flatten this for use as a foundation to a pavement around or beside the house and forego the use of the hidden topsoil. Nowadays machines can quickly complete these sorts of tasks and new soil is easily obtained from a local garden centre. If there is no access to the garden from the street, levelling will have to be done by hand.

Steps

Informal gardens and those with irregular boundary lines benefit from natural slopes and undulations, but steps may be necessary where the gradient of the slope is steep. The maximum gradient for a handmowing machine is forty-five degrees and for powered machines about thirty-three degrees. For the air-cushion type of mower the angle can be much greater. Steps can be semi-circular either in stone or splayed brick and become an important architectural feature. They should be easy to climb or descend, with wide treads and low risers (ideally in a proportion of three or four to one). In formal gardens steps lead straight from one level to another with a half-landing and return if more than ten steps are necessary, but in a more casual scheme the steps may curve gently on a long incline. Ramps make it easy for

77 *left above* Comfortable shallow brick steps lead up to a stone paved area where plants seed freely in cracks giving an air of maturity. Thick planting covers the supporting walls.

78 *left below* A well-thought-out garden, where steps, paving stones and grass make an attractive and balanced picture. Plants in containers, in the walls and in the beds unify the whole.

79 *right* Round a sundial plants are encouraged to seed informally and to spill over stone edges.

80 *below* Contrasting brick and stone surfaces reflect light in different ways. Here, after rain, attractive terracotta pots are arranged for emphasis. Pots can often be rearranged to suit the seasons.

machines and wheelbarrows but seldom look attractive. Steep terraces provide the opportunity for hidden borders and for using different sorts of soil at each level. Plants from beds beside steps should tumble over the edges and where possible should be encouraged to grow in cracks in masonry where they will quickly mask the rather stark appearance of new cement joints. At this stage of planning, be generous with your hard materials; they will help the framework of the garden to provide an ideal background to the plants, which will be seen to their best advantage against brick or stonework besides benefiting from the extra heat provided.

Paths

Having connected various points with paths on the scale plan, now think of the paths as important axial lines which may define edges of beds and borders as well as being aligned on doors or windows. In a rectangular town garden, paths will normally look most functional if run parallel or at right angles to boundary fences or walls. On the other hand, a curved design leads the eye away from rigid boundary lines and helps to screen them. When directions must be changed plants or pots, or features such as a seat, a statue or a pool, can accentuate the interchange by providing a focal point at the end of a stretch. A path can change direction with a gentle angle leaving some favourite plant on the corner, and can even lead nowhere but be a visual trick to entice the eye forward. A path of mown grass through uncut meadow,

especially if emerging from shade to sunlight, is a simple invitation to go further.

Where dry access is important, paths should be constructed of stone or concrete slabs, tiles, bricks or gravel (with edging). The material chosen should be the same as that for the pavement near the house, and should have an affinity with the building material of the house. If the house is of brick, use brick for paths, pavements and edging. Stone flags are now expensive and difficult to obtain but cement blocks come in attractive colours, with rough or granulated surfaces. They are easy to lay, being regular in depth and outline. In a small backyard frost-proof quarry tiles or more modern glazed tiles can be used. As with steps the soft foliage of plants flows over the hard edges of paths and pavements. Paths also connect compartments giving continuity between one and another, leading on through an opening or series of openings and giving a deceptive air of distance and space (see page 64 for false perspective).

Paving

A flat area next to the house undoubtedly helps to anchor it securely to its site. The actual width depends not only on the visual aspect but on convenience. As a paved area it becomes an outside room, and borders for plants and flowers may line the boundary walls, either level with the house and paving or in beds raised against the house walls. This may be the full extent of a very small garden or of a front garden, but in a larger site paving will be a

81 *below left* Boundary fences and new paving need softening with leaves and flowers. The Welsh poppy, *Meconopsis cambrica*, has fresh fern-like leaves and orange and yellow flowers. (PB).

82 *below* The architectural leaves of the giant mullein, *Verbascum bombyciferum,* and the silver-leaved *Convolvulus cneorum* make a setting for a small statue. Brick paving and foliage plants make a very attractive garden.

flat surface which leads one on beyond, or may be extended into a path leading to a sitting-out area. This sitting area can be created merely by widening the path in a suitable spot.

Visually there is a relationship between the size and height of a building and the pavement next to it, but no hard and fast rule is possible as it will depend on the aspect of the site. The walls of the house make a warm background to important planting, whether in sun or in shade, but as long as initial excavation is deep and good soil is provided, the space for a bed can be very narrow. Roots will travel downwards and outwards under the paving and be kept cool and moist. (The winter-flowering Algerian iris and fig trees actually prefer poor builders' rubble and a confined root space.) The keen horticulturist may well want to plant his best plants by the house and of course a raised bed in full sun is ideal for alpines which require good drainage. Plants with scented flowers and aromatic foliage are also valuable near the house, and particularly beside paths and gateways where they will be constantly touched in passing. If levels change beyond the flat paving, a low wall makes a good dividing line and should be broad enough to make a comfortable seat, but a low fragrant hedge such as box, lavender or rosemary would be attractive. Pots arranged in a row also act as a formal division.

Paths, paved areas and flowerbeds are easiest to maintain if set at right angles to each other, but when this is not convenient the angle should be as wide as possible. Acute angles drawn on paper always appear sharper when reproduced on the site, and planting is difficult if the corner bed narrows to a point and people tend to take short cuts over bed or grass. Where a sharp angle is unavoidable a heap of attractive cobbles in this corner can look good and discourage walking. Cobbles laid in a traditional pattern can be part of a horizontal area with smooth-surfaced paving to emphasize a sense of direction. If rectangular paving is used for paths or pavement the direction in which it is laid affects the feeling of length and width. Stone and cement slabs and tiles laid lengthways increase the impression of distance, but it should be remembered that narrow paths look mean and are unsatisfactory and uncomfortable to use. There are many good frost-proof tiles available today, some the traditional size of bricks (they can be thin pavoirs), some double, and some square shaped and it is important to match the scale to the area. Too many joints give a fussy air and reduce the feeling of spaciousness. The smaller the area of the whole garden, the fewer should be the paths or tricks of pattern and design.

You should always try to establish the hard masonry framework before introducing the soft plant material, which continually changes, not only with the seasons but as trees and shrubs grow large and as perennials spread into wider clumps.

83 The sword-shaped leaves of irises emerge from the sprawling leaves of the variegated dead nettle, *Lamium maculatum* 'Roseum'. The free drainage at the top of a wall is ideal for these plants and the lamium hangs like a curtain down the edge of the steps. Both thrive in quite poor conditions. (HS).

84 *right* A metal frame covered in roses frames an opening into a secret garden beyond. Casual planting gives a deceptive air of cottage-garden simplicity, but the plants themselves are choice.

Chapter Eight

THE LIVING FRAMEWORK

Lawn and grass

The lawn has the power to unify, is pleasant, cool and restful to look upon. Indeed a green grass lawn set among beds and borders seems almost like a lake. The shape should be simple with few fussy curves and the central area uncluttered by flowerbeds. In a long rectangular garden you could have two circular lawns, each of different radius, but they must relate to the plan and purpose of the whole garden. Lawns are bounded by beds, paths or pavement and the curve of the bed; the direction of the path and the line of the pavement will all be determined by the shape of the lawn.

The most restful effect is achieved by concentrating the lawn in one area, but grass paths can lead off it enticing one to explore other areas of the garden and acting as visual links between them. A tightly mown path between rougher grass looks attractive and spring and autumn bulbs can be naturalized in the longer grass, which needs cutting only three times a year. Alternatively, the mown path leads simply to a 'woodland' garden in sun or shade where grass is long, and wild flowers as well as bulbs are encouraged. Cow-parsley, moon daisies and willow herbs will flower in season. Even the smallest 'wild' area gives a rural air to a town garden.

When space is very restricted it may be best to have no lawn at all. Grass needs considerable maintenance and is never satisfactory in deep shade, and if there is already an area of pavement it may be more practical to extend this, or to use another attractive surfacing which blends with it (see page 80).

Preparation for a good lawn should be thorough. The area must be adequately levelled and if the soil is heavy clay or the site a damp one, preliminary tile drainage is essential. A foot's depth of good soil over well-drained subsoil makes a good foundation and two inches (5cm) of sand on the surface prevents any future water-logging, as well as encouraging grassroots to travel downwards to the richer layer. Seed mixtures vary for sun, shade and soil type and selection can be made from a wide choice. The quickest but more expensive method is to use turf, which can be purchased as sods and carefully laid. It is not often possible to obtain a particular grass mixture but undoubtedly the lawn becomes established more easily if you use turf. For either method, work can begin in early spring or late summer. Sprinklers (if allowed by the local authority) can be used in periods of drought. The first cut should be made when the grass is about three inches (7.5cm) high and should not be too severe. Gradually set the blades of the mower lower until the required length is

reached. Most lawns look attractive at about one inch (2.5cm) but the perfectionist requires them shorter. The more you cut the more you must feed as roots are fighting for survival with little green growth to support them. Normally lawns need cutting an average of twenty-nine times a year, at weekly intervals in the growing season, and as required in warm winter spells. In a wet spring and summer, mowing may have to be more frequent as it seldom pays to allow grass to grow too long.

In large areas much time is saved by leaving the mowings on the grass where they act as a mulch against excessive drought and as fertilizer. In a very small garden this may look untidy and bits of grass are carried by feet

85 *below left*   The new extension in Plan 8 (pages 112 - 113), showing the curve of granite sets making a wide path to the partially hidden tool area. On the right is an *Abutilon vitifolium* in flower.

86 *right*   Shrubs with variegated leaves are useful for emphasis in garden design but should be used sparingly where space is restricted. *Pieris japonica* 'Variegata' has an attractive habit of growing in tabulated layers and has white lily-of-the-valley flowers in spring. (PB).

87 *below*   *Tiarella cordifolia* makes useful groundcover. Here it is growing in a raised peat bed, but in fact it will thrive as groundcover in any soil. (HS).

on to hard areas and into the house. The mowings are useful for compost and can be mixed with organic kitchen and garden rubbish (see page 54). Mowing is made easier if flowerbeds are edged with stone or brick set an inch below the level of the grass, and hard paths and pavements should also be designed, if possible, to be below the grass level. The machine can be taken right up to and over the edges without damage and there is no need for final hand trimming. Regular maintenance means fertilizing, selective weedkilling and periodic raking to remove dead mosses and roots and to aerate the soil, but many garden owners and users find all this a bit fussy, and most lawns look amazingly well as long as mowing is regular.

88 *below* In a small backyard very close planting of bold foliage plants gives a rich effect. Hydrangeas, London pride *(Saxifraga umbrosa)*, variegated hostas, foxgloves and camellias all combine to make a lush picture in rather unpromising circumstances.

89 *right* The statuesque *Yucca gloriosa* in full flower. The stiff pointed leaves are an asset to any garden throughout the year. Here herbaceous flowering plants and hosta leaves soften its stark outline and the irises in the foreground carry through the theme.

Other groundcover

Sloping banks which are difficult to mow and horizontal surfaces in shade can be covered with dense low-growing evergreen shrubs or perennials which make an alternative to grass and, massed together, look well with paving or gravel. They are also a useful design feature. Sloping grass banks as a continuation of a lawn can look wonderful and create interesting light and shadow effects at different times of the day, but the awkward steep bed next to paving or adjoining borders is much more easily maintained by carpeting plants. In shade, creeping ivies (either with plain or variegated leaves), lamiums, St. John's wort, epimediums, and periwinkle all make excellent cover and need less attention than grass. In sun, cranesbill geraniums, drought-resistant ornamental grasses, polygonum, creeping thyme and many others are equally successful. Prostrate growing shrubs make strong weed-proof cover and their branches mingle together happily. Junipers make good horizontal evergreen shapes and the low-growing cotoneasters such as *Cotoneaster dammeri* and the variegated form of *Cotoneaster horizontalis* have attractive berries in autumn. (A list of selected shrubs and perennials for groundcover is on page 185.)

When perennials are used next to grass the shapes of beds can be cut out by the mowing machine and no other edging is necessary. Some of these plants are very rampant and look best planted in solid masses of one type. Like a lawn they help to unify a garden and form a restful background to more mixed colours in formal beds. Most need to be planted about twelve or nine inches (30 to 23cm) apart and initial outlay on plants is high. For the first few years hand-weeding between them is essential even if light mulches are given. They must on no account

90 *left above*   Creeping jenny, *Lysimachia nummularia* 'Aurea', sprawls at the base of a stone wall but can equally well be used as groundcover under shrubs. It prefers a moist soil. (PB).

91 *left below*   Plants grown in a mass are often very effective as groundcover. A clump of variegated *Iris pallida* makes an excellent foil to dark-leaved plants. They love full sun, good drainage and warmth. (PB).

92 *right*   Even concrete paving slabs mellow with age and sprawling grey plants can be encouraged to hide ugly edges. The little *Tanacetum haradjanii* will soon spread; here it revels in the reflected heat from the hard surface. (PB).

93 *below*   Contrasting plant shapes and colour and texture of leaves demonstrate the importance of careful planning for satisfactory plant association.

be planted unless the ground is clear of perennial weed. It is worth losing a growing season in careful elimination of invasive weeds by digging or herbicides. Ground elder, creeping buttercup and bindweed need selective spraying and this must take place when the bed is empty of perennials. Usually I use a contact herbicide which is absorbed through the leaves and kills or weakens the root system; the type of weedkiller which sterilizes the soil for a year or six months is not necessary (see page 188 for recommended sprays).

Once the plants have grown together there is virtually no maintenance except for an annual clip with shears for those that straggle. This form of massing of plants is particularly suitable for front gardens which need to look well kept but are not sat in or walked upon.

94 *left*   Strong foliage shrubs use a trellis as a background and give colour and interest in this shady corner of a flower-arranger's garden.

95 *below*   Roses, honeysuckle and bamboo frame steep wooden steps which lead down to a back garden. This is another corner of the garden on page 20.

96 *right*   Shining glossy leaves, brickwork and trellis make a dramatic garden picture where there is little natural light. *Fatsia japonica* is making new growth and the bergenias and camellias both thrive in filtered light. (See details on next page.)

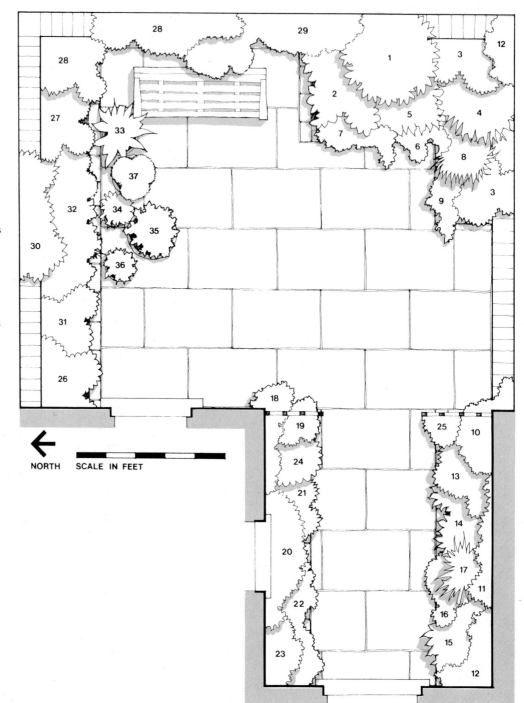

NORTH   SCALE IN FEET

A SHADY BACKYARD

*The main section (15 × 12ft : 5 × 4m) of this very small
L-shaped garden gets sun for two or three hours a day in
summer but the smaller part (9 × 7ft : 3 × 2.3m) is in
complete shade. Being in London near the river, the garden
has virtually no frost and high walls protect from normal
winds, although occasional violent gusts blow between the
buildings. When acquired the garden was a concrete yard.
Now raised beds line the walls round a centrally placed garden
seat and a trellis screen divides the two parts and gives an
illusion of greater space. Seen from the kitchen window a
curtain of green plants covers the trellis, hiding unattractive
back window sills of houses opposite.*

*The planting is very close and the warm humid
atmosphere encourages growth. Although there is little direct
sun overhead, light draws the plants upward and the effect is
of a rich and exotic jungle. Plants climb into and onto each
other and tumble over the brick walls of the raised bed.
Architectural foliage plants such as* Fatsia japonica,
Melianthus major *and* Cordyline australis *thrive and
contribute strong lines.*

*New topsoil was brought into the garden in sacks down
steep area steps and through the sitting room, and hard core
removed where the concrete was broken up for beds. The walls
behind the raised beds were rendered with special waterproof
plaster to prevent seepage, and the area for walking and sitting
is now attractively tiled. Frequent feeding and spraying
against aphids and disease are essential in this enclosed
garden. The result is an oasis of mingled greys and greens,
filled with the scent of flowering plants and aromatic foliage.*

Water

Water lying still reflects sky, building, trees and plants. In the wind it ripples and the surface is patterned with new and ever-changing shapes. The movement of running water holds eternal fascination for the onlooker and whether a slow stream or swift waterfall seems to appeal actively to the senses and induce contemplation and restfulness. The spray from a steep cascade sparkles in the air adding a new dimension of light and sound. On a hot day the noise of rushing water or its gentle gurgle soothes and cools.

A natural stream running through a garden offers great opportunities for adding visual interest to the garden and for growing ornamental moisture-loving plants round its edge, along its banks, or partly submerged. Slow-running water can be dammed and the widened pool will assume natural contours and curves, the surrounding land sloping naturally towards it. PVC or butyl rubber sheeting can be laid to help retain the water and the edges covered realistically with soil. Lawn can run smoothly to the edge or plants merge in masses between grass and water, some half-submerged and floating, others upright, making a vertical line to contrast with the horizontal surface of the water. If there is space, stepping stones or a bridge become a feature and overhanging trees and plants give new reflections as well as shade and movement.

In a small space it is difficult, if not impossible, to make an artificial area of water appear natural. Sinuous curves and attempts at imitating nature by informal planting cannot persuade the mind that the water is in a logical place, and the whole effect becomes unreal. The formal perfection of a well-designed geometric pool is different, however, as no attempt has been made to copy nature. The pool is a definite feature in the design and its success depends on the appropriateness of its situation in the garden and on the excellence of its construction.

Water will become the focal point of light in a small area and in full sun the formal pool appears at its brightest; reflections are most exact and vivid. However, attractive patterns are formed by moving light and shadow on a shaded pool and dark water gives an extra sensation of coolness on a hot day. Overhanging trees or bushes moving in the lightest breeze are reflected, while in the open the stillness can be modified by the spray of fountains breaking up the calm surface. In winter the shaded pool will make the garden feel cold, so it is best to tuck it away in a separate compartment. In full light

97 *left*   Water gives beautiful reflections and adds an extra dimension to a garden. Here water lilies and irises completely cover the clear surface. They should be severely cut back. (HS).

98 *above right*   Waving feathery grass seen against the sky. *Miscanthus sinensis* 'Zebrinus' likes to grow in moist soil round a natural pool. In a small garden grasses take the place of bamboos giving a feeling of airiness to the design. (HS).

99 *right*   The pink and orange tinted flowers of *Rosa mutabilis* planted in a framework of grey foliage plants attract the eye and the golden leaves beyond make another focal point.

water tends to give extra warmth and colour by reflecting what sun there is. From a practical point of view there are few days in this country where heat becomes oppressive.

The shape chosen for the formal pond will depend on the design of the whole garden but a circle, square or rectangle, surrounded by stone edging is most suitable for a traditional garden plan. A modern house may call for a geometric curving pool outline. The stone edges can overlap the water so that a new line of shadow is reflected in the pool, or the edge can be raised and made wide enough to form a continuous seat, and thus the pool becomes an extension of the paved sitting area. If it is on a lower level than the surrounding garden, steps can lead down to the water, the last step disappearing invitingly under the surface.

Where space is severely limited and it is impossible to excavate to any depth, a very shallow pool can be made and filled with pebbles or smooth cobbles barely covered with water. A pump can be installed to keep movement constant and to give all the sensations of changing light and shadow on the surface of the water, as well as a constant background murmur, just as if it were a much larger and grander piece of formal pond. A jet of water or a carefully angled spray thrown by a fountain over a designed and sculptural stone background makes a very elegant feature in any garden; it could be a focal point at the end of a narrow path. Water runs off into a prepared rill and expensive construction of water-holding cement cavities is avoided, but you still have the pleasant sensation of hearing and seeing water. If there are small children any pond is dangerous and in a limited space you may feel that a lawn for playing on is more useful and practical than an ornamental pool.

100 *above*   A curving pond with lilies and water plantain *(Alisma plantago)* is overhung by *Magnolia x soulangiana*. Note how the leaves of the evergreen bergenia and an attractive dogwood reflect light in different ways.

101 *below*   Trees overhanging water make a cool area in summer. This pool is rectangular and set in formal paving. Spiky vertical leaves contrast well with the horizontal line of water.

102 *right*   A moist corner in a London garden. Enriched acid soil is ideal for rhododendrons which contrast here with the large rough leaves of *Peltiphyllum peltatum*.

Chapter Nine

PLANTS IN DESIGN

We have so many plants to choose from that making rational selections becomes almost impossible but, in general, when tempted to diversify think constructively in terms of shape and colour harmonies rather than contrasts. In exactly the same way as you made a list of requirements for garden use, draw up another list which will help you to clarify in your mind the functions plants are going to fulfil.

First and most obviously, select only those plants which will thrive in your particular soil and aspect. If you choose an exotic plant put it near the house, or in a surprise corner, and not where it will jar against neighbouring landscapes or the adjacent garden. A garden is meant to be restful and not a showcase of rare plants. Remember that trees and hedges and certain individual plants give shelter from wind as well as seclusion and privacy. They also hide unattractive features outside or within the garden. But plants which shelter also cast shade and, in a small area, this is an important consideration. Shade can be a design feature, space being emphasized and defined by moving from sunlight to darkness or vice versa, or it can be for coolness on hot days. Dappled shade makes a canopy for woodland or tender plants. Some trees cast a dense impenetrable shade in summer and should be avoided. Planes, maple and robinias make light shade and patterns which move in the wind; being deciduous, they are perfect features around which early spring bulbs can flower and flourish. Aconites, cyclamen and little anemones look pretty grouped around tree trunks in grass. Taller plants can be used for clearly defining boundaries and for making inner space divisions and compartments. These in their turn protect from wind, give privacy, cast shade on flower borders and make rigid lines of greater or lesser density, comparable almost to masonry in their effect on the framework.

In planting small areas, foliage shapes and contrasts should be as simple as possible. It is best to adopt a theme and then expand upon it rather than try to fit in too many different ideas. Architectural plants with very definite shapes, such as New Zealand flax *(Phormium tenax)* with its fan shape of sword-like leaves, horizontal and weeping plant shapes and very brightly coloured foliage have to be used carefully to emphasize a point without attracting too much attention. Conflicting shapes and colours distract the eye and instead of uniting a design into a satisfactory and cohesive picture serve only to make it restless. In general, plant lines are soft and flowing and provide contrast and continuity between the hard lines of masonry and the curves of flowerbeds and lawns.

All plants – from trees and shrubs down to the smallest creeper or bulb – should be arranged to have some relationship with another plant or group of plants as well as balancing with the architectural structure of the house and the general layout. It is not enough to know the shape a plant assumes; it is also important to understand its rate of growth and its needs, so that the proportions between different plants and beds of plants can be kept more or less constant. Arranging plants is rather like

103 *left* A background of permanent planting of *Cornus alba* 'Elegantissima' and grey-leaved *Hosta sieboldiana* is enlivened by the summer-flowering annuals, petunias and impatiens.

104 *below* A satisfactory garden can be made with well-designed pots, fine plants and well-chosen paving and brick. Meticulous tidiness is necessary in a small space.

105 *right* In full sun ivy-leaved pelargoniums trail from a wooden window box. Best effects are often obtained by using only one type of plant. (PB).

arranging furniture in a room where the framework has already been provided by the shape of the walls and the colour of the paintwork; in the garden an extra dimension is added by the fact that the plants grow and change continually.

Plants appear dense and solid or light and delicate depending on the structure and surface of the leaf as well as on the colour. Evergreen trees and shrubs give an air of solidity all the year round and their positions in a garden or in a bed or border should be carefully chosen to make a balanced picture. Deciduous shrubs become denser in summer, but give skeleton structure in winter and when the branches grow closely together create excellent winter effects with their pale brown or grey barks and shapely arching stems or trunks. A formal garden which, as we have seen earlier, has an exact and often repeated geometric pattern inside it, makes considerable use of dense evergreens such as box, Portuguese laurel, conifers, yews and grey-leaved plants with rounded contours, such as *Phlomis fruticosa,* lavender and santolina. (The air of formality can be increased by clipping into rigid shapes.)

Grey-leaved plants – the leaves appear grey because they are covered with small hairs which protect them from excessive sunlight – thrive best grouped together in warm sunny borders. The varying shades of grey-green chosen make an agreeable planting scheme and a restful background to seasonal flower colour.

Herbaceous plants also play an important role in garden design and foliage plants such as *Acanthus mollis, Alchemilla mollis,* irises with sword-shaped leaves, grasses with delicate drooping rush-like habit, and eryngiums with prickly thistle-like foliage all help to compose beds with strong architectural shape. Archangelica, the giant hemlock, *Heracleum mantegazzianum,* and the large silver thistle, *Onopordon arabicum,* are biennials with exciting and formidable sculptural leaves. Hostas, ligularias and rheums are grown for their value as foliage plants in a garden scheme as much as for their attractive flowers. The tender South African plant, *Melianthus major,* sel-

106 *below* A composition of good foliage plants in a shady yard. *Elaeagnus pungens* 'Maculata' and variegated hostas look lovely with paving and brickwork, and bergenias, camellias and tellima can seed in pavement.

107 *right* Old stonework makes a perfect background to good plants. Here *Rosmarinus officinalis* sprawls happily against a pillar in full sun. (HS).

dom flowers in this country, except in the south-west, but has huge sea-green pinnate leaves and loves full sun and good drainage. Ferns thrive in damp shade particularly if the soil is good peaty loam.

If most or part of a garden is shaded then use plants which increase the feeling of cool greenness and give light and colour with different shades of green. Some golden foliage becomes less gold out of the sun's rays, but many silver-variegated plants shine in a dark corner. *Cornus alba* 'Elegantissima' is a deciduous shrub with red stems in winter and pale variegated leaves in summer, the little lamium, *Lamium* 'Beacon Silver', glows as a groundcover in deep shade. It is always satisfactory to look through shade into sunlight and particularly so if a

108 *left*　A well-balanced garden design. Trees, climbers and shrubs give height and privacy to a garden laid out in compartments.

109 *right*　Anchusa and blue iris show the importance of using blue in the garden. It is an admirable flower colour to mix with pale grey leaves. (See details of plan on next page.)

110 *below*　Plants such as *Alchemilla mollis*, a variegated cornus and the dark-leaved *Cotoneaster horizontalis* illustrate the possibilities of leaf colour contrast.

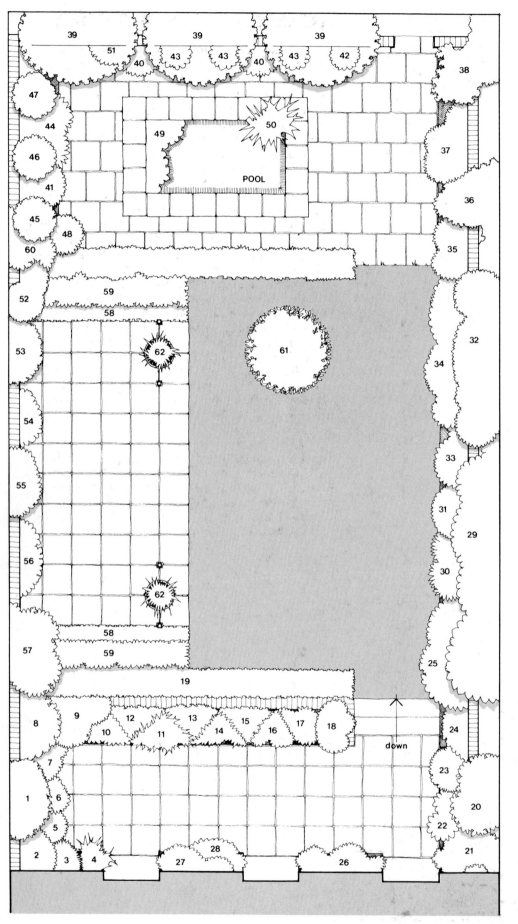

NORTH

SCALE IN FEET

1 *Cytisus battandieri*
2 *Crinodendron hookeranum*
3 *Daphne odora*
    'Aureamarginata'
4 *Iris unquicularis*
5 *Convolvulus cneorum*
6 *Cestrum parqui*
7 *Convolvulus cneorum*
8 *Rhamnus alaterna*
    'Argenteovariegata'
9 *Ceratostigma willmottiana*
10 *Convolvulus mauritanicus*
11 Iris, mixed German blue
    and yellow
12 *Anchusa* 'Loddon Royalist'
13 *Rosmarinus officinalis*
14 *Caryopteris clandonensis*
    'Ferndown'
15 *Rosmarinus officinalis*
16 *Teucrium fruticans*
17 *Phlomis chrysophylla*
18 *Buxus balearica*
19 *Lavandula angustifolia*
    'Hidcote' (18)
20 *Rosa* 'Mermaid'
21 *Hedera helix* 'Glacier' (5)
22 *Bergenia stracheyi*
23 *Cotoneaster adpressa*

A GARDEN IN COMPARTMENTS

This is a town garden with acid soil, fifty-seven ft long and thirty ft wide (18m × 10m), which has been divided into three compartments, the central one at a lower level. Some of the garden is in deep shade cast by pleached limes at the far perimeter and also by a neighbouring Quercus ilex and a sycamore to the south-west. The aim has been to show a strong contrast between pale-leaved plants with blue and pink flowers in full sun and dark sombre plants in shade. This increases the feeling of depth.

Originally the garden sloped gently upwards away from the house and levels were adjusted by digging out the middle section, extending the height at the end and building up a platform outside the house. A path links the three areas along the line of the steps, leaving space for a border against the outer wall where shade-tolerant plants and climbers give bulk and interest. While earth-moving was in progress a small rectangular pool was fitted in to the paved shade area.

Low walls are combined with evergreen hedges, lavender at the house end in sun, and Osmanthus heterophyllus at the shady side. Planting of grey-leaved shrubs and blue-flowered perennials in an informal bed at the edge of the paving near the house allows glimpses through to the lavender hedge and the rose-arbour, which covers a further paved area against the warm wall in full sun. Box and beds of pink roses give fragrance and colour. Inside the simply constructed open framework tender wall-shrubs and climbers take advantage of the favoured microclimate.

This is a garden where maximum advantage has been taken of the extremes of hot sun and sheltered wall beds and cool dark areas of shade beyond. Relatively little maintenance is needed, although the area of path which is part of the sunken lawn may get unduly worn. If it does, the garden might well be improved by paving this stretch, thus making the visual link between compartments stronger.

111 *above* Honeysuckle, clematis and the fragrant philadelphus are planted informally to give a rich display without jarring colour contrasts.

112 *above* Pillars of an old balustrade divide a vegetable patch from the garden proper. Behind the grey-leaved *Senecio* 'Sunshine', gooseberry bushes mark the transition from the ornamental to the more strictly useful.

113 *below* Hardy geraniums, foxgloves and the variegated *Euonymus fortunei radicans* make another attractive foliage group.

114 *right* A rose arbour, framing the house in the distance, leads to a circular bed of Iceberg roses edged with lavender. Straight lines and geometric shapes emphasize a firm design and make a background to rich planting.

dark path leads from one area into another. Trees and shrubs with pale and golden foliage such as *Robinia pseudoacacia* 'Frisia', golden philadelphus and the variegated dog-woods can give the effect of sunlight and the ground beneath them can be covered with golden ivies, golden grasses, gold-leaved hostas and golden marjoram and thyme. Ivies with attractive mottled leaves of any shapes, sizes and colour will lighten shade as well as tightly covering the ground in a dense mat.

Vivid coloured foliage and flowers are at their best in a hot sunlit position, but look harsh and lose their glow in darkness. Bright reds and scarlets foreshorten distance so plant these near the house, while misty mauves and blues fade away and give the impression of greater length to a border and of space stretching far away. It is very noticeable how white and pale flowers show up well in evening light, but can look insipid in the sun at noon. A garden which is seldom occupied except at dusk could be planted with just one or two pastel shades. Quiet related colours give a feeling of depth and richness which can be marred by coloured foliage and flowers, which attract the eye and distract the mind.

Bright colours and unusual shapes may be used as focal points to accentuate elements in a design and to give surprise around a hidden corner, but the use of too much deliberate colour contrast is exhausting and planting schemes are most successful when colours harmonize and enhance each other. Bold sophisticated planting

should be near to the house. Containers full of plants with exotic leaf shapes and a profusion of flowers help to soften the hard lines of masonry. As the garden recedes from the house the planting should be simpler. Exotic plants at the bottom of a garden tend to draw the eye and obscure the design, giving a feeling of restlessness and insecurity. If there is space for a separate inner compartment this may well be used for a specific scheme such as roses, herbs, a single specimen tree or a formal water garden.

Many of the smaller conifers with very definite columnar and pyramidal forms have to be sited where a strong vertical emphasis does not look ridiculous. Too often they are placed singly on a corner or curve of a bed when bulk would be better given by a rounded shape or mound. In general, they are best planted in groups to contrast with bushy shapes, or a pair can emphasize and frame a gateway, path, or distant seat. Small bushes such as hebes, lavenders, *Senecio* 'Sunshine' (this can grow quite large or be cut back annually), associate well in full sun with irises and phormiums. In shade the prostrate *Viburnum davidii* makes a spreading bush with a firm outline and contrasts with hypericums, vincas and hellebores. Weeping trees in small gardens encourage the eye downwards so should be carefully placed, if possible on a steeply rising slope. Alternatively, one tree could be the sole ornament of a formal space, surrounded by grass, paving or a mass of prostrate groundcover.

In a garden with sheltering high walls, evergreen shrubs with a regular pyramid profile can be used as buttresses to give architectural effects. They thus take the place of trees which would, in a larger space, be used to give a sense of balance (see page 107). The bay tree (*Laurus nobilis*), *Abutilon vitifolium*, *Pittosporum tenuifolium* and its various coloured foliage types, and upright conifers can thrive in full sun, while camellias, eucryphias, *Fatsia japonica* and the variegated buckthorn, *Rhamnus alaterna* 'Argenteovariegata', are suitable for shade.

Many plants have attractive leaves and flowers which associate well with masonry and fall attractively over the low edges of walls and steps. Some can be encouraged to seed in unexpected cracks in stonework or in corners of beds and give a natural air of profusion and casualness. The little viola, *Viola labradorica*, with its dark bronze leaves and purple flowers crops up spontaneously in odd places, as do alchemillas, eryngiums and euphorbias.

115 *above* Plants such as these grey thistles, *Onopordon arabicum*, are architectural features in any garden. They are biennials and seed freely *in situ*, looking attractive in paving joints and gravel. (PB).

116 *below* The bold sculptural leaves of the giant rhubarb, *Rheum palmatum*, accentuate the corner of a steeply descending woodland path. (HS).

Small campanulas sprawl across stone edges and spread in walls, while sedums, red and white valerian and the white *Cerastium tomentosum* may have to be controlled. For areas of damp shade the creeping Curse of Corsica, *Helxine soleirolii,* is ideal, spreading in pavements and round the stonework of pools. In a new garden, harsh masonry, austere pavements and gravel paths can benefit from softening plant shapes which disguise stark cement joints and give the garden a sense of age and maturity which cannot be planned. These days, when the use of weedkillers is essential for easy maintenance, the seedlings of some of these old favourites are inevitably destroyed. A simazine-based herbicide applied to gravel paths and pavements in early spring will sterilize the top inch of soil and prevent seed germination; weeding is thus eliminated for the year but some of the the best garden seedlings are also lost.

117 *above* Mixed colour borders are united by a restful grey tone. Grey-leaved plants love sun and good drainage and make excellent edging plants. Here *Stachys lanata* carpets the soil and hides an ugly edge. (HS).

118 *below* The bronze leaves of *Rodgersia podophylla* are rough textured and strong, contrasting with soft pale foliage. (HS).

Chapter Ten

TREES FOR THE SMALLER GARDEN

The first planting choice for a small garden is that of the right tree or larger shrub. Walk out into the garden and pick the site bearing in mind the following factors: a tree or large shrub screens unsightly objects from view, either at the boundary or middle distance; the eventual size to which it will grow must be in keeping with the scale of the surrounding layout. In a garden about the size of a tennis court the ideal ultimate size might be anything between seventeen and thirty-nine feet (5.5 and 11.5 m), just comfortably stabilized so that you lift your eyes to see the crown without craning your neck, and so that the outline of the plant frames the skyline (in a very small garden surrounded by buildings the tree will be framed by these). Remember too that if, as is so often true of town gardens, the site lies level with a basement, then the view from the living rooms on the floor above is important.

Shade may or may not be desirable but nearly every garden benefits from the extra dimension created by shadows cast by trees or the larger plants, covering different areas during the day as the sun moves from east to west and giving a feeling of movement whenever a breeze stirs the leaves. Many plants thrive under a canopy of light shade and even in our temperate climate the sitting area for a family is more comfortable if partly shaded. Shelter from prevailing winds and from wind-funnels produced by nearby walls and hedges is also important for the survival of tender plants. The most useful spot for a tree may then be best determined by practical experience in the garden rather than by an abstract decision on paper.

A specimen tree or shrub could be used as a focal point in the garden. It should be chosen for its suitability rather than for its rarity. The country garden should merge into the landscape and trees on the boundary should resemble indigenous plants and not strike a bizarre note. Suitability will depend on the soil and

aspect of the garden and the climatic conditions. Neighbours must be considered, bearing in mind the ultimate height and outline of the tree as well as the question of invasive roots, which can damage drains and foundations besides taking a large share of moisture from other plants. The north or east side of your garden may well be the south or west aspect of your neighbour's, and although he may welcome plants which give a light foliage canopy, or shape and purpose to his garden design, he may bitterly resent the use of a dense evergreen or a tree such as the common lime, *Tilia europea*, which makes a black deposit on plants near it. As a safety

119 *left*   The golden-leaved tall tree, *Robinia pseudoacacia* 'Frisia', gives a feeling of lightness to this garden. Campanulas and lamiums seed freely and the very distinguished variegated form of *Fatsia japonica* grows under a shady wall.

120 *right*   *Cercidiphyllum japonicum* is a fast-growing small tree preferring moist soil. In spring its young leaves are pale pink, and in autumn the foliage turns yellow and orange.

precaution choose a planting spot where the distance from the tree to your house and to your next-door-neighbour's is equivalent to the ultimate height of the tree. Remember that poplars have very vigorous and far-reaching invasive roots which can easily damage the foundations of masonry, while birches and rhododendrons are shallow rooting, stealing moisture from other plants, and needing rich mulches to compensate.

Having chosen what seems to be a suitable site after due consideration of all these factors, return to the house and reconsider its appropriateness while looking through the windows or standing in the doorway which best frames the garden. If possible get someone to move a stake which represents the tree until the position is exactly right, or the ideal compromise is reached. Mass and structure of trees should be dense enough to achieve an architectural quality which balances visually with the house or other buildings on the site as well as with the neighbouring house, walls and trees. All trees and large shrubs have very definite habit and shape, and their varying silhouettes will be seen across your line of vision, standing out against the skyline or framed against surrounding trees and buildings. It is important therefore to get the balance right.

Evergreens make excellent screens and give the garden winter interest and structure but, except for conifers, tend to grow rather slowly. Leaves are shed all year round as new growth develops and these can look untidy on gravel and pavements. Certain forms of holly *(Ilex*

121 *left* This elegant foliage tree, *Robinia pseudoacacia* 'Frisia', is overhung by large lime trees and is in an inner secret compartment of a London garden.

122 *above* *Smilacina racemosa* will thrive even in the shade of a large tree, but will benefit from a moisture-conserving mulch. (HS).

123 *below* A magnolia casts light shade over a comfortable sitting area. The brick paving matches the curve of the lawn.

aquifolium and *Ilex × altaclarensis*) have particularly good leaf variegations and shape and make large pyramid bushes. Arbutus, eucryphias, camellias, and abutilons combine flower with attractive leaves. *Phillyrea latifolia* is a valuable small evergreen tree superficially resembling *Quercus ilex* (which grows much too large for a small area). Other more shrubby phillyreas, as well as osmanthus, elaeagnus and *Garrya elliptica*, will all give height where there is insufficient space for a tree.

Conifers, especially upright types, are best reserved for growing in formal repetitive patterns which hold together a good design, as the strong vertical emphasis of the trees and their dense green or blue foliage tend to be unrestful. In a rural garden they look inappropriate if outlined against the skyline and need particularly careful siting. Indigenous ones such as yew and juniper merge best into the countryside. In a town conifers can be framed against surrounding buildings, or clipped and shaped as if part of a formal topiary scheme. Most are readily available as quite large specimens for immediate design effect. A tendency for the base to be spoilt by dead brown wood and leaves means that they have to be replaced regularly when any unsightly deterioration begins.

The basic shape of small trees varies enormously, from round umbrella heads on a bare trunk, to fastigiate, weeping, fan shaped with branches starting from the base, and horizontal branched trees with their wedding cake effect. Some have heavy dark leaves, others a more delicate framework of light foliage in summer and an attractive skeleton outline during the winter months. The shape, of course, also affects the contour of the shadow cast during the day. Slow-growing deciduous trees which can reach heights of over sixty feet (18m) in as many years can be planted for present enjoyment even though they will ultimately be unsuitable. Forms of oak, ash, elder and sycamore which do not grow too large exist, and even the fast-growing poplars, nothofagus and eucalyptus may be initially satisfactory because they give such swift results even if they have to be removed after twenty years or so.

Weeping shapes are attractive and the familiar grey pear, *Pyrus salicifolia* 'Pendula', is one of the most beautiful. Another pear, *P. elaeagrifolia*, is rarer and more erect. The common weeping willow is too large for a small area but *Salix caprea* 'Pendula' seldom exceeds twelve feet (4m). Horizontal branches make *Cornus controversa* and *Idesia polycarpa* interesting structural trees and forms of *Viburnum plicatum* and *Viburnum davidii* have similar outlines at a lower level.

Fruit trees including apples, pears, almonds and all sorts of ornamental prunus generally do not grow too big. Birches, catalpas, dogwoods, gleditsia, hornbeam, laburnum, magnolia, various types of maple and mountain ash, white beam and yew are all possible choices. Also to be recommended are *Robinia pseudoacacia* and in particular its popular form 'Frisia' with golden foliage, *Cercidiphyllum japonicum* – providing there is adequate moisture - *Ginkgo biloba*, *Acer griseum*, which has exciting peeling bark, and *Betula jacquemontii* with white parchment bark. The best and most suitable are included in the select list (see page 146, and also page 184).

Leaf colour, shape and texture are important and there is the added attraction of spring or autumn tints. Gold or purple variegated leaves which are outstanding as they unfurl may become dull in late summer, while others contribute most to the October garden with vivid scarlet and crimson colouring. Some have exciting barks (types of *Cornus alba* and willows are grown only for their winter coloured stems and cut down every March for best results) which are most evident in winter when leaves have fallen. Coloured leaves need careful siting as they tend to attract the eye and dominate the garden; they are best near the house or hidden from immediate view. Texture of leaf reflects light in different ways, some being glossy like laurel and camellia, others matt like yew or dull green like rhododendron. Plants with grey leaves often dislike polluted city atmosphere as the small hairs on the surface catch and hold dirt. Large leaves create very dense shade under which little will thrive, and any discolouration or hole (pecked by bird or eaten by caterpillar) attracts undue attention in a small space. The light graceful foliage of birch, gleditsia, mountain ash, and the Kentucky coffee tree, *Gymnocladus dioicus*, makes a perfect canopy allowing light to filter through to plants beneath.

Flowers and fruit are fleeting and perhaps in a small garden less important than other features, but if combined with structure and beauty of leaf are welcome too. In spring (or winter) flowering prunus and fruit trees enhance the garden. *Malus floribunda*, magnolias, acacias (if the garden is warm and sheltered), followed by later flowering magnolias, laburnums, eucryphias and the September scented flowers of *Clerodendron trichotomum* and its bright blue fruits also look very handsome. Arbutus, crab apple, and *Sorbus aucuparia* and its various cultivars all bear excellent coloured berries.

124 *above* Trees which cast dappled shade are useful where space is restricted. *Koelreuteria paniculata* has light elegant pinnate foliage and bears yellow flower trusses in July. (HS).

125 *opposite* *Stranvaesia davidiana* is a useful small tree or wall shrub and the leaves and berries are very decorative. (HS).

A final word on trees: if one already exists in your garden do not remove it in haste. Equally, do not hesitate to remove an ugly or diseased specimen. Carefully consider whether a previous owner had a special reason for planting it and, even if disproportionately large, review the possibility of severe pruning and lightening of the head before removing it. It may have added character and strength to neighbouring gardens and be much missed. A good tree takes many years to mature into a beautiful specimen and is hard to replace. It is possible to get large trees transplanted for quick effects but this is a professional and skilled task and the tree will inevitably be temporarily checked.

126 *above*   An old mulberry tree gives a feeling of age and maturity to any garden. It normally has an attractive irregular outline and habit and, moreover, the fruit makes an excellent jam. (PB).

127 *below*   *Magnolia stellata* slowly grows to make a small tree and is charming in spring when covered with star-like flowers. (HS).

110

Chapter Eleven

HEDGES FOR SHELTER, PRIVACY AND DESIGN

Hedges are planted to protect gardens from cold winds, to define outer boundaries and create inner compartments, to increase the feeling of space, to add interest to the design and for convenience and privacy. Besides fulfilling all these functions plants for hedges should delight us with their foliage, flowers and fruit, and provide a handsome and suitable background to beds, borders and seats or statuary. The best hedging plants are those which give least trouble, last for many years without renewal, are content with an annual trim and do not encroach greedily on flowerbeds taking goodness from other plants.

Shelter

The area of shelter inside a hedged enclosure will be about seven times the height of the surrounding hedge. The most favourable spot is the area covered by about twice its height. Prevailing local winds will vary according to nearby hills, woods, clumps of trees or buildings, and narrow gaps between houses may well be wind-funnels. In a small garden it is very easy to discover the

128 The silver-leaved cotton lavender, *Santolina incana*, makes an excellent hedging plant, especially for inner compartments. It looks lovely falling gracefully over the edge of paving. (HS)

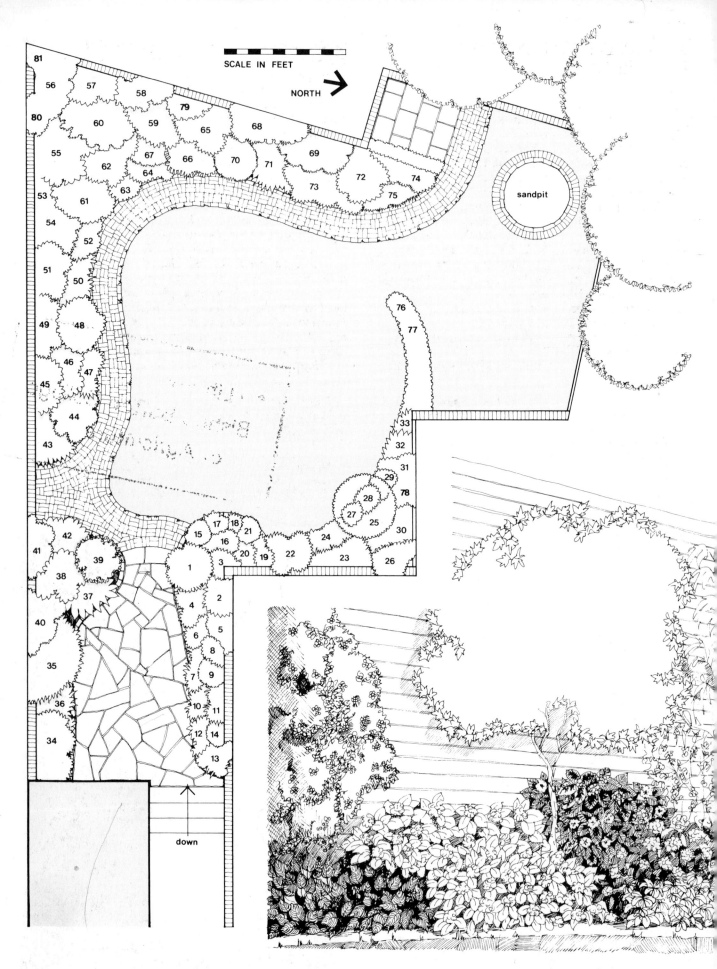

SCALE IN FEET

NORTH

81
56 57 58
80 79
60 59 65 68
55 67 66 70 69
62 64 71 72 74
53 63 73 75
54 52 sandpit
51 50
76
49 48 77
46
45 47
44
43
42 33
41 39 32
38 31
40 37 29 78
35 15 17 18 21 28 30
16 27 25 24
36 3 20 19 22 23 26
34 1 4 2
6 5
8
7 9
10 11
12 14
13

down

112

A GARDEN WITH A NEW EXTENSION

Mrs Millward describes below her own garden extension, giving details of constructional work. The result is an outstandingly successful garden for family use.

Our original garden, to which we came in 1975, was a standard London patio garden measuring 20ft by 15ft (6m × 4.5m). Reached by steps up from the basement, it was paved with York stone and surrounded by narrow borders.

We had always hoped to extend this garden by buying a piece of the derelict yard behind and after three years' bargaining acquired a plot approximately 40ft by 45ft (12m × 13.5m). As this plot extends sideways behind neighbouring houses it cannot all be seen from the house, and we have tried to emphasize the change from the enclosed space of the original patio to the wider garden beyond by planting trees and evergreen shrubs either side of the paving leading from one to the other. (See plate 129, below right).

The new area was covered in granite setts, Sussex squares, engineering bricks and soft reds, the setts being underlaid with 10in (25cm) of concrete. We drilled, pick-axed and dug the whole area re-using the engineering bricks for the foundations of the new boundary wall and re-laying the setts on sand to form a path. We sacrificed some border width to have dry access to our compost heap and washing line. The path has had the unexpected advantage of keeping the children's tricycles off the grass. They prefer the noise they can make by riding over the setts!

Having filled eight skips with rubbish, which incidentally could not conceivably have been done had we not had rear access to our new plot, we then dug down 18in (45cm) where the borders were to be and filled in with best topsoil. This considerable expenditure has been a sound investment. Where the turf was to be laid we dug less deeply, filled in with inferior topsoil from a local building site and finally added a layer of lawn compost. We laid the turves in March and six months later we had an excellent lawn, achieved by weekly mowing with clippings left on, and one spring fertilization.

In order to provide maximum playspace for two children and their friends, we confined the borders to the perimeter. A hornbeam hedge visually screens the children's activities from the rest of the garden and the Caragana arborescens 'Lorbergii' planted at the end of the hedge helps to hide the climbing frame and sandpit without casting any shade.

1 Choisya ternata
2 Abutilon vitifolium
3 Solanum crispum
4 Ballota pseudodictamnus
5 Clematis 'Pennell's Purity'
6 Cotoneaster hybridus 'Pendulus'
7 Artemisia absinthium 'Powis Castle'
8 Ceanothus 'Delight'
9 Hebe salicifolia 'Kirkii'
10 Artemisia stelleriana
11 Artemisia schmidtiana
12 Geranium renardii
13 Helianthemum 'The Bride'
14 Parahebe cataractae
15 Hebe pinguefolia 'Pagei'
16 Cotinus coggygria 'Flame'
17 Cytisus kewensis
18 Hypericum moserianum
19 Santolina neapolitana
20 Abelia grandiflora
21 Oenothera missouriensis
22 Laurus nobilis 'Aurea'
23 Cytisus battandieri
24 Cistus 'Elma'
25 Malus toringoides
26 Jasminum stephanense
27 Stipa gigantea
28 Salvia officinalis 'Icterina'
29 Potentilla fruticosa 'Elizabeth'
30 Elaeagnus pungens 'Maculata'
31 Bupleurum fruticosum
32 Hosta plantaginea 'Grandiflora'
33 Chaemycyparis pisifera 'Filifera Aurea'
34 Elaeagnus pungens 'Maculatum'
35 Prunus (weeping)
36 Hosta crispula
37 Helleborus orientalis
38 Camellia williamsii 'Donation' (2)
39 Paeonia 'Joseph Rock'
40 Clematis viticella 'Ascotientis'
41 Pyracantha
42 Hydrangea petiolaris
43 Hosta sieboldiana
44 Tiarella collina
45 Cotoneaster lacteus
46 Camellia reticulata 'Mary Williams'
47 Astrantia maxima
48 Acer palmatum 'Dissectum'
49 Anemone hupehensis
50 Hosta crispula
51 Cornus alba 'Elegantissima'
52 Viburnum plicatum 'Nana'
53 Clematis alpina
54 Viburnum × burkwoodii
55 Hydrangea 'Blue Wave'
56 Clematis orientalis
57 Stranvaesia davidiana
58 Hedera colchica 'Dentata Aurea'
59 Cotinus coggygria 'Notcutt's'
60 Gleditsia triacanthus 'Sunburst'
61 Acer japonicum 'Aureum'
62 Viburnum plicatum 'Lanarth'
63 Chiastophyllum oppositifolium
64 Hakonechloa macra 'Albo-Aurea'
65 Cornus alba 'Spaethii'
66 Penstemon hartwegii 'Garnet'
67 Fritillaria imperialis
68 Carpentaria californica
69 Elaeagnus macrophyllus
70 Hebe 'Fairfieldii'
71 Hosta sieboldiana
72 Liriodendron tulipifera 'Fastigiata'
73 Cistus cyprius
74 Philadelphus coronarius 'Aureus'
75 Fuchsia magellanica
76 'Versicolor'
76 Caragana arborescens 'Lorbergii'
77 Carpinus betulus
78 Lonicera brownii 'Fuchsioides'
79 Clematis armandii
80 Clematis macropetala
81 Hedera colchica 'Paddy's Pride'

windiest spots and then design and plant accordingly. Remember that leaves with gaps between them filter winds much better than a dense hedge making a solid barrier. If access is needed in a length of hedge, then the hedge line can be broken and overlapped. Scale is important and in a restricted area it may be best not to use a high outer barrier such as holly, beech, yew or hornbeam but to plant a mixture of smaller shrubs thickly. Box, lavender and santolina all make delightful and fragrant small hedges which give shelter to tender small plants. High hedges may still be necessary, however, to screen unsightly dustbins or washing lines.

Privacy

A natural desire for privacy may well conflict with the satisfaction of having an open view onto countryside, or indeed with the need to make use of some pleasant and attractive aspect of the next-door-neighbour's garden. In a town, particularly with terraced houses, adjoining gardens will probably contain some tree or shrubs which will appear to be part of your background planting, or climbers from a neighbour's wall will mingle with wall plants in your garden. Where there is no boundary wall a flowering hedge will discreetly enhance the two garden sites which it divides and will hide any ugly wire or fencing which may be necessary to keep children and animals in and out. Evergreen honeysuckle, variegated ivy and shrub roses can be trained on wire or wood to look as permanent as hedge plants and will make an effective barrier. Children can be deterred by the thorns of shrub roses or berberis, but very few small animals will fail to find a way through unless wire netting or some form of closely woven fence is used as well.

A high evergreen hedge in a small front garden obviously screens the windows from passers-by, but may make the house gloomy and dark. In a garden with an open and exposed aspect it is possible to plant round a small sitting area which will then be screened from wind as well as from neighbours. If the hedge is primarily for privacy near the house then planting in the immediate or middle foreground rather than at the boundary limit will achieve quicker results (as when planting a tree to hide some unsightly object from view – see page 105). Thick dense hedges, particularly evergreen ones, also make sound barriers and the noise of heavy traffic is muffled.

Design

Inner hedges and paths can pull together an informal design and their rigid lines contrast well with the rounded and billowing shapes of flowering plants. Often the most satisfactory garden is one with a strong framework which looks casual because of mixed beds of contrasting plant material, such as good foliage shrubs, herbaceous groundcover and cleverly blended flower colours, but which in fact has a sharply defined pattern. The three-dimensional hedges serve as vertical background to borders, beds and grass. Moving between inner compartments, or being able to glance into an enclosure, adds interest even in the smallest garden.

Ideally, each separate area might be used for growing one type of plant, or the line of the hedge may just emphasize the change from pavement to grass or flowerbed. The sunniest area of a garden can have a hedge dividing it from shade, and plants used in each part can be distinctive. Grey-leaved shrubs and aromatic herbs prefer strong sunlight, whereas woodland plants with large green smooth leaves thrive in shade. The garden will appear larger as well as more interesting if both types are kept in their own compartments. In a small formal garden squares of interlocking low hedges such as box, santolina and lavender, which respond well to tidy clipping and shaping, might contain roses, annuals or even grass or gravel.

Most gardens have some straight lines and sometimes these can be made the main design feature, the theme being carried through with hedges, beds and borders. In other situations it may be satisfactory to distract the eye from the boundary and make the lawn or central area into an oval or circle with curves of flowerbeds following a similar radius. A curving inner hedge continues and cuts off the garden at one end, completing the pattern already begun by beds and grass. Hedges can be like stage wings curving round and varying in height. If there is a focal point at the end of a path leading from the centre then the eye can be carried through from far away, but if the shape of the garden is very irregular this focal point may be visible only after approaching the hedge, and a seat could be placed so that it can be seen through the gap. The vegetable plot, garden shed or compost heap will be hidden from view by the hedge.

If the garden is a perfect square or rectangle a circle or oval hedge can run inside it, but this should be planted as a carefully planned exercise and not at random. The smaller the area concerned the more important it is to get proportions and measurements exactly right. At this stage the designer has to be more of an artist than a gardener, but when the plans have to be implemented knowledge of the habit and growth rate of hedging plants becomes vital.

Preparing and planting

Mark out the line of the hedge with pegs and string (if it is to be a curve use a hose pipe, see page 60) and dig a trench the whole length, at least a spade's depth and two feet (60cm) wide. Loosen the lower soil (with a pick-axe if necessary, as it is essential for roots to penetrate into subsoil) and plant in a single line. Double and staggered rows are really unnecessary and add considerably to the expense. Be very careful to plant evenly and straight, using a measure to get spacing accurate. The smaller the plants the cheaper is the hedge and usually young plants grow more quickly and will overtake those which were planted when larger. It is tempting to use large specimens for quick effect, but they are more likely to be checked and take a year or so to settle down and start growth again.

Feeding and weeding

A good mulch added on the top surface will help keep down annual weeds, and a contact herbicide (which kills through the leaves) should minimize the need for hand-weeding. The emergence of annual seedlings can be controlled by safe simazine-based weedkillers which sterilize the top few inches of the soil (see page 188). Continue to feed regularly, using organic farmyard manure and dried blood and bonemeal. Slow-acting artificial fertilizers can be scattered in granule form and will encourage healthy growth and vigour. In a town garden feeding through the foliage with a pressure sprayer keeps the leaves clean as well. Water well in periods of drought (see page 43).

Pruning

Fast-growing hedges need cutting most often and the smaller the garden the more important it is to have things neat and shapely. But there are types of hedge which need only an annual trimming and an occasional cutting right back into old wood. A traditional evergreen hedge such as yew can be cut to architectural shapes with sloping and tapering sides and top, but the less formal type of shrub rose, berberis and potentilla just need loose shaping in winter. Among the conifers the fast-growing Ley-

130 *right* Senecio monroi has crinkly-edged grey leaves and is useful for hedging. If pruned regularly every April it will remain tidy and compact for many years. (HS).

131 *below* Iceberg roses make an informal hedge at the top of a dividing wall. In the background more roses are used to mark a further division, where perhaps a low evergreen hedge might have been more satisfactory.

land (*Cupressocyparis leylandii*) is popular and responds well to cutting but other cypresses resent being trimmed back and the bottom of the hedge gets bare and unsightly. Box is easily kept in shape and, as it roots readily from cuttings put straight into open soil, can be planted with little expense. If time is no object, trimmings can be obtained from a neighbour's hedge. Pruning base, sides and top encourages new shoots, so do this rather fiercely, after planting if the hedge is deciduous, and in April when the worst frosts are over if evergreen.

Types of hedging plants

If the hedge is the background to a border it will compete with the ornamental plants for food and moisture. Some plants such as yew, lonicera and privet are notoriously greedy and if they are used it is wise to leave a space between them and the bed, which may not be easy in a small garden. On the other hand yew is the most attractive and solid of all hedges; it will grow six to nine inches (15 to 23cm) a year and if pruned regularly and carefully makes a solid thick barrier right down to the ground. Privet and lonicera are excellent in the polluted atmosphere of cities and the golden-leaved forms of both make colourful boundaries in dark and dry areas.

It is possible to sink a piece of corrugated iron into the soil to prevent roots spreading, but it may be better to choose less demanding hedge material with deep tap roots instead of invasive surface ones. Roses, holly, beech and box are ideal and most of the deciduous shrubs give shelter for small bulbs and creeping plants at their base. Cyclamen will thrive in dry shade under box, and *Anemone blanda* and scillas multiply under deciduous rose hedges. Low-growing herbaceous plants such as cranesbill geraniums or London pride *(Saxifraga umbrosa)* make a neat flowering edge between a hedge and a path. Violets and dicentras all spread and make a colourful display

132 *above* Rosemary, santolina and atriplex make a soft background to the vivid *Rosa mutabilis* and act as an informal hedge which divides the garden from a covered entrance way.

133 *below left* Thick planting of strong foliage plants makes an informal hedge, and a trellis gives immediate height to form an inner division.

134 *below* Informal mixed planting can be used to divide a garden into inner divisions. Here upright climbers arranged on a frame make a screen, and below, flowering perennials give seasonal colour.

135 *right* A combination of grey leaves and white flowers is always restful. Pale colours glow at night and are therefore particularly appropriate for sitting areas. (See details of plan on next page.)

in light shade. The dangerously invasive dead-nettle (*Lamium galeobdolon* 'Variegatum') will carpet the ground under yew or privet but should rarely be given a place in a small garden.

If you are keen to have an elegant design but have little time to spare it is possible to make an attractive garden with some trees (if space allows), a few formal lines given by strong hedges, which need little attention, and clever planting with evergreen creepers such as the lamium, ivy, periwinkle and epimedium, which will flourish where grass is difficult.

Outer boundary hedges need to be more substantial than those which form inner compartments, and if they are the outer bastion for wind-protection must be fairly

tough. In a sheltered town garden the choice is much less restricted. The small seaside garden has other problems of extra wind and salt spray (but less frost). Yew, lonicera and privet have already been mentioned (with warnings); the last two are fast growing and cheap to acquire, and popular for these reasons. Forms of holly (*Ilex aquifolium*) are slow but make stately hedges and need little attention. The Leyland cypress is the quickest and tallest of all evergreen hedges and will screen to a height of fifteen feet (5m) within a few years, but makes a hard rigid line whereas you may prefer a softer more gentle shape.

Elaeagnus in variety and evergreen cotoneaster can be shaped to make hedges, although they are happiest if

AN AWKWARDLY SITED GARDEN

This suburban garden (approximately 38 × 42ft : 12.5 × 14m) is heavily shaded on the south west by a London Plane tree outside the garden, and on the south by an evergreen Ligustrum lucidum, which was planted to screen an ugly block of flats beyond the garden fence. The north side of the site has a sheltering warm brick wall which provides space for tender climbers. A sitting place in front of the south-facing wall looks diagonally across the lawn towards the Ligustrum lucidum, behind which there is space for a compost heap and a gate leading into a back lane. The greenhouse and the fruit and vegetable area are cut off from the lawn by a diagonal

hedge of rugosa roses, R. Blanc Double de Courbet, which look decorative for most of the year with white scented flowers in summer. Betula ermanii, which casts very light shade, helps to hide the ugly buildings to the east and south. Its shining and peeling bark looks attractive from the windows of the house in winter, and Abelia grandiflora and Kalmia latifolia help to frame this vista. Round the paving area in front of the warm wall, grey-leaved plants with white, blue and yellow flowers are planted in profusion.

Most of the planting is for minimum upkeep. Maximum space has been allotted to lawn for children to play on. In the bed to the west, evergreen flowering shrubs and good groundcover plants will look attractive all year.

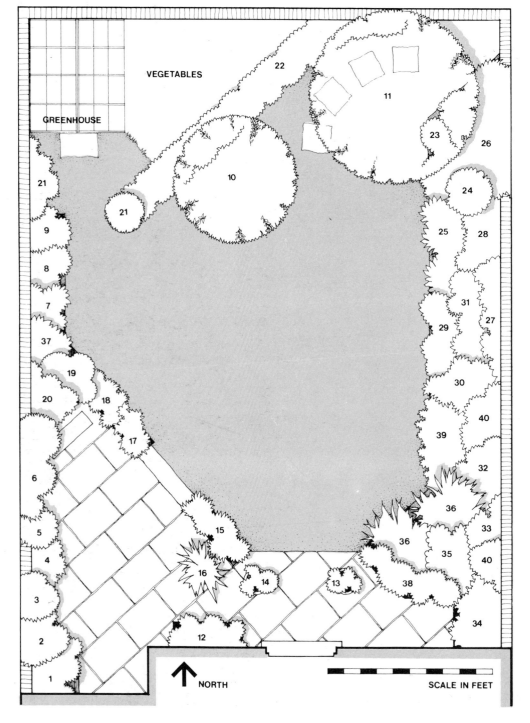

1 Myrtus communis 'Tarentina'
2 Laurus nobilis
3 Cytisus battandieri
4 Eucalyptus glaucescens
5 Vitis coignetiae
6 Pyrus salicifolia 'Pendula'
7 Phlomis chrysophylla
8 Rosa 'Golden Showers'
9 Sophora tetraptera
10 Betula ermanii
11 Ligustrum lucidum
12 Bupleurum fruticosum
13 Kalmia latifolia
14 Abelia grandiflora
15 Phlomis fruticosa
16 Cordyline australis
17 Teucrium fruticans
18 Iberis sempervirens
19 Armeria maritima
20 Cistus cyprius
21 Senecio monroi
22 Rosa rugosa 'Blanc double de Courbet' (6)
23 Epimedium rubrum (9)
24 Choisya ternata
25 Pulmonaria angustifolia (5)
26 Hedera colchica 'Dentata Variegata'
27 Hydrangea petiolaris
28 Mahonia aquifolium (5)
29 Brunnera macrophylla (5)
30 Osmanthus delavayii
31 Mixed planting of small spring bulbs
32 Ligustrum ovalifolium 'Aureum' (3)
33 Eucryphia glutinosa
34 Mahonia 'Buckland'
35 Camellia williamsii 'Donation', 'Jermyns' and 'November Pink'
36 Arundinaria nitida (3)
37 Hosta sieboldiana (3)
38 Juniperus sabina 'Tamariscifolia' (2)
39 Alchemilla mollis
40 Elaeagnus macrophylla

NORTH

SCALE IN FEET

allowed to develop a more open structure. Berberis have arching prickly branches which repel invaders. Varieties of *Berberis darwinii* and one of its hybrids, *B. × stenophylla,* grow to different heights and have attractive leaves and yellow flowers in spring. They should be pruned immediately after flowering if at all. Pyracantha can be grown as a hedge, but is often best trained along a fence where it can give a very formal effect with its stiff growth, and if pruned judiciously can provide a froth of white blossom in early summer and bright berries in winter. In shade laurustinus (*Viburnum tinus*) and the more prostrate *Viburnum davidii* with its beautiful turquoise fruits are excellent.

In a country garden the traditional hedgerow haw-thorn (*Crataegus monogyna*) makes an easy visual transition from the garden to the fields beyond and a strong barrier against animals.

Among deciduous plants, beech, hornbeam and shrub roses are outstanding. Espalier apples and pears are both attractive in shape and flower as well as useful. Obviously it is more sensible to use fruit trees for inner hedges if you want to harvest the fruit yourself, but a happy agreement could be made with a neighbour to share planting, pruning tasks and staking costs as well as the fruit. Espaliered fruit trees evoke pleasant memories of old walled kitchen gardens. If erected on stout posts and wire they can be easily tied and trained.

Rugosa roses are perfect shrubs for perimeter hedges.

They have fresh apple-green leaves, attractive fragrant flowers, double or single, ranging in colour from wine-red to pink and pure white. Most varieties also have huge hips, the single-flowered 'Frau Dagmar Hastrup' being one of the most freely fruiting. The very thorny stems make an impenetrable barrier, and if grown as cuttings on their own roots they will also sucker to make the base of the hedge thick and bushy. Hybrid musks can be trained on a frame to make a narrow hedge, or allowed to grow naturally taking up more space; 'Buff Beauty' has creamy-buff flowers and bronze leaves and 'Penelope' pink-apricot flowers. Both flower twice if dead-headed. Inner hedges can be of repeat bush types such as 'Iceberg' and 'Chinatown', which can be pruned hard to keep them to a moderate size, or non-recurrent gallicas such as the striped rose, 'Rosa Mundi' (amazingly bountiful with its flowers for two weeks at the end of June but dull the rest of the summer). The continuous flowering 'Natalie Nypels' grows to two feet (60cm) and with its rose-pink scented flowers makes an admirable spreading bush suitable for a hedge.

Usually a protected town garden is several degrees higher in temperature than one in the country, and the choice of suitable hedging plants is therefore greater. Among the evergreens, pittosporums, senecios, griselinias, escallonias and hebes all have attractive foliage; the last two also have a long flowering season. (For specific varieties to choose see plant list.) Among the olearias, which in general make good seaside hedges, the hybrid *Olearia × hastii* is the hardiest with grey tough leaves and white daisy flowers. It makes a neat four-foot (1.2m) hedge.

Evergreen herbaceous plants such as bergenias and silver-leaved artemisias all give winter colour and need little attention. Bergenias also make splendid edging to protect spring bulbs. Catmint is very nearly evergreen and if trimmed in mid-summer after flowering will bloom again in early autumn. There are many good shrubby potentillas, all varieties of *Potentilla fruticosa;* they have a long flowering season and can be used as hedging in places where shrub roses would be too high. Rosemary needs an annual spring pruning to prevent the plants from becoming woody. A pink-flowered variety, *Rosmarinus officinalis* 'Roseus', is attractive and very low-growing.

136 The splendid daisy bush, *Olearia macrodonta*, has green undulating holly-like leaves and can be planted as a free-standing specimen or grown as a wind-resistant hedge in warm counties.

Chapter Twelve

CLIMBERS

Some gardens, especially town ones, do not have enough space for a small tree or free-standing shrub, but still need tall vertical plants to screen unsightly objects and raise the eye upwards. Many backyards or patio areas are partly surrounded by high walls of neighbouring houses on which it is possible to train vigorous climbing plants which can often reach a height of twenty feet (6m) in a couple of seasons. A small tree can take as long as twenty years to achieve the optimum height for the scale of the garden and as we have seen (Chapter 10) a fast-growing specimen seldom stabilizes at a suitable point and often has invasive and damaging roots.

Where there is sufficient space a simple pergola, in middle distance or at the end of the garden, can be constructed and covered with climbing and twining plants. Leafy plants trained on wires stretched between the upright pillars make a shady arbour or walk. Fences and trellis attached to the top of boundary walls can be clothed with vigorous climbers which need little space

137 *below*   In a narrow sunken front area an ivy, *Hedera helix* 'Goldheart', a clematis and a cotoneaster climb from tidy containers, giving a feeling of profusion. New soil and fertilizers should be added annually to permanent container planting.

138 *right*   A well-pruned climbing rose, 'The New Dawn' has healthy green leaves and double pale pink flowers. If the dead heads are removed this rose will flower twice in a season. (HS).

for their roots. Gardening upwards increases scope when the growing area is limited. An ugly shed or garage roof can have its sloping surface hidden by twining stems and leaves turning it into an attractive feature instead of an eyesore. Many of these climbing plants prefer to have their roots in cool shade and their leaves and flowers in an open sunlit position, and plenty of water and fertilizer should be given if the site is a dry one at the base of a wall.

What to choose

For very high plain walls it is best to choose climbing plants which attach themselves securely by self-clinging devices such as aerial roots or adhesive pads, and need no artificial support. Among the former are some of the most vigorous and ornamental plants, but a word of warning about their use. The aerial roots seeking soil and moisture will force their way into joints and cracks and over a long period these thin tendrils grow and swell and can damage ornamental masonry. This is a problem easily dealt with in a maintained garden, but in an empty or neglected site a strong-growing plant such as ivy may well be almost supporting a wall and trying to clear it may lead to collapse.

Ivies, and in particular *Hedera canariensis* (and its variegated forms) for sun and *Hedera colchica* for shade, have large leaves and will form a dense curtain on a wall or shed-roof. Grown horizontally they will cover the ground in a weed-proof mat. The smaller-leaved common ivy, *Hedera helix,* has many excellent forms and looks attractive over low walls, twining round pillars, and trailing downwards from containers and balconies. *Hydrangea petiolaris* and the very similar *Schizophragma hydrangeoides* both use aerial roots to anchor themselves, but are very decorative with their large flat flower heads which hang on for many months and make attractive winter features. They will grow in sun or shade and are happy on a wall or forcing their way upward through a tree.

Pileostegia viburnoides is seldom seen but once established will grow to twenty feet (6m) in shade or on a north-facing wall, almost free-standing, but stabilizing itself with its aerial roots. The climbing vine, now classified as *Parthenocissus,* adheres by pads and does no damage to stone or brick. Varieties of the two species *P. quinquifolia* (the true Virginia creeper) and *P. tricuspidata* (the Boston ivy) are attractive foliage plants which ramp up tall walls; their green spring foliage turns to brilliant scarlet and crimson in autumn even when in shade. *Parthenocissus henryana* thrives on a north wall and has bronze leaves with silver veining.

The regular climbing plants which twine with stems and tendrils need wire trellis (of wood or plastic) or a host plant for support. Wire, held taut by vine-eyes, is inconspicuous but diamond or square-shaped trellis is more adaptable when the plant needs to be temporarily removed for wall maintenance. There is a wide choice of suitable plants if artificial support can be given.

Some climb upwards using twining stems and curling tendrils, others cling by leaf stems (petioles) or, like roses, have hooked thorns; most need extra support early on with string or twine. Among the most decorative (and this is necessarily a select list) are various forms of vine (including *Ampelopsis*). The luxuriant five-lobed leaves of *Ampelopsis brevipendunculata* give a light shade comparable to the fruiting vine, *Vitis vinifera*, when trained over a pergola. Fruits varying from pale to bright deep blue are borne freely after a hot summer. *A. brevipendunculata* 'Elegans' is much less vigorous but has striking mottled foliage and is suitable for a warm garden. *Celastrus orbiculatus* will climb to thirty-three feet (10m) and bears startling brown fruit which splits to reveal yellow and red seed and is borne against a background of pale yellow leaf colouring. Clematis are another indispensable climbing genus, some with evergreen leaves, but all with attractive flowers. The flower form varies from small-flowered stars and lantern shapes in species, to large-flowered hybrids of many vivid colours. All like a cool root run and most benefit from

139 *left* *Rosa helenae* cascades through the purple-leaved *Prunus pissardii* giving height in the corner of a garden and colour and background to a rose border. The eucalyptus in the adjacent garden fills the skyline.

140 *below* Roof gardens need plenty of wind protection and an inner trellis provides a frame for climbers.

plentiful feeding. Pruning and tying are important and each type requires specific care.

Actinidia kolomikta is a striking foliage plant with strange tri-coloured green, pink and white leaves which needs a place in full sun. *A. chinensis*, the Chinese gooseberry, has large heart-shaped hairy leaves and will flower and bear fruit in a good year. Although most decorative in a small garden the leaves seem to be popular with birds and caterpillars and its appearance can be ruined for the whole season if the large individual leaves are damaged. Jasmine and honeysuckle are old favourites and bear fragrant flowers throughout the summer. The common white jasmine, *Jasminum officinale*, has forms with gold and silver leaf variegation and is less rampant – very useful when space is limited. The evergreen honeysuckle, *Lonicera japonica* 'Aureorecticulata', is one of the most effective climbers for screening (it also makes a good prostrate groundcover) and *Lonicera j.* 'Halliana' has sweetly scented flowers.

Wisteria prefers a rich soil and a position in full sun. *Wisteria sinensis* grows very large and its long purple or white racemes look magnificent on a pergola or on a warm wall. Perhaps the spectacular and rather less vigorous Japanese wisteria is most suitable for a restricted area. *W. floribunda* 'macrobotrys' has delicious scent and very long three-foot (90cm) racemes. These rampant climbers are so desirable that it may be worth allowing one of them to be the sole climber in a small garden. *Vitis coignetiae* has very handsome heart-shaped leaves which turn fiery red in autumn. The golden hop, *Humulus lupulus* 'Aureus', *Eccremocarpus scaber* and various sorts of tropaeolum all behave like herbaceous plants, dying to the ground, but making attractive summer climbers. In a very warm garden *Cobaea scandens*, usually treated as an annual, will survive the winter. It is easily grown from seed and very fast. The tender *Trachelospermum jasminoides* and *Ficus pumila* are excellent evergreen climbers for a very sheltered and warm garden. The former is slow growing but the strong scent amply repays patience.

Vigorous climbing roses should be considered as part of foundation planting. Many of the old ones are still best value for healthy and fragrant flowers. The pale yellow Banksian rose (there is a white form too) flowers in May, but needs a sunny sheltered wall. 'Mermaid', with single yellow flowers, will thrive against a north-east wall and flowers spasmodically all summer. 'Félicité et Perpétué' has small white flowers and also thrives surprisingly well in half-shade. 'Madame Grégoire Staechelin' flowers only in June but is magnificent with double pale pink heads, and 'The New Dawn' has pink flowers in June and again in September. 'Climbing Cecile Brunner' is perfect in a confined space, with its small pale flowers, and is not too rampant. The old 'Gloire de Dijon' grows to fifteen feet (4.5m), has buff to apricot scented blooms, and flow-

141 *below far left* Perhaps the most beautiful of all flowering climbers, the wisteria can grow happily in quite a small space, giving weeks of scented bloom and amply repaying time spent on feeding and careful pruning. (HS).

142 *below left* The white-flowered *Solanum jasminoides* loves a small enclosed yard in full sun. It needs a supporting frame against a wall but will quickly twine and clamber, needing little attention. (HS).

143 *right* Pyracantha are among the sturdiest evergreen shrubs for north and east exposures, flowering and fruiting very freely. They can be trained formally against a wall or allowed to make a natural shape. (HS).

144 *below* Against a warm sheltered wall wisteria and the spring-flowering *Clematis armandii* give a long flowering season.

ers continuously from June. The huge Musk ramblers such as *filipes* and *longicuspis* are lovely for cascading into and over trees, but tend to get out of control unless they are kept firmly in a wild corner. They flower in July with wonderful apple-scented fragrance. *R. paulii* 'Rosea', *R.* 'Max Graf' and *R.* 'Raubritter' are more modest and trail happily down banks and over walls.

145 *below* *Rosa* 'Félicité et Perpétué' will flower happily in shade, but the Banksian rose on the right needs warm sunlight. In the foreground *Rosa* 'Raubritter' is grown in a sunken bed and needs firm pruning.

146 *right* The architectural leaves of *Fatsia japonica* clothe the walls of a front area with green foliage. In a small space it may be best to keep the central area empty and concentrate planting round the edges.

147 *below right* The golden hop, *Humulus lupulus* 'Aureus', is an herbaceous climber useful for rapid summer screening. It is effective and colourful and can be grown in pots. (HS).

Chapter Thirteen

WALL SHRUBS

Good wall shrubs can shape and dominate a design and if the scale is right they can be as important as true climbers. Some can be pruned and tied to grow flat against a wall, where they save space and benefit from the extra warmth and protection. In these truly micro-climatic conditions many shrubs flower and fruit better if pruned regularly and the soft wood of more tender types ripens and hardens. Evergreens usually need more shelter from wind than shrubs which shed their leaves in winter and are, of course, ideal for giving shape and body to small gardens. Their foliage enhances the garden throughout the year and walls, hedges and fences will screen them against cold and drying gales.

Shrubs with pleasing architectural and formal shapes balance the garden framework when viewed against a vertical background. Those with a regular conical or pyramid ouline contrast with more rounded bushes, and with the sprawling habit of many climbers. Spiky sword-shaped leaves give emphasis next to soft foliage and have more permanent interest than the fleeting season of flower colour contrasts and harmonies. Pyramid

148 Thick planting of shrubs in curving beds distracts the eye from straight boundary walls. Grey foliage plants and blue-flowered ceanothus make a pleasant group.

shapes arranged judiciously along a wall or in front of a hedge bring an air of quiet formality to an otherwise loose design of mixed planting. If the border is straight and narrow these shrubs can act as buttresses, forming bays of shelter at regular intervals. The design is held together by repetition but different types of planting can take place in the sheltered separated beds. Conifers (but not those which grow into forest trees) can be used in this way. Too often one vertical cypress or juniper is set in the curving angle of a bed and becomes a distracting focal point rather than serving to unite the design of the garden as a whole. The smaller the area the more important is the need to keep plants with strong accents in places where a wall or hedge can make a background, rather than place them against bare sky or against a view into distant landscape.

Tough reliable shrubs are essential in a planting framework. Among these the old-fashioned *Chaenomeles speciosa* (better known as *Cydonia* or more familiarly as 'Japonica') will thrive and bear flowers in early spring even if in shade. They respond to being cut back and shaped immediately after flowering. Many cotoneasters will make an elegant curtain against a wall and need little pruning to encourage a formal outline. Some are deciduous, bearing red berries late in winter months while others such as the *salicifolius* forms have attractive evergreen leaves as well as scarlet fruits. Some of the garden varieties of escallonia are particularly suitable for a small site as their pendulous branches arch forwards. The common fig, *Ficus carica*, although needing warmth for fruit-bearing, will grow even in the colder counties. It needs hard pruning to control its spread and can be trained and tied. *Garrya elliptica* has leathery evergreen leaves but in a cold area the leaves are often scorched by

149 Most plants love the extra warmth and protection of a wall and can be pruned hard in a small garden.

wind so it benefits from wall protection. It thrives in sun or shade and is unaffected by atmospheric pollution, or by the salt winds in a seaside garden. Prune after flowering, cutting hard back to a branch system which can be trained against a wall. Less well known is an attractive evergreen shrub, *Itea ilicifolia*, which benefits from having its branches tied back and carefully shaped.

Many hydrangeas form large shrubs which can be pruned to make a permanent framework and *Hydrangea quercifolia* benefits from being grown against a wall as it tends to straggle in the open. Its strongly lobed leaves have magnificent autumn tints and the large flower heads are attractive. The evergreen *Magnolia grandiflora* and the deciduous *M. × soulangiana* grow to enormous dimensions but are so handsome that they deserve a place if at all possible. Ruthless and skilful pruning will restrict them to a rigid pattern but plenty of space must be allowed for their invasive roots. Other suitable magnolias are those in the liliflora group with stiff erect flowers, and *M. × loebneri*, which has pretty star-shaped flowers resembling the better known *M. stellata* (this, of course, is an excellent shrub for a small garden).

The firethorns are closely related to cotoneaster but are all evergreen and have aggressive thorns. However, they have pretty hawthorn-like flowers and red or yellow fruits in late summer. They are tolerant of shade, air-pollution, and almost any soil condition and can be stylishly pruned like espalier fruit trees with symmetrical and horizontal branches. They can be very effective on roof and balcony gardens as they stand up to exposure to wind and sun, and will grow to considerable size, even when the roots are in restricted containers. One of the best is *Pyracantha coccinea* 'Lalandei' which has orange-red fruits. Rather similar is *Stranvaesia davidiana* which can be tied back into a fan shape; the older leaf growth turns a vivid scarlet in autumn.

The winter-flowering scented *Viburnum farreri* (better known as *V. fragrans)*, makes a vase-shaped shrub against a wall and responds vigorously to pruning. The evergreen *V. rhytidophyllum* is a coarse plant with corrugated leathery leaves and is tough, shade tolerant and effective because of its very strong characteristics. Also, it breaks freely from the base when hard pruning is necessary.

In warmer areas or in favoured town gardens there is a wide choice. Both *Buddleia auriculata* and *B. crispa* flower on wood of the current season's growth so can be tightly cut back in spring. However, they like the protection of a wall and the reflected heat. The former has strongly fragrant winter creamy flowers, while *B. crispa* flowers in June with terminal panicles of lilac borne freely against the very attractive grey felted foliage. *B. alternifolia* is very rewarding against a wall if space is limited, but needs considerable care and skill to get the best results. Many forms of ceanothus can be carefully trained and all benefit from wind protection. This is especially true of the spring-flowerers and no garden should be without at least one. They should be planted very close to the wall and given support and fan or horizontal branching encouraged. Otherwise they send out shoots towards the light and are easily rocked by wind or damaged by snow falls.

One of the hardier of the early flowerers is the evergreen *Ceanothus* 'Cascade' which has an elegant habit, while *C. papillosus roweanus* is tender with very brilliant dark blue flowers. *Coronilla glauca* likes wall shelter and full sunshine, and will make a bushy shrub needing little cutting and attention. It blooms intermittently throughout the year, although most freely in spring, and its pale yellow pea flowers can brighten a winter garden. Cestrums with orange-red flowers like to scramble up climbing shrubs. The pineapple-scented Moroccan broom, *Cytisus battandieri,* like ceanothus, benefits from being fastened securely to some form of wall support as it is fast growing and unstable. Hard pruning encourages new vigorous growth and prevents the development of too much bare wood. *Fremontodendron californicum* is an exotic tender evergreen which likes to be firmly anchored to a supporting wall in full sun. *Punica granatum,* the pomegranate, flowers well and even fruits if encouraged with supports against a warm wall. The additional heat from the stone or brickwork makes all the difference to this plant, although it will readily survive quite low temperatures in the open. The main branches can be tied out fanwise. As well as carrying vivid scarlet flowers and bright fruit the pomegranate has very attractive bronze glossy foliage which colours well in autumn after a hot summer. One of the flowering currants, *Ribes speciosum,* is semi-evergreen with very beautiful fuchsia-like slender flowers, and needs a warm wall. Old wood needs cutting out regularly and the young shoots from the base can be tied to supports.

Another shrub which could be a bush or encouraged to grow against a wall is the upright rosemary, *Rosmarinus officinalis* 'Fastigiatus'. Less substantial shrubs such as *Artemisia arborescens* and the half-hardy *Senecio leucostachys* can be encouraged to weave in and out of wall plants and make admirable foils to duller green.

A firm symmetrical plant outline along the boundary wall or fence will help you to feel that the garden has a definite plan. Too many gardens appear to have grown in a haphazard fashion where little attention has been paid to design and balance. Resist the impulse to plant at random. Generally speaking, the conical shape of a plant broader at the base and tapering to a point contrasts well with less regular plant profiles, but a horizontal tiered effect or a definite weeping outline can also be appropriate. Some bushes have gentle rounded forms which soften harsh backgrounds of modern building and masonry. Others, of course, can be clipped to make desirable shapes and patterns. I believe that the most successfully planned gardens have loose natural planting inside a quite rigid framework of plants and/or architecture; a framework which should not obtrude but which enhances and unites the informal planting.

Many shrubs, and particularly evergreen ones, benefit from wall protection, and as a result have a natural but regular habit which they might never achieve if buffeted by winds. *Abutilon vitifolium* will keep an attractive pyramid outline if regularly pruned after flowering. Camellias with glossy evergreen leaves prefer semi-shade and a good acid loam, and are an ornament to any dull corner. They are tolerant of city pollution, but revel in extra heat and the early spring flowers are less likely to be frosted in bud if in a sheltered position (not east-facing, see page 38).

Crinodendron hookeranium is another acid-loving evergreen making a large dense bush with heavy green foliage. It is tender when young, but once established able to endure low temperatures. *Drimys winteri* likes very similar conditions but is tolerant of lime soil. It may grow too large for a small garden, reaching at least twenty-five feet (7.5m) if given a sheltering wall, but it is very worthwhile with scented ivory flowers and rhododendron-like pale leaves. Eucryphias too, both evergreen and deciduous, make elegant spires and flower in August and September, when good flowering shrubs are few. *Eucryphia × nymansensis* 'Nymansay' is lime-tolerant, and *E. milliganii* makes quite a small shrubby bush suitable for the smallest garden. Hoherias flower in mid-summer, and the evergreen *H. sexstylosa* has very attractive but variably shaped leaves, which partly conceal the profusely carried white flowers. They tend to have a fastigiate habit but the deciduous species have a broader form.

150 Climbing plants cover walls and help to make a small garden secret and remote.

There are many hollies which will naturally retain a dense shape but which also respond especially well to pruning. *Ilex × altaclarensis* hybrids have beautiful large leaves, often almost untoothed, and many of the *Ilex aquifolium* forms have colourful leaf variegation. They all grow slowly but are reliable hardy plants, retaining unblemished foliage throughout the year. The bay tree, *Laurus nobilis*, grows naturally into a symmetrical pyramid, but can easily be shaped and pruned to suit a restricted space. *Pittosporum tenuifolium* has wavy leaves of apple-green, some with silver-white variegation, and there is also a purple-leaved form. These conical bushes have a delicate light structure without the heavy density of many evergreens, but they do prefer a sheltered garden and cannot endure low temperatures. One of the buckthorns, *Rhamnus alaterna* 'Argenteovariegata', is an admirable hardy evergreen for sun or shade which can be cut and pruned into shape. A variety of cherry laurel,

Prunus laurocerasus 'Zebaliana' throws out horizontal branches and can be used on corners or for framing a path or gateway. The deciduous *Viburnum plicatum* 'Mariesii' also has regular tiered branches, which in early summer are covered with broad flat heads of creamy-white. This is a very valuable plant but tends to grow rather large; its branches spread to fifteen feet (4.5m) after ten years or so. The variegated laurustinus, *Viburnum tinus* 'Variegatus', is more tender than the type but makes a well-structured bush, clothed down to the ground with attractive green and white leaves borne on red stems, and winter flowerheads.

Many conifers are suitable for use in garden design. *Chamaecyparis lawsoniana* 'Ellwoodii' and *C. l.* 'Kilmarcurragh' do not grow too tall and the feathery grey-green foliage of the former and dark sombre green of the latter are useful. Both make a conical shape, while *Juniperus virginiana* 'Sky Rocket' has a narrow pencil-slim columnar habit. *J. communis* 'Hibernica' resembles an Italian cypress and is more suitable for our cold wet climate. Most of the true cypresses although of excellent regular shape grow too large for use as wall shrubs, and as they grow the green leaves at the base die back. Small conifers have a wide range of foliage colour and texture which affects their density in a planting scheme, and they retain these qualities through all the seasons with only minor variation in spring when there are new growing tips of a

151 *left* Wall shrubs can be fiercely pruned to keep them in shape. A vine scrambles through a tree and in the background is *Solanum jasminoides* which flowers in summer. The variegated elaeagnus gives colour all the year.

152 *below* Where space is limited, shrubs such as *Osmanthus delavayii* can be pruned severely after flowering in April. Its small dark green leaves are attractive all year. (HS).

paler colour. They take and keep a rigid formal shape from the start, they are readily available and easy to look after. However, their very artificiality should counsel caution. It seems simple to solve a planning problem by their use, but a garden with too many vertical exclamation marks becomes fussy and restless.

Conventional rounded plant shapes contrast well with these conifers and with the pyramid-forming shrubs already discussed. *Choisya ternata* and *Osmanthus delavayii* carry flowers in shade among their deep green leaves. Aucubas, *Euonymus fortunei*, ligustrums, phillyreas, skimmias and *Viburnum davidii* all make strong bushy shapes against a shady wall or at the front of a bed.

In sun the hardiest of the abelias, *Abelia × grandiflora*, has an arching habit and glossy leaves with bronze autumn tints. Artemisias prefer full sun and their silvery foliage (both evergreen and deciduous) looks attractive with other greys or with conventional green. *Artemisia absinthium* 'Lambrook Silver' has silky grey divided leaves, and other prostrate artemisias cling and scramble over stone edges and low walls. *Ballota pseudodictamnus* has rounded felted leaves and if clipped in spring will make a shapely mound. Like the artemisias, ballota needs good drainage. *Bupleurum fruticosum* has blue-green glaucous foliage and makes a superb rounded bush; its valuable leaf colour is enhanced by the yellow flower umbels which hang on as decorative seed heads until the spring. *Euonymus japonicus* has shining leaves and phlomis species grey felted ones, both can be cut back hard in spring. The evergreen senecios have lax

grey foliage, and potentillas, although deciduous, look attractive in winter with brown arching stems and seed heads. Shrubby euphorbias, hebes, myrtles, lavenders and santolinas are all sun-loving, welcoming shelter from cold winds and thriving in warm gardens – ideal plants for giving structure throughout the seasons. On a very small scale heliantheums with grey-green and felted yellow foliage and thymes with aromatic leaves make rounded shapes almost at ground level.

Many herbaceous plants lack real form and structure and although they have showy flowers their foliage is undistinguished. Most are seen at their best in beds of mixed planting where shrubs give bulk and height and a feeling of permanence, but some perennials and, of course, particularly evergreen ones do have an architectural habit or sculptured leaf which makes them worth having especially when space is limited. Acanthus, bergenias, iris and *Stachys lanata* all keep foliage through most of the year while alchemilla, rodgersias, rheums and veratrums contribute in the summer season. Hostas in shade, or in sun and moist soil, have large glaucous green or variegated leaves from May until September. Macleaya, artichokes, archangelica, grey Scotch thistles and eryngiums have exciting carved leaves which are carried on high stems and immediately attract attention. Some of these are biennials which self-seed and give an unplanned and unexpected lift to a dull corner.

153 Fatsia, acanthus, hosta, geraniums and *Euphorbia robbiae* provide restful green leaves and a background to pelargoniums in pots. A honeysuckle trails down behind the statue.

Chapter Fourteen

CONTAINER PLANTING

General rules

In any garden attractive pots contribute significantly to the overall design, giving extra interest and colour as well as providing a suitable home for plants of permanent and seasonal interest. Well-made stone or terracotta containers are as important as ornament, statuary or seats, and their choice and subsequent positions should be carefully planned and thought out. Simple architectural shapes and pleasing materials are best and should blend with existing walls and pavement. In a very small town garden, and on a balcony or roof, pots may be the only place for plants to grow and imaginative arrangements help to extend the visual interest. By constantly changing and shuffling round the foreground planting you can ensure that the best is always on show. Tubs, troughs and pots of a large variety of materials and of size and shape can be grouped and regrouped as the seasons change and as some plants pass their peak the tired flowers and foliage can be hidden behind those in full flower and health.

In the country garden containers are a luxury which adds to the whole garden scheme - framing gateways, edging pavements, giving architectural interest to a vista, or simply enabling the owner to increase his range of plant types by using different varieties of specially prepared soils. There is generally more space for storage and even perhaps a small greenhouse where tender plants can be overwintered and annuals grown from seed. Extra pots can be kept to facilitate change-overs, and compost and fertilizers mixed and prepared.

Permanent shrubs and perennials can be grown alone in pots or mixed with bulbs and annuals. Formal shapes such as clipped bay trees and box, fan-shaped phormiums with sword-like leaves, yuccas and agaves with fleshy pointed foliage, will enhance your scheme and trailing and flowing plants can spill over pot edges, breaking up hard rigid lines. Obviously, formal clipped shapes need high quality containers of good design, but with soft flowing plant lines inexpensive plastic and other synthetic materials or old metal pots and troughs can be used skilfully so that the plants themselves hold the eye and the pot material is not obtrusive. In a small town garden where sunlight is very restricted pots can be moved backwards and forwards in and out of shade and sun, to suit not only the requirement of the plants but to increase the pleasure of the casual visitor as well as the owners. The pots can be built up to form a picture like a flowerbed. They can be arranged on steps, benches, or other upturned pots, to give extra height and depth to the scheme. Ugly plumbing or domestic details can be hidden and disguised by movable containers in places where permanent beds would be out of the question.

Basement front areas, backyards, balconies, roof gardens and window-boxes are all dependent on containers and these can vary from built-in and fixed raised or sunk

154   A mixture of containers planted with contrasting foliage plants turn a sunken front area into a garden for all seasons. In the summer flowering annuals will be added for colour and fragrance.

beds to decorative pots. Fixed container beds are difficult to empty and refill – essential tasks when the soil becomes old and tired – but can provide a larger space for root run. Balconies and roof gardens have the additional problems of weight. Containers can be hung on walls which then take the bulk of the extra stress, but these too are often troublesome to empty and feed.

All plant roots in pots are more vulnerable to prevailing weather extremes than when in flowerbeds. The soil, exposed to wind and sun, dries out more quickly especially at the edge of containers where the tips of growing roots are found. Excessive heat and low temperatures on balconies and roofs make extra care essential and plants need daily watering in summer and ample feeding. The extra light on a roof encourages flowering and drought-resistant annuals are most suitable, but their roots may need shading in very hot sunny periods. Roots stop functioning if the temperature around them rises above 90°F (32°C) and growth stops when temperatures fall below 42°F (6°C).

The basic care of all container-grown plants consists of adequate watering and sufficient nourishment to compensate for unnatural root restriction. The soil must be suitable for the chosen type of plant and adequate provision made for drainage. Scrupulous attention to cleanliness is necessary to prevent spread of disease and protective measures against pests should be taken to ward off infestation. Healthy plants resist disease and pests much better than sickly ones. (This is true in any small area and the plants in open beds in enclosed sunny or shady yards need similar cherishing.) All dead flowers and blemished and dry leaves must be carefully removed and dust and grease rinsed off glossy leaves. Weeds, which compete with plants for food and water, must be regularly removed and the soil kept loose and friable. When cleaning containers wash them in a solution of formalin and keep tools spotless. Fungus growths, bacterial diseases and viruses can all be treated, but a plant is inevitably set back by an outbreak. Similarly, aphids, red spider and slugs can be controlled by spraying, but preventive care is better than subsequent treatment.

Watering, nourishment and soil mixture are all interdependent. When plants get dry around the roots they cease to be able to take up nutrients and begin to wilt so watering is most important. Water from hose or can should reach the plant like gentle rain, rather than as a fierce gush which hardens the soil surface. The skill in watering comes from experience and most amateurs tend to underwater in summer, when plants are in full growth, and overwater during the winter resting period. Ideally, the temperature of the water should be the same as the surrounding temperature so that normal root functioning is not interrupted. It is best to water in the morning or evening; for very exposed sites it may be necessary twice a day. Even when there appears to be adequate rainfall the soil in containers can dry out as thick foliage prevents moisture penetrating to the soil. However, the frequency of watering also depends on the plant or plants, their age, the type of container and the soil used.

Position your containers so that the drought-resistant plants (of the type we call Mediterranean, often with grey or aromatic leaves, which withstand fierce sun and prevent excessive evaporation) will be in the sun. Tender

155 *opposite* The shape of good containers effectively enhances the plants in them. The simple lines of these terracotta pots make a striking group. The plants to the right are protected by glass.

156 *above* A variegated holly, *Ilex* × *altaclarensis* 'Lawsoniana', makes a decorative pot plant with a strong regular pyramid shape. Ilex can be used as an alternative to bay trees and will thrive in shade. (PB).

plants need protection in winter, either by fronds of evergreens (better than plastic sheeting as this allows too much heating up in hot sun followed by rapid fall in temperature as the evening air cools), or they may be moved into cool but light winter quarters, perhaps a veranda or porch with some overhead protection. A good moisture-retentive compost (see page 139 for details of suitable soil mixes) and the use of mulches such as damp peat and gravel, which keep the surface warm as well as moist, are essential. Plants such as alpines resent moisture around their crowns and gravel allows free drainage into the soil below.

Slow-acting fertilizers can be incorporated in the original soil mix, but during the growing period plants in containers need extra nutrients. After plants have been potted allow a few weeks for the roots to become estab-

lished and then use liquid diluted feeds at intervals of fourteen days during the summer. Foliage feed applied with a pressure spray from overhead is very useful; not only is it quick and easy to use but it also helps to keep leaves clean in polluted atmospheres. During the dormant period of all perennials, bulbs, trees and shrubs, no extra nourishment should be given and water should be applied sparingly. Care must be taken to ensure that there is adequate drainage and that the roots of plants do not stand in saturated soil in wet periods or during the winter months.

The material of which a container is made affects evaporation of moisture and its insulation against heat and cold. Terracotta allows evaporation, which keeps plants healthy, but the pot needs frequent watering. Plastic, on the other hand, conserves the moisture and extra care must be taken to provide good drainage. Other materials such as stone, cement, asbestos and fibreglass have varying degrees of suitability, but it is hard to beat wood for attractiveness, simplicity and for plant comfort. It needs more maintenance but initial preparation ensures a long life. Teak and oak are suitable unpainted while softer woods need priming, an undercoat and top-coat inside and out. A non-toxic preservative should be used when paint is inappropriate and varnish can be applied over a natural finish. Wooden troughs and barrels can have castors attached for easy moving.

Having decided on the pots, now choose a suitable growing medium. For most purposes a mixture of two parts sterilized loam (which is composted soil) and one part each of peat and sand, and if possible one part of well-rotted animal manure, is best. The standard John Innes Potting Compost No 3 is good for most plants and has a normal pH of about 6.5. It is possible to get ready-made mixtures for plants which cannot thrive in such high rates and the compost recommended by the Royal Horticultural Society's Gardens at Wisley has a pH of about 5.5. This is the recommended mix for plants such as camellias and is basically seven parts acid loam, three parts peat and two parts gritty lime-free sand. Bonemeal and hoof and horn are added. Loamless soils are popular where weight must be avoided, and also perlite, which is light and absorbent but prevents water-logging.

Nutrients must be given to all mixes by the addition of fertilizers and by frequent liquid feeding during growing periods. Where only annuals are grown replace the soil yearly, but when trees, shrubs and perennials are in permanent containers try to replace the top few inches of soil as often as feasible and mulch well. Fill the containers to a few inches below the rim to allow for watering and top-dressing. Crocks must be carefully laid over drainage holes which should be made at nine-inch (14cm) intervals, and for permanent planting a layer of upturned turves is then added. For plants which prefer very free drainage an additional layer of coarse sand above the crocks ensures that roots will not rest in saturated soil. It is possible to mix your own soil in the country, but in a small town garden it is much simpler to buy suitable mixes in conveniently sized bags.

157 *far left* Roses, miniature conifers and pelargoniums brighten up an austere steep staircase. More adventurous planting could be used for a more exciting effect.

158 *left* Standard and trailing fuchsias are mixed with zonal pelargoniums to give a colourful summer-flowering display. (PB).

159 *left below* A very formal and symmetrical arrangement of colourful petunias and trailing variegated ivy makes an effective scheme for a window box.

160 *below* Petunias and the silver-leaved *Helichrysum petiolatum* make a happy planting combination for pots above a front area. Neither of these plants needs frequent watering or rich feeding.

Planting straight from containers into larger pots can take place at almost any time of the year but, just as in an ordinary garden, plants like to get their roots well established before the first frosts in the autumn, and as early as possible in the spring. The optimum moment for permanent plants will depend on the special conditions in your garden as well as when a plant is available. If offered a gift of something desirable never turn it down because it is the wrong moment to move it, accept it and take a little extra trouble in settling it into a new home. Most evergreen and tender plants are much better planted out into pots in late spring. Flowering annuals should be planted in the open only when all danger of late frost is over, preferably in the last half of May. Recently, garden centres have started to offer boxes of sizeable seedlings as early as late April but these should be resisted. Cold nights prevent growth and reduce the health of a plant, the leaves turn yellow and the setback is permanent. You would do better to wait. Plant bulbs in autumn with the hardier small trees, shrubs and perennials.

In a large ornamental container a mixture of plants can be grouped together in exactly the same way as in a flower border, although additional care must be taken to ensure that all the plants thrive in the same soil mixture and need similar amounts of sun, water and nourishment. It is useless to put drought-loving petunias and grey-leaved helichrysums with large climbing plants which require much moisture. Plants requiring acid soil such as azaleas, pieris, and enkianthus all need semi-shade and adequate water.

Plants to choose

If you have a veranda, porch or wide indoor windowsill, or of course a small greenhouse, it is possible to over-winter one or two tender shrubs which, in early summer, will add a touch of exctic interest to the garden. Tender scented rhododendrons and azaleas, the fragrant white-flowered *Pittosporum tobira*, the common myrtle and

oleanders make admirable pot plants, but are normally too vulnerable to frost for all but the most sheltered gardens. Fuchsias, shrubby and herbaceous artemisias and salvias are worthwhile if a minimum of winter protection is possible. The lemon-scented verbena, *Lippia citriodora*, and the very fragrant *Trachelospermum jasminoides* make excellent growth in pots. In warm gardens the latter can be allowed to climb against a sheltered wall.

Quite large hardy shrubs can be permanently grown in tubs as long as the receptacle is at least sixteen inches (40cm) high and wide, and adequate soil and feeding is given. Root restriction leads to curtailment of ultimate size but often encourages flower, as the energy of the plant goes into forming flower heads rather than into lush vegetable foliage. In shade aucubas, camellias, *Choisya ternata, Fatsia japonica*, elaeagnus, hydrangeas, mahonias and osmanthus are all suitable and almost any vigorous deciduous shrub. Climbers such as *Hydrangea petiolaris*, the mermaid rose, and types of Virginia creeper (*Parthenocissus*) will adapt to more difficult conditions, quickly covering vertical space up the side of terrace houses. In sun evergreen shrubs such as bay, box, phillyrea, senecio and rosemary can all be clipped into quite formal outlines, while phormiums, yuccas, bamboos, and ornamental grasses provide their own elegant architectural form. Wisteria will thrive in a pot but will grow less vast. Most clematis are adaptable, although they strongly resent root disturbance.

Japanese maples such as *Acer palmatum*, 'Dissectum',

acid-loving *Pieris forrestii* and *Enkianthus* species make tabulated layers with their branches and the exotic Japanese angelica tree, *Aralia elata,* with golden and silver variegated leaf form are all possible in containers. It is always interesting to grow plants which would normally be outside the range made possible by your garden soil, even if you do have plenty of conventional bed space. Conifers can adapt themselves readily to root restrictions and are suitable for formal planting, especially for framing doorways or an entrance to a path.

Pots can overflow with trailing ivies, artemisias, variegated catmint and perennial campanulas, as well as having spring-flowering bulbs. The foliage plants will hide decaying leaves of bulbs. Tulips, hyacinths, narcissi, anemones, scillas and fritillaries and the more difficult early iris species grow happily in containers and can be left from year to year, or cleared away to provide space for summer annuals. Lilies, which flower in midsummer and onwards, look best alone. Herbaceous plants with strong foliage and attractive flowers are particularly appropriate when pots can be rearranged to bring seasonal plants into the foreground. You can choose from *Acanthus mollis* with sculptural shining

161 *opposite*   In a warm town garden oleanders will flourish in containers. *Nerium oleander* has pink or white flowers and needs plenty of water for growth. (PB).

162 *below*   *Osteospermum × ecklonis* looks most effective if planted alone in a pot. (HS).

leaves, *Alchemilla mollis,* forms of the leathery-leaved bergenias, hostas with green and variegated ribbed foliage (excellent in pots where they cannot be reached by slugs and snails), the biennial archangelica, the hardy arum, *Zantedeschia aethiopica* (requiring plenty of moisture), periwinkle of both *Vinca major* and *V. minor* forms and many cranesbill geraniums, which can be cut back after early flowering and will form new leaves and flower again in late summer. Annuals can be mixed with perennials but remember to choose plants with similar horticultural requirements.

Fragrant annuals such as petunias, pelargoniums (some with delicious scented leaves), tobacco plants *(Nicotiana)*, heliotrope *(Heliotropium peruvianum)* and night-scented stock *(Mathiola tristis)* can be planted near windows and doors. Brightly flowered ageratums, alyssum, begonias, salvias, and the white-flowered marguerites also look attractive in pots near the house. Violas and dianthus flower almost all summer. They can be mixed with soft grey-foliage plants such as helichrysums, senecios, artemisias, gazanias with grey and variegated leaves, and the blue-grey rue, *Ruta graveolens,* all of which prefer full sun and need little watering. If you have space grow annuals from seed and take cuttings of half-hardy woody plants. Remember that many of these old favourites will seed themselves in pavements and walls as well as in their containers (or neighbouring ones). Many annuals can be sown straight into their final places. Herbs can have a sunny spot near the kitchen door, either as individual plants in separate pots, which looks functional, or grown together in one large pot.

Herbaceous and annual climbers in containers can make startling growth during one season and any essential wall maintenance can be done during winter months, when the plants have been cut down. Many climbers actually prefer their roots in shade where soil is cool and moist. The golden hop, *Humulus lupulus* 'Aureus', will scramble to twenty feet (6m) and is happiest on some sort of frame. *Eccromocarpus scaber* will climb through plants or up a trellis and has orange or red flowers. Many of the large-flowered late hybrid clematis need severe pruning in February, and most like a situation where the flower head can reach full sun. *Cobaea scandens* is tolerant of some shade and the little known *Senecio scandens* is quite hardy but dies down to the ground each year. *Ipomea hederacea* loves full sun.

On balconies and around roof gardens permanent trellis provides a framework for hardy climbers and will screen from wind and excessive sun. Overhead arbours help to increase the feeling that the area is an extra room and on an open roof lessen the sensation of giddiness from space around or below. Pots can contain jasmine, honeysuckle and roses for climbing, and senecios, sun-loving hebes, potentillas, brooms, cistuses and annuals

for foliage and colour. On a shady balcony hydrangeas, osmanthus, ivies and other evergreens with variegated leaves will add interest and are little trouble.

Obviously, balconies and roof tops have more extreme temperatures than a sheltered yard and the primary consideration will be to introduce wind-resistant shrubs (even small trees) which will give protection to other planting. Pyracantha would be a good choice, with its frothy white summer flowers and red or orange autumn berries; also it adapts well to some root restriction. Varieties of *Rhus typhina,* the slow-growing *Cotinus coggyria* and cotoneasters are all suitable, and able to endure drying winds and harsh sunlight.

Permanent raised beds on roofs can be constructed of some light building material such as Thermalite concrete blocks, rendered with sand and cement and painted. Soil can be a light compost containing perlite which gives bulk but acts also as an insulator (see page 139). Leave extra space below the level of the rim for moisture-conserving mulch which will help prevent the soil drying out. If possible, use permanently fixed perforated hoses laid into rectangular raised beds, and an overhead spray system would be ideal to keep foliage and soil cool and damp. All shrubs and climbers need careful staking and tying to sturdy supports as winds will not only be strong but will come in unexpected gusts, and shallow-rooting trees and shrubs – which adapt best to containers – are easily overturned.

Window boxes generally cannot be very deep and need low-growing plants which do not obscure the light, so bulbs and annuals are most suitable. They are exposed to wind and sun but often projecting eaves and ledges prevent them getting their full share of rain. Choose good moisture-retentive soil mixtures or plants which enjoy drought conditions. It may also be a good idea to install some kind of peforated hose and drainage pipe to take off excessive moisture and to prevent dripping onto the pavement or people below.

163 *above left* An inner floral walk on the roof of a modern block of flats. Pots are raised in stages to give the maximum effect, but need frequent rearrangement and replacement to keep the display at its best.
164 *left* Specially prepared soil can be obtained for containers. Here rhododendrons, pelargoniums and herbs thrive in suitable mixtures.
165 *right* Money spent on good solid masonry as a background to planting is never wasted. Brick walls and stone flags blend together satisfactorily. (See details of plan on next page).

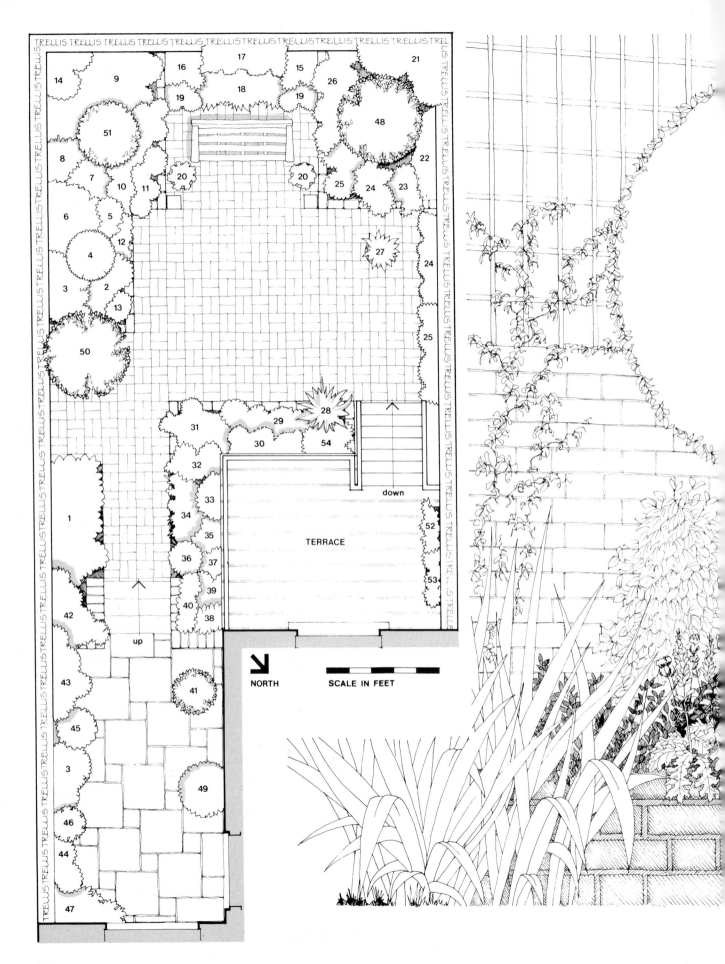

TRELLIS TRELLIS TRELLIS TRELLIS TRELLIS TRELLIS TRELLIS TRELLIS TRELLIS TRELLIS TREL

14   9   16   17   15   21

51   19   18   19   26   48

8   22

7   20   20   25   24   23

10   11

6   5   27   24

4   25

3   2

13

50

31   28

29   54

30

32

52

33

TERRACE   53

34

1   35

37   down

36

39

40

38   up

42

NORTH   SCALE IN FEET

43

45

41

3

49

46

44

47

144

A DIFFICULT TOWN GARDEN

The problems here are inherent in the plan of the maisonette which is on basement and ground-floor level and surrounded by unattractive houses. A raised terrace leads out from the kitchen and is used for eating and sitting out. The garden itself lies below but is seen mainly from the terrace and the surrounding trellis is closely covered with coloured foliage and scented climbers. Three quick-growing trees will eventually screen the adjacent houses. The paved garden is reached by descending three shallow steps below the main garden level. The illustration is an imaginary view of how the steps and surrounding plants will appear.

The focal point of the garden is the arbour covered with roses which shelters a white painted seat. This will attract the eye and invite a glance from the eating terrace above. Other planting in perimeter beds is also designed to be viewed from above. In full sun tender plants and climbers are mixed with low sprawling herbs and attractive paving holds the design together. Rectangular troughs can be fitted round the edge of the terrace and filled with summer flowering annuals.

1 *Hydrangea petiolaris*
2 *Senecio monroi*
3 *Rosa* 'Penelope'
4 *Eucryphia intermedia* 'Rostrevor'
5 *Abelia grandiflora*
6 *Actinidia kolomikta*
7 *Clematis spooneri*
8 *Weigela florida* 'Variegata'
9 *Choisya ternata*
10 *Phlomis fruticosa*
11 *Acanthus mollis*
12 *Dicentra formosa* 'Boothman's'
13 *Bergenia cordifolia*
14 *Lonicera japonica* 'Aureorecticulata'
15 *Rosa* 'New Dawn'
16 *Rosa* 'Félicité et Perpétue'
17 *Clematis orientalis* 'Bill Mackenzie'
18 Hostas, mixed
19 *Pachysandra terminalis*
20 Agapanthus Headbourne hybrids
21 *Lonicera japonica* 'Halliana'
22 *Clematis armandii*
23 *Hedera helix*, mixed and variegated forms
24 *Vinca minor*
25 *Hypericum calycinum*
26 *Cotoneaster dammeri*
27 *Yucca filamentosa* 'Variegata'
28 *Phormium cookianum*
29 *Lavandula angustifolia* 'Hidcote' (3)
30 *Jasminum officinale* 'Aureovariegatum'
31 *Ruta graveolens* (3)
32 *Teucrium fruticans*
33 *Buddleia auriculata*
34 Herb garden
35 *Eupatorium ligustrinum*
36 *Francoa sonchifolia*
37 *Prunus lusitanicus* 'Variegatus'
38 *Lilium regale*
39 *Sequoia sempervirens* 'Prostrata'
40 *Bergenia stracheyii*
41 *Laurus nobilis*
42 *Ficus carica*
43 *Viburnum farreri*
44 *Parthenocissus henryana*
45 *Hedera helix* 'Angularis Aurea'
46 *Fatshedera lizei*
47 *Euonymus fortunei radicans* 'Silver Queen'
48 *Malus floribunda*
49 *Rhamnus alaterna* 'Argenteovariegata'
50 *Acer palmatum* 'Senkaki'
51 *Cercidiphyllum japonicum*
52 *Vitis vinifera* 'Brandt'
53 Assorted pelargoniums
54 *Rosa* 'Climbing Cecile Brunner'

A SELECT LIST OF PLANTS

A

Abelia × grandiflora An evergreen shrub with glossy leaves tinting bronze in autumn. Arching branches carry pink and white tubular flowers over a long period in late summer. Height 5ft (1.5m). Underplant with variegated ajuga.

Abies koreana Slow-growing silver fir taking many years to reach 15ft (5m). Green linear leaves, silvery-green beneath. Carries bluish-purple candle-shaped cones even when young. Branches more or less horizontal, tree eventually conical.

ABUTILON Evergreen shrubs making elegant pyramids to 13ft (4m). *Abutilon vitifolium* has open saucer-shaped flowers of pale mauve. The form 'Album' is attractive in a white garden. The hybrid *A. × suntense* has clear dark mauve flowers. Both need cutting back after flowering. Good in an open situation in warm garden, but needs wall protection in cold areas. Sun or semi-shade.

ACACIA Small evergreen trees thriving in sheltered gardens, preferably with wall protection. The best and hardiest are *Acacia dealbata* with silvery green fern-like leaves, and *A. pravissima* which has strange flattened pale leaves. Both have fragrant yellow puff flowers in early spring and need sun and a well-drained soil.

ACAENA The New Zealand burr is a hardy perennial, almost prostrate in habit, and a useful foliage plant in well-drained soil. *Acaena buchananii* (1-2in: 2.5-5cm) has grey-green ferny leaves and should trail over paving or grow in cracks in stonework. *A. microphylla* (2in: 5cm) has bronze pinnate leaves with crimson burr flowers in summer.

Acanthus mollis A perennial with deeply divided green sculptural leaves to 8in (44cm). Purple hooded flower spikes in late summer. The species *A. spinosus spinosissimus* has even more finely cut leaves with silvery points. All acanthus look marvellous with stone or brickwork and in a warm garden are more or less evergreen. Should be planted on corners and look effective in pots.

ACER A very large genus of trees and shrubs, nearly all hardy and easy to grow but preferring a good acid loam.

Acer griseum grows slowly to 20ft (6m) with cinnamon-coloured peeling bark, neat foliage and decorative fruits. *A. pennsylvanicum* grows to 20ft (6m) and is an erect tree with green bark, striped white. The attractive leaves colour yellow in autumn. *A. negundo* 'Variegatum', the well-known box elder, is not fussy about soil and grows quickly to 20ft (6m). It has pale leaves with broad white border. *A. palmatum* 'Senkaki' is a smaller tree with coral-red young stems showing best in winter. Has delicate cut leaves of light green with orange tints in October. *A. palmatum* 'Dissectum' makes a rounded humped bush. Leaves very vivid in autumn. *A. japonicum* 'Aureum' is a slow-growing shrub for moist acid soil.

Achillea × taygetea A perennial with silver-grey pinnate foliage and flat heads of pale yellow, borne from June to September (18in: 45cm). Needs full sun but any soil. Useful for flower arrangements and for drying.

Actinidia chinensis A deciduous climber (30ft: 9m), not for the very small garden. Has most striking heart-shaped leaves and red hairy young shoots. Quick-growing twiner for pergolas or trellis. Flowers and fruits in hot sunny situation. *A. kolomikta* can grow to 20ft (6m) but rarely. Likes full sun and has unusual tricoloured leaves of green, creamy pink and white. A choice plant and not difficult.

AGAPANTHUS The African blue lily is an indispensable late summer flowerer for borders or containers, with blue spherical heads above strap-shaped leaves. *Agapanthus campanulatus* and its form 'Albus' grow to 2ft (60cm), and the hardy Headbourne hybrids are the best. Need full sun and rich feeding and moisture in early summer. Blue and grey borders are almost dependent on these fleshy-rooted perennials. Grow with *Caryopteris clandonensis* and ceratostigma.

AGERATUM Useful annuals for pots and window-boxes. Blue-grey flowers usually 12in (30cm) and many good garden forms. Need regular dead-heading for continuous flowering. Do not plant out until mid-May.

Ajuga reptans is an evergreen perennial bugle (4-12in: 10-30cm). Forms with exciting coloured foliage make useful edging and groundcover under shrubs, or can be grown in prostrate massed groups. 'Burgundy

146

Glow', 'Purpurea' and 'Variegata' are all attractive, the latter with pretty marbled leaves.

Akebia quinata can climb to 30ft (9m). This semi-evergreen twining plant will grow through shrubs or on trellis and has fine lobed leaves and fragrant dark purple flowers.

ALCHEMILLA The scallop-shell leaves of all alchemillas are very graceful. The best known, *Alchemilla mollis*, lady's mantle, is an invasive seeder with lime-green starry flowers in summer, and again in autumn if cut back after flowering. No garden should be without it. Thrives in sun or shade, in paving or in beds. *A. conjuncta* is much smaller and the backs of the leaves are covered in silky hairs. Lovely and spreading in a small space.

166 *Alchemilla mollis.*

ALLIUM Onions with attractive flower heads suitable for growing through low groundcover. *Allium aflatunense* has fine spherical flowers of deep lilac on 3ft (1m) stems in late May. *A. bulgarium* (syn. *siculum*) has strange creamy-green bell-shaped clustered flowers, hanging from drooping stalks. The 3ft (1m) seed heads are valuable and decorative. Grow next to strong grey-leaved hostas.

ALNUS Alders are erect conical-shaped deciduous trees which eventually grow large but are suitable for establishing the shape of small gardens. *Alnus cordata* has dark shining leaves and dark upright fruits. Leaves flutter in a breeze. Easy to grow successfully in moist soil. *A. glutinosa* is similar but with yellow catkins in March. A common native of brooksides with duller green leaves, but happy anywhere.

Alstroemeria ligtu hybrids are the most useful of the Peruvian lilies. Once established they will spread rapidly. Pale pink and flame-coloured flowers on 2ft (60cm) stalks with grey leaves. They need full sun and look good on fronts of border trailing onto stonework.

Alyssum maritimum A small self-seeding annual, branching with grey-green leaves and rounded racemes of white flowers. Quite a few improved garden forms exist with coloured pink and red flowers, but naturally seeds revert to the type, which is a charming cottage-garden type of flower.

Amelanchier canadensis A deciduous tree or large shrub growing to 15ft (5m). Profuse white flowers in spring and superb autumn leaf colour. Very easy plant for any soil.

Ampelopsis aconitifolia A twining vine-like plant with divided leaves of deep green. Uses tendrils to cling to wires or trellis (20ft: 6m). For sun or shade. *A. brevipendunculata* is a more luxuriant climber resembling hops. Very large leaves and bears blue fruits after hot summer. Its form 'Elegans' has startling variegated foliage, mottled pink and white. A little tender, but ideal for sheltered town garden as not too vigorous.

Anaphalis triplinervis A perennial with compact growth and pale grey foliage to 12in (30cm). White pearl flowers in August. Trouble-free plant for white and grey borders.

Anchusa azurea Herbaceous perennial with greeny-grey rough hairy leaves. The best forms have bright blue flowers and look splendid with grey foliage plants or in blue border. June to August flowering. Need renewing every few years. Sun and good drainage.

ANEMONE Large genus offering early spring-flowering tuberous plants and the Japanese hardy perennials which are invaluable for late summer flowers. *Anemone appenina* and *A. blanda* have blue daisy flowers on short stalks in early spring and are lovely naturalized in wild garden areas. *A. pulsatilla*, the beautiful Pasque flower, has ferny leaves, hairy flower buds and pink and mauve cup-shaped flowers. It needs dry soil and sun. *A. hupehensis*, the hardy Japanese anemones with rose-pink or white flowers on 3ft (1m) stalks, are happy in shade and multiply quickly to make large clumps.

Angelica archangelica Architectural biennial with broad divided leaves, bearing flat heads of clustered yellow-green flowers in summer (5ft: 1.5m). Seed heads are attractive. The hollow stems can be preserved in syrup.

Antennaria dioica Perennial which spreads into a prostrate mat (6in:15cm). Has grey-green leaves with small white or pink tufted flowers. Ideal for dry walls or creeping over masonry edges.

Anthemis cupaniana (18in:45cm). Makes mounds of finely cut silver-white foliage, with distinctive musk fragrance. In spring covered with white marguerite flowers. Lovely over low walls, but needs frequent trimming for tidiness.

Aponogeton distachyos A perennial aquatic plant with greeny-white flowers for an ornamental pool. Known as the water hawthorn. Plant 9 to 24in deep (23 to 60cm). Needs acid soil.

Aquilegia alpina 'Hensol Harebell' Perennial with deep blue flowers in May and June (12in:30cm). Will flower in sun or shade. Many other aquilegias are useful, including the long-spurred hybrids which are best treated as biennials.

Arabis albida Evergreen perennial (9in:23cm) which creeps and spreads over sunny wall, bank or pavement. Flowers of type are white and carried from February to June, but red garden forms exist which are less invasive.

Aralia elata, the Japanese angelica tree, rarely makes a large specimen. Its variegated forms, *A. elata* 'Aureovariegata' and *A. elata* 'Variegata', are particularly attractive, spreading sparsely branched shrubs, usually to 9ft (3m). They have huge pinnate leaves and large panicles of white flowers in late summer.

Arbutus unedo An ericaceous tree or large shrub which tolerates lime soil. Evergreen with pale young growth and white dangling pitcher-shaped flowers, followed by strawberry-like fruits. Can be pruned back hard to suit a small garden. Looks lovely against a dark background.

Arenaria balearica is an evergreen perennial making a bright green almost prostrate mat for low walls in shade. White starry flowers in late spring.

Argemone platyceras (2ft:60cm) A white crested poppy with spiny glaucous leaves and white papery flowers 2in (5cm) across. Needs full sun and well-drained soil, and will seed freely. Reputedly tender but seedlings grow quickly where they fall, and flower in same year. Very unusual and attractive.

Armeria maritima and *Armeria corsica* make tufted grassy mounds studded with typical thrift heads, about 6in (15cm). Evergreen and should be encouraged in paving and on walls. Full sun.

ARTEMISIA Mostly grown for silvery-grey aromatic foliage. Perennials, shrubs and sub-shrubs. *A. absinthium* 'Lambrook Silver' is a sub-shrub with silver-white feathery leaves (2ft:60cm), ideal for grey foliage border and lovely with pink or blue colour schemes *A. arborescens* 'Faith Raven' – hardiest form of

this rather tender evergreen wall plant – has filigree silver leaves. *A. schmidtiana,* another sub-shrub, only 3in (7.5cm) high, is suitable for well-drained position, trailing over low wall or edge of pot. *A. ludoviciana* 'Latifolia' is the best wide-leaved form of this vigorous running perennial (2ft:60cm). Attractive as grey mass in borders with agapanthus, dianthus and under evergreen cistuses. *A. stelleriana* has ovate lobed silver leaves and is prostrate, rather less rampant than *A. ludoviciana.* All need full sun and well-drained poor soil.

Arum italicum 'Pictum' has spear-shaped leaves attractively marbled in grey and cream, best in full sun, and attractive in winter (1ft:30cm).

Arundinaria nitida and *A. murielae* Excellent elegant clump-forming bamboos for shade or for containers. The former has distinctive purple stems (9ft:3m). *A. pumila* and *A. pygmaea* are dwarf grassy bamboos, ideal for groundcover.

Asperula odorata Woodruff provides charming scented groundcover for woodland to 6in (15cm).

Asphodeline lutea (3ft:1m) Stems above grey-green grassy leaves bear strap-petalled straw-yellow flowers in spring. Seed spikes are attractive. Plant in front of border in full sun.

Aster × frikartii The best aster for a small garden as it has a very long period of autumn flowering. Clear lavender-blue rayed flowers on 3ft (1m) stems. Any good soil and full sun, completely hardy.

ASTILBE. Panicles of red, pink and white feathery flowers are carried above elegant divided foliage. For moist corners in sun or shade. Innumerable good garden forms of different heights and flower and leaf colour. Lovely with hostas, rodgersias and alchemillas.

Astrantia major Perennial with tripartite divided leaves. Carries branching stems with star-like greenish-pink unusual flowers. *A. maxima* has pink flowers and there is an excellent variegated form. All grow to 2ft (60cm) and prefer moist soil. Should be planted in large clumps where the flowers can be appreciated.

Atriplex halimus Evergreen shrub with silver-grey shining leaves to 3ft (1m). Can be cut to ground each spring and shaped to make compact bush. Withstands salt winds and can be used as seaside hedge. Not tender as will always shoot from base but often ungainly in cold areas. Full sun.

Aucuba japonica This plain evergreen with shining glossy leaves is not grown often enough. In a small space it is a useful alternative to ordinary cherry laurel. The aucuba survives pollution and drought and can be grown in dark backyards. Sponge down leaves if necessary to keep glow.

Azara microphylla Very elegant tall narrow evergreen shrub with attractive leaves and fragrant vanilla-scented flowers in early spring. Grow near a window or doorway. A variegated form is exceptionally beautiful but difficult to get satisfactorily established. They prefer acid soil.

B

Ballota pseudodictamnus has attractive felted grey leaves and is an excellent low-growing evergreen shrub for sunny borders. It makes a good foil to glossy green leaves and flowers of any colour. Can be severely clipped with shears after last frosts. Hardy if good drainage and full sun.

Begonia evansiana A small hardy perennial begonia for sun or half shade. Very suitable for smaller garden with its glistening heart-shaped leaves and flesh-pink flowers from June till October. Up to 18in (45cm).

BERBERIS Genus of evergreen and deciduous prickly shrubs suitable for hedges and as specimens. Adaptable to any soil. Flowers usually pale yellow to orange, followed by showy fruit. For a small garden *Berberis candidula* makes a dense dome-shaped bush or low hedge (3ft: 1m) with bright yellow flowers and leaves with blue-white undersides. *B. darwinii* is an early flowering species with excellent shining evergreen leaves. Makes an impenetrable thorny outer hedge (5ft: 1.5m). *B. thunbergii* 'Rose Glow' is deciduous and has interesting purple leaves with silver-pink mottled variegation. Can be pruned to make dense bushy shape. *B. verruculosa* is evergreen with neat glossy dark green leaves, white underneath. An unusual berberis is *B. dictyophylla* 'Approximata' which has grey-green leaves with white bloom on them in spring, and an attractive arching habit. Unfortunately, difficult to obtain but well worth searching for. It is a smaller version of *B. temolaica,* which is equally beautiful but too large for small gardens.

BERGENIA Most useful evergreen perennial. Wonderful green shining leathery leaves for sun or shade. Useful for edging next to stone and brick and for growing as tight masses under trees or as prostrate cover in place of grass. Mainly spring flowering. The Ballawley hybrids have large rounded leaves and crimson flowers on 2ft (60cm) red stems. *Bergenia × schmidtii* is a pink-flowered hybrid growing to 1ft (30cm) and flowering in February and March. *B. cordifolia* has rounded wavy-edged leaves, burnished red in winter, and vivid purple flowers of 18in (45cm). *B. stracheyi* is a dwarf with tidy small leaves and short stems with pink or white flowers. *B.* 'Abendglut' has maroon-coloured leaves in winter, the backs of which are plum-red.

BETULA *Betula pendula,* our native birch, is as graceful as any and has silvery bark and leaves of mid-green, but all birches are important small trees which look attractive even in winter with their delicate branch tracery outline and glowing barks. *B. ermanii* (20ft: 6m) has

orange-brown bark and *B. albo-sinensis septentrionalis* pink and red bark with a glaucous bloom. Perfect trees for small space, but they dislike drought.

Brunnera macrophylla A very robust perennial for groundcover in shade. Bright forget-me-not blue flowers over coarse dark green leaves (18in: 45cm). Lovely under the grey weeping pear or pale pink roses. There is an attractive variegated form, but it is slow to spread as it needs dividing, and reverts easily to the plain green-leaved type.

BUDDLEIA A large genus. Among the best for a small area is *Buddleia alternifolia* which makes a large shrub or small tree with arching branches of narrow grey-green leaves covered in scented lilac flowers in June. Can be specimen tree or trained against wall. Prune after flowering. *B. auriculata* has leaves with white felted undersides and very fragrant flowers in winter. Needs wall protection but very worthwhile. *B. crispa* is a 6ft (2m) wall shrub with pale grey felted leaves. Pink flowers with orange throats are carried all through mid to late summer. Needs severe spring pruning and tying back to wall supports. Not tender but likes care and encouragement. Must have full sun. *B.* 'Loch Inch', one of the best August-flowering deciduous buddleias, has grey-green leaves and scented conical blue flowers. Prune in February.

Bupleurum fruticosum Excellent evergreen shrub with sea-green glaucous leaves and umbels of yellow flowers, which also make attractive seed heads. Can be pruned neatly to retain a rounded shape or tied back against a wall. Looks lovely with soft grey foliage of plants such as *Cytisus battandieri* and euphorbias. Drought resistant. A biennial *Bupleurum falcatum* is seldom seen but has attractive sickle-shaped green leaves and pale yellow cow-parsley flowers on 3ft (1m) stems for most of the summer. Seeds freely in warm sunny border.

BUXUS Evergreen shrubs with aromatic foliage revelling in hot sun and suitable for hedges and for clipping into compact shapes. *Buxus balearica* has bright green smooth leaves and makes a tall thin shrub, best against a warm wall. *B. sempervirens* has innumerable forms with varying leaf shapes and growing to different heights. *B. s.* 'Suffruticosa' is most often used as dwarf edging to 18in (45cm) for sun or shade and its variegated form is also attractive. *B. s.* 'Handsworthensis' grows taller and makes a dark dense screen to 5ft (1.5m).

C

CAMELLIA Fine glossy-leaved shrubs for woodland or for shady backyards in town gardens. Also thrive in pots if given good loam with a pH of about 5. Early spring flowers can easily be frosted. Bewildering choice of good species, hybrids and garden forms. *Camellia × williamsii* hybrids have single and double free-flowering forms suitable for any situation. The tender *C. saluenensis* has attractive smaller leaves and lovely silver-pink single flowers, and the *C. sasanqua* cultivars have scented flowers and are excellent for warm gardens and do not mind being tied back to a wall.

CAMPANULA Indispensable perennials and biennials for all gardens, where they will scramble and seed freely. All have blue (or white) harebell flowers. *Campanula carpatica* (1ft:30cm) is a perennial with bright green leaves and large cup-shaped flowers from white to dark blue. Good for border edge or any dry sunny spot. *C. garganica* makes a splendid creeping wall plant, with compact tufts and blue open-petalled flowers (3in:8cm). *C. portenschlagiana* and *C. poscharskyana* are rapid colonizers for edges and over low walls. Pale blue flowers over fresh green leaves (12in:30cm).

Campsis grandiflora is a deciduous late-flowering climber with pinnate leaves and orange-red trumpets. Usually flowers at top of supporting wall so useful round windows of upper floors (30ft:10m).

Caragana arborescens 'Lorbergii' A small shrubby deciduous tree, with graceful narrow grass-like leaves, casting little shade but making a delicate outline against the sky. Yellow flowers in early summer. Not fussy about conditions.

167 *Bupleurum fruticosum* has attractive umbels of pale yellow flowers and translucent foliage.

CARDAMINE *Cardamine latifolia* is a very useful herbaceous groundcover for moist soil around ponds. Rich green leaves and mauve flower heads (18in:45cm). *C. pratensis* 'Flore Pleno' is double lady's smock, very pretty with pale lilac flowers above deeply cut foliage (1ft:30cm). Prefers semi-shade and damp.

CAREX The golden sedges are most useful and attractive. *Carex morrowii* 'Variegata Aurea' grows to 10in (25cm) in a moist border and *Carex riparia* 'Aurea', Bowle's golden sedge, has soft grass-like foliage to 2ft (60cm).

Carpenteria californica is a sun-loving evergreen shrub with saucer-shaped white flowers, distinguished by prominent yellow anthers. Will grow to 5ft (1.5cm) against a wall. Hardier than supposed but dislikes open situations.

Caryopteris clandonensis 'Kew Blue' is the best form of a small twiggy shrub with aromatic leaves and vivid blue flowers in late summer. Useful in a blue border in hot sun, but needs regular shaping in April. Height 2ft (60cm).

CASSINA Heath-like evergreen shrubs with leaves dense and crowded. *C. fulvida* has golden foliage with white terminal flowers in July; *C. leptophylla* is more erect and has thin grey leaves and flowers a little later. Both need hot sun and severe pruning in May.

Cautleya robusta Rather exotic canna-like perennial with spikes of dark yellow flowers with maroon bracts. Long green leaves. Plant in deep moist soil in sun or shade. Height 2ft (60cm).

Carpinus betulus, the deciduous hornbeam, grows very slowly to 60ft (18m) but in the first thirty or so years will not exceed 25ft (7.5cm). Develops fine smooth fluted bark early on and a regular crown of beech-like foliage. *C. betulus* 'Fastigiata' makes a symmetrical cone-shaped small tree. Also useful for hedging and arbours.

Catalpa bignonioides, the Indian bean tree, is deciduous and grows to 25ft (7.5m). It prefers good soil which is not too dry, and a sunny and sheltered site. Large leaves appear in June followed by white flowers with yellow and purple markings, shaped like foxgloves. The golden form is popular but dominates a small garden, and is best in a hidden compartment. Very slow growing.

CEANOTHUS These evergreen shrubs all like sun and a protecting wall or warm site. *Ceanothus* 'Cascade' is hardy with bright blue spring flowers and an almost weeping habit. *C. thyrsiflorus* has paler blue flowers and an attractive prostrate form. *C. thyrsiflorus repens* is useful for a small garden growing into a dense hummock 4ft (1.2m) high and 8ft (2.4m) wide. Looks attractive in front gardens over a warm sunlit pavement. *C.* 'Burkwoodii' makes a medium-sized rounded shrub with rich dark blue flowers in late summer. Lovely with other blue flowers such as ceratostigma, caryopteris and perovskia.

Celastrus orbiculatus A deciduous climber up to 30ft (9m). Inconspicuous flowers but the brown seedpods open to reveal glistening orange-yellow and scarlet fruits. The mid-green foliage turns pale yellow to set them off.

Celmisia coriacea These New Zealand perennials need a warm garden in the south or west, but will survive low temperatures providing there are no mild spells to start premature spring growth. Attractive tuft with leathery grey pointed leaves and handsome flowers. Requires acid soil, fairly well drained, and full exposure to sun.

Centranthus ruber The common valerian has pinky-red flowers and seeds everywhere. The white form is more select. Very useful for old walls and modern pavements where masonry looks stark.

Cerastium tomentosum, snow-in-summer, very invasive but charming perennial for walls and banks (6in:15cm). Has woolly silver leaves and small white cup-shaped flowers all through May and June.

Ceratostigma willmottianum Sub-shrub for full sun. Intense bright blue flowers from July until winter over

bronze-tinted leaves. Cut back brown stems in spring. Grows to 2ft (60cm).

Cercidiphyllum japonicum A very elegant tree with pink young leaves turning to green in spring, and splendid autumn colour, varying between pale yellow and pink-red. Probably prefers moist soil, but otherwise easy to manage.

Cercis siliquastrum, the Judas tree, has rosy-pink flowers covering the branches in May, before the leaves. Rather slow growing but worthwhile. Full sun.

Cestrum parqui Another sub-shrub with a strange musky aroma from small yellow-green flowers, which are freely borne all summer onwards. Usually needs cutting down in spring and shoots from the base. C. 'Newelli' has orange-red flowers and clambers through wall shrubs.

CHAENOMELES Deciduous shrub for sun or shade. *Chaenomeles speciosa*, the old-fashioned japonica, flowers early against a wall before the leaves unfurl. As a shrub

168 *Convolvulus cneorum* in the foreground.

151

in the open makes nice spreading shape. Useful for containers in town gardens and especially for exposed roof gardens. Red, pink or white flowers. Likes sun or shade.

CHAMAECYPARIS, the false cypress, makes a useful conifer in a small garden where some regular vertical accent is needed. There are a number of good foliage forms. *C. lawsoniana* 'Ellwoodii' has grey-green leaves, *C. lawsoniana* 'Erecta' bright green, *C. l.* 'Fletcherii' blue-green and *C. l.* 'Stewartii' pale yellow to yellow-green in winter. They all grow large eventually and will have to be replaced as they get out of scale. *C.l.* 'Kilmacurragh' is very narrow and columnar with dense dark foliage – one of the best where space is severely limited and hardier than the true Italian cypress, *Cupressus sempervirens*.

CHEIRANTHUS The perennial wallflower *Cheiranthus* 'Bowles Mauve' is a very pretty mauve flowering plant with rich green leaves. Its variegated form is particularly delightful if a little tender. Grows to 2ft (60cm).

Chiastophyllum oppositifolium is a small creeping evergreen perennial with broad rosettes and yellow flowers on red stalks (6in: 15cm). Ideal for edging in sun or shade. An alternative to London pride *(Saxifraga umbrosa)* or the larger leaved bergenias.

Choisya ternata One of the most delightful, attractive and useful evergreen shrubs for sun or shade. Makes dense rounded glossy-leaved bush bearing sweetly scented white flowers in spring, and sometimes again in September (5ft: 1.5m). Tender in cold counties if exposed but most smaller gardens will offer adequate protection.

Chrysanthemum parthenium 'Aureum', golden feverfew, has pale divided leaves all year round, making golden clumps in shade or sun. Carries sprays of white daisy flowers in summer (12in: 30cm). *C. parthenium* 'White Bonnet' has double white daisy flowers and green leaves, and *C. rosmariensis* stiff narrow grey-green foliage, like rosemary, and large white flowers on long 10in (25cm) stalks. Needs full sun, in front of trough or well-drained border.

CISTUS Evergreen shrubs which revel in full sun and Mediterranean conditions. Do not feed. Many excellent species and hybrids, some with green sticky foliage, others with grey felted leaves. Lovely with grey-leaved plants, myrtle and dianthus. Hardiest is the fragrant *Cistus laurifolius* with large papery white flowers, yellow centred. *C.* 'Peggy Sannons' is of medium size, with grey leaves and pale pink flowers. *C.* 'Silver Pink' is fairly hardy and flowers all summer, and *C.* × *lusitanicus* 'Decumbens' makes a prostrate hummock 3ft (1m) wide and 18in (45cm) high. Large white flowers with crimson inner blotches.

CLEMATIS A mainly deciduous and climbing genus with many good species and hybrids. Plants to flower from early spring to late autumn can be chosen. *Clematis*

armandii is an evergreen climber with long leathery leaves – a very fast grower for town walls and trellis. White spring flowers, intensely fragrant, are carried in clusters. *C. cirrhosa balearica* flowers from December with delicate pale yellow flowers and fern-like evergreen foliage, a little tender, but will thrive in a warm corner. *C. spooneri* is a vigorous deciduous species with white flowers (a good pink form exists), ideal for covering a shed or old tree stump as it quickly makes a dense tangle of stems. *C. macropetala* has blue flowers in spring. *C.* 'Nelly Moser', a large flowered hybrid, flowers twice – in spring and late summer; flowers are of palest mauve pink with crimson stripes. *C. orientalis* has a form 'Bill Mackenzie' with drooping yellow flowers over a long autumn period. *C. flammula* is almost herbaceous, but will climb to 12ft (3.5m) making a dense mass of attractive fresh leaves and bearing panicles of white scented flowers in late summer. All prefer roots in cool shade and will happily intertwine with each other and through other climbers.

Clerodendron trichotomum A large shrub or small tree, deciduous, with fragrant white flowers in August and September, followed by bright blue berries. Not planted often enough. Very attractive with evergreen shrubs and underplanted with Japanese anemones and colchicums.

Cobaea scandens is a useful half-hardy climber with green flowers changing to violet, followed by large seedpods. Can be sown in early spring. Treat as an annual and allow to scramble over trellis, balconies, etc.

Convolvulus cneorum A small (1ft: 30cm) silverleaved evergreen shrub needing full sun and good drainage. Pink funnel-shaped buds open to pure white. A graceful plant. *C. mauritanicus* is more or less a perennial, shooting annually from the base. Lavender-blue flowers are borne above clear green leaves. Almost prostrate, sprawling over warm bricks or stone. Grow next to grey and silver plants.

Cordyline australis The hardiest of the New Zealand cabbage trees. Usually makes a single trunk with branches crowned by sword-like leaves. A purple-leaved form is a little more tender. Makes an ideal pot plant for sophisticated town gardens, otherwise best in warm counties. Plant near soft foliage plants which look splendid next to them. Older plants have large creamy white trusses in early summer.

CORNUS Mostly deciduous small trees or shrubs with elegant foliage, coloured stems and beautiful pale flowers. *Cornus alba* 'Elegantissima' has striking white-variegated leaves in summer and red stems in winter. Can be cut down in spring. *C. alba* 'Spaethii' is similar with golden-variegated foliage. *C. alternifolia* 'Argentea' is an excellent architectural shrub with tiered branches and delicate silver-variegated leaves. Grows up to 39ft (13m). *C. kousa chinensis* can be a specimen tree in small garden, white flower-bracts covering the branches in June. All prefer a good rich loam and woodland conditions of dappled shade.

Coronilla glauca is a medium-sized evergreen shrub for the warmer garden, best with some wall protection. Glaucous green leaves and pale yellow flowers in early spring, and spasmodically through the winter. Very attractive foliage and effective with *Fuchsia magellanica* 'Versicolor' and above *Convolvulus mauritanicus* and *C. cneorum*. A variegated form is a little less hardy, but the more sprawling prostrate *C. valentina* withstands low temperatures.

169 *Coronilla glauca* tied back against a wall to benefit from winter protection. (PB).

COTONEASTER Useful hardy evergreen and deciduous shrubs, usually with decorative berries. *Cotoneaster conspicuus* 'Decorus' is an evergreen, making mounds to 3ft (1m). Grow on banks and over low walls or to hide manholes and drains. White-pink flowers loved by bees. *C. adpressus* and *C. dammeri* are prostrate and creep forward over paving or up rough walling. Both have bright red berries. *C. horizontalis* makes an elegant herring-bone pattern against a shady wall or at the edge of broad steps, but can grow large. Its variegated form is much less vigorous and suitable for a limited space.

Corylopsis pauciflora is a deciduous spring-flowering shrub. Grows to 5ft (1.5m). Reputedly only for acid soil, but seems to do well in a pH of 7. Very pretty and graceful twiggy bush with fragrant primrose March flowers. Young leaf growth is pinkish. Grow *Alchemilla mollis* or omphalodes under it, and keep roots cool and moist.

Cotinus coggygria, the smoke bush, is a large shrub, best as a specimen in a small garden. Will reach 12ft (4m) in height and breadth. Smooth rounded leaves and bronze to scarlet autumn colours, particularly in *Cotinus obovatus*, an American species which has a more compact habit. Unfortunately less easy to obtain. Grow solid evergreen groundcover plants under cotinus and daylilies in foreground. A purple form of *C. coggygria* is an effective foliage plant, and blue clematis looks lovely twining through it.

CRATAEGUS Cheerful deciduous trees of about 15ft (4.5m) and easy to grow. Mostly with thorns so do not let them overhang paths. Flowers fragrant, followed by good autumn fruit. Leaves colour well too. *Crataegus crus-galli*, an old thorn, has a flat top, white blossom, scarlet fruits and red autumn leaves. *C. monogyna*, our common native thorn, has many good forms, and *C. tomentosa* has large corymbs of white flowers and handsome orange fruit.

Crinodendron hookerianum is a large evergreen shrub of 10ft (3m) with dense dark green long leaves and crimson lantern flowers in May and June. It has survived recent hard winters and is more lime-tolerant than usually stated. Basically a woodland plant, but happy against a warm wall in exposed gardens.

CROCUS Small corms, very hardy, mostly with flowers which stand up to bad weather. Any well-drained soil in sun or shade. The smaller up to 3in (7.5cm) are the best and easiest. *Crocus tomasinianus* (February) has lavender-lilac flowers and seeds everywhere. *C. chrysanthus* has some splendid garden forms, notably 'E. A. Bowles' with yellow and bronze flowers and 'Snow Bunting' with white and purple. Flowering in October is *C. speciosus*, lilac-blue with hybrids of various colour.

Cryptomeria japonica 'Elegans' is a tall bushy conifer with soft feathery foliage which goes bronze in winter. Prefers acid soil and does not grow too big.

Cupressocyparis leylandii There are many good forms of this useful hedging conifer, but it is used rather too frequently and grows so fast that it can make ugly rigid boundary lines. Very wind-resistant and thrives in any soil. Makes a perfect dense screen. Probably spoils more small gardens than it helps.

CYCLAMEN Small tuberous plants with very attractive marbled foliage and sweetly scented red, pink and white flowers. *Cyclamen hederifolium* (syn. *neapolitanum*) is seen most often, flowering in September after leaves have disappeared. Thrives in shade and pretty in broad masses around tree trunks or in woodland clearings. *C. repandum* has more rounded marbled leaves and flowers in spring, the leaves emerging later. Cyclamen species can flower in almost every month of the year, but these two seed freely and are charming when appearing spontaneously in odd shady corners. They will flourish under box hedges and in rough grass.

Cynara cardunculus, the cardoon, makes a magnificent herbaceous plant for important corner positions or for grey foliage in border of mixed planting. It is 3ft (1m) high with long silvery-grey divided leaves and luminous blue thistle heads. Full sun.

Cyperus vegetus A grassy perennial for moist soil, with tightly packed plumes of greenish flowers (18in: 45cm). Seeds prolifically.

CYTISUS All brooms love poor soil and full sun, and can manage with little moisture. The evergreen *Cytisus battandieri* is a splendid wall shrub growing to 12ft (3.5m) with silver laburnum-like leaves, very silky, and cone-shaped pineapple-scented flowers in June and July. Needs regular pruning and staking and looks attractive with roses such as 'Golden Showers', and underplanted with glossy leaves of *Acanthus mollis*. *Cytisus × kewensis* is a deciduous almost prostrate broom, covered in cream-coloured flowers in May. Very useful for falling forward over steps or paving. *Cytisus praecox* is happy in sandy soil to 3ft (1m) and very floriferous. White and yellow flowering forms.

D

Danae racemosa Small evergreen shrub with arching branches of glossy narrow leaves. Hardy but loves heat and shade. Perfect for a dark corner in a town garden and for growing in containers – the foliage looks most elegant with stone or terracotta.

DAPHNE Small evergreen and deciduous shrubs. Best-known old favourite is *Daphne mezereum* with very sweetly scented purple flowers in February (there is also a good white form) before the leaves. *D. odora* 'Aureo-marginata' has evergreen leaves with creamy margins and deliciously scented flowers in April and May. Grow in narrow border by house walls. *D. cneorum* 'Eximia' is an almost prostrate evergreen with crimson flower buds opening pink in May. Supposed to be difficult, but a great treasure and can be grown in containers. *D. × burkwoodii*, fast growing to 3ft (1m), is semi-evergreen with pale pink scented flowers. All daphnes are happy in semi-shade. None is long living.

Desmodium praestans A semi-evergreen tender shrub for the warmer gardens. Silky leaves and purple pea flowers in summer. Good for growing in containers in full sun. Height 10ft (3m) against a wall.

Deutzia chunii A deciduous shrub to 6ft (2m) with narrow willow-like leaves and attractive pink flower panicles in July. *D. setchuenensis* has similar height but is narrow and upright with flat heads of clustered white stars in July and August, later than most of the genus. Very useful in summer shrub borders and hardy in most gardens.

DIANTHUS Pinks are useful and attractive for edging and groundcover in full sun. The flowers are very sweet smelling. *Dianthus deltoides* has starry carmine flowers

170 *right* *Dicentra formosa* has feathery green-grey foliage and pink flowers.

above mats of dull green leaves. Associates well with thyme and helianthemums, seeding informally in gravel or paving. The fragrant *Dianthus* 'Swan Lake' has intensely grey leaves and 'Loveliness' is an Allwood pink with graceful lacy flowers.

Dicentra formosa has very beautiful ferny grey leaves and makes pretty groundcover under roses, needing a cool but not necessarily shady position. The forms 'Boothman's' and 'Langtrees' are particularly good with very glaucous fretted leaves and pale pink flowers. Grows to 18in (45cm). Perennial.

Dictamnus fraxinella, the burning bush, is a most attractive perennial (2ft: 60cm) with aromatic flower heads rich in volatile oil, which can be ignited on a still evening. Glossy green leaves and purple flowers. The white form is suitable for an all-white border in sun.

Dierama pulcherrimum has graceful arching stems above tufted grassy leaves. Flowers are trumpet shaped and pink-red. Looks marvellous hanging over ponds or formal water. Needs well-drained soil enriched with leaf mould. Height 2ft (60cm).

DIGITALIS The ordinary woodland foxglove is valuable in rough corners, it self-seeds (treat it as a biennial) and gives a natural air to any planting. *Digitalis lutea* has attractive yellow flowers and short stems (2ft: 60cm) and will thrive in dry shade.

Dorycnium hirsutum Evergreen hairy-leaved silver shrub growing to 2ft (60cm). Charming pink and white pea flowers followed by brown seedpods. Needs well-drained border or pot in full sun. Will seed in paving and wall cracks. Trim in May to prevent leggy growth.

171 *above* Phlomis italica, perhaps the prettiest of the genus with pale pink flowers and grey leaves. (See page 171).
172 *below left* Eucryphia glutinosa.
173 *below* Euphorbia griffithii 'Fireglow'.

Dryas octopetala An acid-loving prostrate evergreen for low walls and edges (4in:10cm). Bears white saucer-shaped flowers in June. Grow spring bulbs through it.

E

Eccremocarpus scaber Vigorous fast-growing climber with green pinnate leaves and orange or red tubular flowers. Not hardy but often shoots from the base and seeds freely in sunny gardens. Excellent for containers on balconies and roof gardens, twining among established climbers over pergolas and trellis.

ECHIUM The large species are too tender for all but the mildest areas, but the low-growing annual *Echium lycopsis* 'Blue Bedder' (18in:45cm) has pale blue tubular flowers and is excellent massed in borders or in pots during July and August.

ELAEAGNUS Useful evergreen and deciduous shrub for its foliage and sweet-smelling flowers. For the small garden is *Elaeagnus angustifolia* (6 to 12ft:2 to 4m), a semi-evergreen with silvery-grey leaves and slightly pendulous habit. *E. commutata* is a deciduous suckering shrub, very variable in height and behaviour but with sweet-smelling inconspicuous flowers in May. *E. macrophylla,* an evergreen with beautiful undulate grey-green leaves, is one of the best for hedges or screening. The hybrid *E.* × *ebbingei* is perhaps tougher, and certainly has hybrid vigour, so do not use in a restricted space. The *pungens* forms can all be cut back for hedging and there are many with good variegation on their evergreen leaves.

Enkianthus campanulatus is a very attractive deciduous shrub needing acid soil. Tabulated layered branches of up to 8ft (2.5m), lily-of-the-valley flowers in spring and brilliant autumn colours. Can be grown in pots in alkaline areas.

Epimedium perralderianum Tough evergreen perennial groundcover (15in:38cm) with yellow flowers in spring. The smaller *E.* × *rubrum* has pretty heart-shaped leaves with coral tints, rose flowers in April. Both will tolerate shade and look best planted in broad clumps.

Eranthis hyemalis, the winter aconite, needs undisturbed space in grass under deciduous trees. Sometimes difficult to establish, but best results come from transplanting quickly as flowers die back in February. Do not allow tubers to dry out. Flowers in February, or earlier, spreading to make a lemon-yellow carpet 6in (15cm) above deeply cut green leaves. Can be mown by April.

Erica carnea Lime-tolerant winter-flowering heather. Many good garden forms. Other erica species need acid loam and there is a wide choice. Personally I dislike massed heather gardens but appreciate one or two well-chosen plants. The tree heath, *Erica arborea,* needs a dry acid soil and hot sun and will grow to 12ft (3.5m); a white form is attractive and fragrant.

Eriophyllum lanatum has silvery-white finely cut leaves and orange-yellow daisy flowers in spring. Looks attractive low and spreading in a grey border. Very drought resistant.

ERYNGIUM A wonderful genus of thistle-like herbaceous plants (some are biennials) with exciting architectural foliage and blue-grey flower heads. Full sun. *Eryngium bourgatii* has deeply cut spiny leaves and white veining and blue thistle flowers (15in:38cm). *E. giganteum* is a free-seeding biennial of great beauty with metallic silver leaves, known as Miss Willmott's Ghost. Looks lovely in any garden. Grows to 2ft (60cm) or more. Good for flower arrangements and can be dried. *E. serra* has evergreen rosettes of doubly serrated leaves, stems to 4ft (1.2m). *E. variifolium*, an evergreen perennial with green and white marbled leaves, will thrive in shade.

ESCALLONIA Evergreen shrubs suitable for hedging or as specimens in small gardens. Can also be trained as wall shrubs. *Escallonia* 'Apple Blossom' is slow growing with pretty pink and white flowers. *E.* 'Donard Seedling' makes a lovely arching shrub or hedge of up to 10ft (3m); flowers are pink in bud opening white. *E.* 'Iveyii' is a very vigorous pyramid-shaped shrub for formal use and can be cut hard. Carries handsome white panicles of flowers in July and August. The tender *E. bifida* has large glaucous leaves and white panicles in late summer. Good wall shrub in warm gardens.

EUCALYPTUS Gum trees are mainly for warm areas but wind protection in small gardens will give them a good start. They are very fast-growing evergreens and often shoot from the base if damaged in a hard winter. Juvenile foliage differs from mature foliage, but if specimens are kept cut back and bushy the paler early foliage is maintained. *E. nicholii* makes a very elegant small tree with narrow delicate leaves of pinky grey. *E. glaucescens* is one of the hardiest with glaucous leaves and attractive bark. *E. gunnii* – hardy with round juvenile leaves changing to a thin strap-shape when mature – is most often grown but can get very large (45ft (14m) in ten years). Less exotic in a country garden is the green-leaved *Eucalyptus subcrenulata* which is hardy and can make an attractive and unusual hedge.

EUCRYPHIA are all highly ornamental shrubs of regular outline. Most prefer acid soil and like warmth and wet. Very successful in town gardens. *Eucryphia glutinosa* is a deciduous shrub of 10ft (3m) or more for acid loam, flowering very freely in August. White flowers 2in (5cm) across with yellow stamens. *E.* × *intermedia* 'Rostrevor', an evergreen with fragrant yellow-centred white flowers in August, will tolerate lime. *E. milliganii* is a tender but delightful miniature, making small shrubby tree, very floriferous even at an early age. Leaves, flowers and habit are on a scale suitable for town gardens and containers. All prefer shade.

EUONYMUS Evergreen and deciduous shrubs. *Euonymus fortunei radicans* is a trailing or climbing shrub with good variegated leaves making a dense mound in shade. *E.*

japonica makes one of the best evergreen hedges for seaside and town planting and has many excellent leaf forms which maintain their good colour and condition in winter. Most of the deciduous species grow rather large for restricted space, but have brilliant autumn colour and attractive orange-red fruits.

Eupatorium ligustrinum (3ft: 1m) Evergreen shrub from Mexico which is best against a warm wall but surprisingly hardy. Attractive glossy leaves and flat heads of small white daisy flowers from summer to late autumn. Loved by butterflies and likes rich feeding in early summer. Easy to grow from cuttings.

EUPHORBIA Most spurges have decorative foliage and lime-yellow flowers. For the smaller garden the forms of *Euphorbia wulfenii* with linear blue-green leaves (splendid in winter) and yellow flower spikes in spring are best. Makes a very architectural shrub. Height up to 3ft (1m). Seed not necessarily true but seedlings are useful in odd sunny corners where they fall. *E. robbiae* is an evergreen runner for shade, known as Mrs Robb's Bonnet, with lime-green flowers in spring. Dead heads need cutting off in summer. *E. griffithii* 'Fireglow' is a hardy perennial with brilliant orange-red flowers in spring. Suitable for a dark corner but dislikes drought. Good with the suckering *Elaegnus commutata* or *Senecio* 'Sunshine'. *E. mellifera*, a tender shrubby evergreen spurge growing to 5ft (1.5m) with brown scented flowers in May, is a very valuable foliage plant, which can be damaged in hard winters but generally shoots again from ground-level. *E. myrsinites* has fleshy glaucous leaves and is prostrate – ideal for warm border edges, raised beds and containers. Needs well-drained soil and full sun. A valuable addition to a small garden.

F

Fabiana imbricata Attractive evergreen heath-like shrub with small tubular white flowers needing well-drained almost neutral soil in full sun. A prostrate form has violet flowers and seems more vigorous than the type, sprawling happily over pavement and down dry banks.

Fatshedera lizei Bigeneric cross between fatsia and ivy (hedera). Splendid for north wall when space too restricted for the former and very tolerant of air pollution. Suitable for containers. Leaves are leathery and palmate.

Fatsia japonica Handsome large evergreen shrub with glossy palmate leaves giving exotic tropical effect. Needs shade and will tolerate poor town conditions. White flower heads in October.

Feijoa sellowiana Useful evergreen with grey-green leaves and crimson and white flowers. Edible fruit in very warm situations. Attractive bush which can grow large but responds to cutting. Full sun.

Felicia amelloides, the blue marguerite, is tender but will survive mild winters and is ideal for growing in pots either as an annual or if brought into cold greenhouse.

Nice bushy shrub (18in: 45cm) with sky-blue flowers from June to August.

FERULA The giant fennel, *Ferula communis gigantea*, has dark green finely cut foliage and a long stalk of up to 10ft (3m). Bears yellow flower umbels in summer. Sounds unlikely for small garden, but it does not flower every year and is so striking it is worth attempting, and its foliage makes it valuable.

Festuca glauca (9in: 23cm) Tufted grey grass, rather bristly, but useful for massed groundcover instead of grass in open area or sunny bank. Equally attractive in grey foliage border.

Ficus carica, the common fig, makes a stately large shrub trained against a wall or a small specimen tree in poor soil. Handsome lobed leaves, untidy as they fall in autumn. Needs full sun to bear fruit. *F. pumila*, a tender climber for very warm gardens in shade, will cling to stone work. Evergreen.

Filipendula ulmaria, the ferny-leaved meadow sweet, is a perennial for damp areas carrying drooping panicles of fluffy cream flowers (30in: 75cm). There are variegated and golden-leaved forms for extra interest.

Fragaria vesca 'Variegata' Wild strawberry plant with splendid healthy variegated foliage of vivid green and cream, almost evergreen. Makes attractive contrast below green, grey or purple leaves. Provides thick groundcover.

Francoa sonchifolia is a hairy-leaved perennial which has graceful wands of small white to pink flowers above the deeply lobed dark green leaves (2ft: 60cm). Almost evergreen clumps spread quickly. In warm counties it can be used as groundcover under roses. In the north and east some protection in winter may be necessary. Francoas make elegant plants for pots. The form 'Bridal Wreath' is the one most easily obtainable. Seeds freely.

Fremontodendron californicum Striking tender wall shrub with three-lobed evergreen leaves. Trained flat against sunny wall it will bear large yellow single flowers throughout summer.

Fritillaria meleagris A small fritillary for naturalizing in grass (12in: 30cm) with delightful hanging bells of speckled mauve or white. More tender species can be grown in well-drained soil in troughs or warm town gardens.

FUCHSIA Tender fuchsias are very decorative in pots, and can be left as bushes or trained as standards. The hardy *Fuchsia magellanica* 'Versicolor' is a spreading deciduous shrub with creamy-white and grey leaves and red flowers. The form *F.m.* 'Alba' has fresh green foliage and palest pink flowers. *F.* 'Sharpitor' has similar pale flowers and light green and white leaves, and is particularly useful in pots. These and other hardy bush fuchsias are cut to the ground each year. Full sun and plenty of water in summer.

G

GALANTHUS The snowdrop *Galanthus nivalis* loves shade and many excellent forms exist. *G. elwesii* flowers in January with single white flowers, deep green on inner petal. The double form is pretty too. Very undemanding genus and space should be found for some representative.

Galega officinalis Old-fashioned goat's rue. Perennial. Charming white or pale lilac pea flowers are carried on 3ft (90cm) stalks. Leaves pinnate. Makes useful clump and needs no staking.

Garrya elliptica 'James Roof' is a large evergreen shrub for a north aspect but can be trained back against a wall. Long grey-green catkins are borne on male plant. *G.* × *thuretii* is a very attractive foliage shrub with dark glossy leaves. Wind resistant. Could be a useful specimen in the smaller garden.

Gaultheria procumbens Acid-loving evergreen shrub for groundcover in shade, suppressing all seedling weeds. Decorative bright red fruits are borne after white lily-of-the-valley flowers. *G. shallon* is a taller shrub (4ft: 1.5m) for woodland.

GAZANIA Tender perennials to be treated as annuals except in the warmest gardens. Neat clumps of grey leaves (also a variegated form) with mainly orange-yellow bright daisy flowers. Can be grown from seed or autumn cuttings, and kept under glass until May. Must have full sun.

Genista lydia Small deciduous broom with pendulous branches covered with yellow flowers in May and June. Prefers acid sandy soil. *G. aetnensis* is much larger and could be a specimen bush, flowering in July and having elegant airy shape.

GENTIANA Find space for some gentians as their blue trumpet flowers are most attractive. *Gentiana acaulis* has brilliant blue flowers in May and June over glossy leaves (3in: 7.5cm). *G. septemfida* has lanceolate leaves and clusters of dark flowers in July and August (9in: 23cm). *G. asclepiadea* is taller with willow-like leaves and prefers moist soil. None of these is fussy about soil but others such as *G. sino-ornata* must have lime-free loam.

174 *above* Geranium renardii.
175 *below left* Hebe andersonii 'Variegata' has violet flowers and attractive leaves.
176 *below* Hosta sieboldiana in full flower. Its leaves stand out among herbaceous plants.

GERANIUM The hardy cranesbills are indispensable perennials offering a wide choice of flower and leaf colour, and suitable for very varied situations in sun or shade, in rockery or in border. They flower very freely in summer. Among the best are *Geranium endressii* 'Wargrave Pink' with bright green leaves (18in:45cm) and pink flowers. *G.* 'Johnson's Blue' has divided leaves and lavender flowers with dark veining (12in:30cm), *G. macrorrhizum* light green aromatic leaves and pink-red flowers for sun or shade. Good groundcover under roses, sea buckthorn, the grey weeping pear, etc. *G. nodosum* will thrive in very dense shade and has mauve flowers and glossy leaves. *G. psilostemon* (syn. *armenum*) is a wonderful tall (4ft:1.2m) plant with dark-centred magenta-crimson flowers. Lovely with hostas. *G. renardii* has silvery-green foliage forming compact (12in:30cm) domes and white flowers with violet veins. Needs full sun and warmth. *G.* 'Russell Prichard' with good bright pink flowers is useful for front of border. Plant near alstromerias. *G. sanguineum* makes small clumps 9in (23cm) high with wide crimson flowers. *G. cinereum* 'Ballerina' is very small, with lilac-pink flowers with dark red veins and centre. Needs full sun and well-drained soil. Very pretty in raised beds.

177 *Verbascum bombyciferum*. (See page 182.)

178 *Viburnum davidii* with its turquoise fruits in winter. (See page 182.)

Ginkgo biloba Unusual deciduous conifer with strange fan-shaped leaves turning pale yellow in autumn. The fastigiate form is most suitable where space is limited.

Gladiolus byzantinus Spreading hardy miniature-flowered gladiolus of great charm. Flower spikes are wine-red in June, above grassy foliage (24in: 60cm). Allow to form casual clumps in narrow borders or among deciduous shrubs.

Glaucium corniculatum, the crimson-flowered horned poppy, has deeply cut grey downy leaves, and is almost prostrate, like *Glaucium flavum*, which has yellow flowers. Both behave like annuals and seed freely *in situ*.

Gleditsia triacanthos Light green pinnate leaves carried on spiny branches make this an attractive foliage tree. The form 'Sunburst' has golden leaves. Both give light shade and are slow growing, up to 20ft (6m). Good town trees.

Grevillea rosmarinifolia Tender Australasian shrub for acid soil. Grows to 3ft (1m) and has splendid crimson flowers in May above strong green linear leaves. Needs moist position with good drainage.

GRISELINIA In mild coastal gardens the evergreen *Griselinia littoralis* will make an attractive small tree with its shining apple-green leaves. More usually it is an eye-catching hedge or neat shrub of up to 6ft (2m). If possible grow it against a dark background and underplant with hellebores, hostas and *Vinca minor*. Variegated forms are less hardy.

GYPSOPHILA The hardy gypsophilas make charming late summer flowering perennials for fronts of borders. They carry a froth of white flowers above grass-like leaves. *G. paniculata* grows to 3ft (1m). Smaller species creep and hang over warm walls.

H

Hacquetia epipactis Small sulphur yellow flowers above attractive wedge-shaped green leaves in early spring (6in: 15cm). Thrives in shade. A choice perennial.

Hakonechloa macra 'Albo-aurea' has soft ribbon or grass-like leaves of vivid variegated gold stripes. Prefers moist shade. A very attractive plant. Grows to 12in (30cm).

Halimiocistus sahucii makes a low wide-spreading bush smothered in white flowers throughout June and July. Evergreen and hardy.

Halimium ocymoides Hardy compact evergreen shrub related to cistus and helianthemum, with narrow grey leaves and bright yellow flowers with dark eyes. A useful shrub for the grey border in full sun.

Hamamelis mollis, the deciduous Chinese witch hazel, flowers from Christmas until late March. The fragrant spidery yellow flowers are attractive. Leaves turn yellow in October. *H. mollis* 'Pallida' has less showy pale flowers. Rather large for small area but scents the garden for many months. Underplant with evergreens such as *Pachysandra terminalis,* which also prefers acid soil. Can be grown successfully in pots and treated like camellias.

HEBE Evergreen shrubs from New Zealand especially suitable for seaside planting, exposed roof gardens and sheltered sites where temperatures do not drop very low. There are many species and garden hybrids of variable hardiness. Most flower over long summer period and all have attractive foliage. *Hebe albicans* (2ft: 60cm) makes a dense rounded shrub with glaucous leaves and 2in (5cm) long white racemes, fairly hardy. *H. × andersonii* 'Variegata' has attractive variegated cream-green leaves with lavender-blue flowers from July into winter (3ft: 1m), and *H.* 'Autumn Glory' dark green leaves on purple stems with violet flowers in late summer (3ft: 1m). *H.* 'Great Orme' is fairly hardy and has dark green leaves and pink flowers in erect spikes (4in: 10cm) from May to July. *H. hulkeana* grows to 4ft (1.3m) and is very attractive with shining leaves and pale lavender flowers in May and June. Needs a warm wall. *H. macrantha* has leathery hard small leaves and white flowers (2ft: 60cm). *H. pinguefolia* 'Pagei' has a height of 9in (23cm) and a spread of 3ft (1m). Makes a useful sprawling shrub with its grey-silver leaves and small white flowers. Will also make groundcover in sun and can be grown over the edge of pots or raised beds. *H. rakaiensis* (syn. *subalpina*) has hard leaves on dark stems and freely borne white flowers, very hardy. Many other good hebes can be chosen depending on site and suitability.

HEDERA All ivies make attractive evergreen foliage either on a wall or as groundcover for sun or shade, thriving in poor soil and unpromising circumstances. Ideal as massed planting on awkward banks. *Hedera canariensis* 'Gloire de Marengo' has large pale variegated leaves and needs full sun. *H. colchica,* the large-leaved Persian Ivy, is rather hardier and undemanding and the form 'Paddy's Pride' has beautiful yellow and pale and dark green markings on the leaf. Twines round pillars or creeps along the ground. There are many forms of *Hedera helix,* including *H.h.* 'Green Feather' with shining digitate leaves, *H.h.* 'Buttercup' with golden leaves, and *H.h.* 'Glacier' with almost white variegation. It is best to use one distinct form in a small garden and not dot different colours about. Very useful for edges of beds and pots and for diguising broken masonry.

HELIANTHEMUMS These evergreen dwarf shrubs are sun lovers and need well-drained soil. Will seed freely in gravel and paving joints. Flower colours range from orange and white to red and pink. Leaves are plain green or silvery. Excellent for giving flowering profusion in the smaller sunny garden. Named forms of *Helianthemum nummularium* will not be true from seed but it is well worth starting with a few of the best ones.

HELICHRYSUM Evergreen shrubs with grey and silver

aromatic foliage. *H. petiolatum* is usually treated as an annual but will live through mild winter. Has grey felted leaves and cuttings are easy. Looks lovely in pots, and falling over edges. Plant with tobacco flowers in new garden while waiting for permanent planting to grow together. *H. serotinum*, the curry plant, is a dense dwarf shrub with narrow silver leaves carrying a strong aroma of curry.

Helictotrichon sempervirens Arching grey-blue grass for a foliage border (3ft: 1m) in full sun. Graceful in pots and drought resistant.

Heliotropium × hybridum, the scented cherry pie, is a very attractive summer bedding or pot plant with dark or pale violet flat heads of tiny flowers above grey-green leaves. Good for foliage border or in pots. Can be grown as a standard. Mix it with half-hardy *Salvia patens*, using the pale and dark blue forms of this plant.

HELLEBORUS Winter-flowering evergreen and deciduous perennials. Choose forms of the Lenten lily, *Helleborus orientalis*, for a shady corner. Flowers from February to April with variable colours of pale cream to warm purple. Seeds freely and hybridizes with neighbouring hellebores. *H. argutifolius* (syn. *corsicus*) has three-lobed evergreen prickly-edged leaves and bears clusters of pale green cup-shaped flowers in February. Grow under deciduous shrubs and feed well for best results.

Helxine soleirolii Half-hardy creeping evergreen perennial for cracks and joints in stonework, especially in cool shade around ponds and fountains. The round green leaves form dense mats. Now correctly called *Soleirolia soleirolii*, but the common name is curse of Corsica or mind-your-own-business.

Hemerocallis flava is a small daylily with pale yellow fragrant flowers above grass-like leaves (2ft: 60cm). It and the old-fashioned *H. fulva* 'Flore Pleno' with orange scented flowers will thrive in semi-shade, not too dry.

Heracleum mantegazzianum, the immense cow parsley, a biennial with very handsome divided leaves and cartwheels of small white flowers. Can be summer feature in small garden, but do not allow to seed.

Hesperis matrionalis, the sweet rocket, a very pretty perennial or biennial plant (2–3ft: 60–90cm). Bears spikes of white, mauve or purple flowers above dark green leaves. Delicious scent in the evening. A double sweet rocket is also desirable. Plant in sun.

Heuchera sanguinea Evergreen perennial of up to 12in (30cm) with rosettes of attractive marbled leaves forming clumps and bearing sprays of light pink flowers from June onwards. Many modern hybrids and varieties. Thrives in semi-shade and good for edging.

Hippophae rhamnoides A very invasive deciduous tall grey-leaved shrub but useful as spiny barrier at end of garden. Very decorative berries in winter.

Hoheria sexstylosa Evergreen pyramid-shaped shrub, excellent against walls or could be a specimen in small garden. Lovely subtle white flowers in late summer. The deciduous *H. glabrata* has pale green leaves and is covered in large white flowers in June and July. Hot sun for best effects.

Holcus mollis 'Variegatus' Small running variegated grass, cream and green (6in: 15cm).

HOSTA Genus of useful foliage plants for country or town garden, thriving in pots in shade or in moist woodland. Leaves very variable from broad corrugated grey-green in the largest hosta, *Hosta sieboldiana*, to small lanceolate green and white. White or pale lilac flowers. If space permits plant in clumps as massed effects are very beautiful. Protect from slugs in spring. Variegated forms are desirable, but it is impossible to be specific as so many new hybrids and forms are now available.

Houttuynia cordata is a hardy perennial for cool moist places. Can be invasive but ideal for watersides, mixing well with astilbes and rodgersias. Only 12in (30cm), with greeny-bronze leaves and white flower heads. A double form is attractive.

Humulus lupulus 'Aureus' Needs full sun to get the best glowing colour. A twining perennial climber it grows to 20ft (6m) in one season. Most useful for pergolas, balconies and roof gardens as can be grown in containers (indeed this is advisable to restrict root spread).

HYDRANGEA Another large genus. Most species prefer some shade and moisture, but are nevertheless very useful in pots. The desirable climber *Hydrangea petiolaris* will self-cling on north or east wall, and has lovely corymbs of dull greenish-white flowers in June. *H. villosa* will flower best in full sun, and its pink-lilac flowers look lovely in an autumn border with clerodendron and Japanese anemones. *H. quercifolia* has rich foliage, bronze tinted in autumn, and trusses of white flowers in August and September. It and the large *H. paniculata* look perfect above flat groundcovers. All *macrophylla* types prefer acid soil but rich feeding will satisfy most hydrangeas.

HYPERICUM The low-growing evergreen *Hypericum calycinum* is useful as well as pretty, covering the ground rapidly and making a 12in (30cm) green carpet, with pale yellow flowers in summer. Trim with shears in spring. *H. × inodorum* 'Elstead' has beautiful red fruits in late summer. *H. olympicum* 'Citrinum' makes a 6in (15cm) cushion with grey leaves and large pale yellow flowers in full sun, in gravel or raised bed. Associates with helianthemums and small campanulas. *H. × moserianum* 'Tricolor' has green, white and pink variegated leaves, grows to 18in (45cm), and needs full sun to retain leaf colours.

161

Hyssopus officinalis Hardy perennial (18in:45cm) with aromatic narrow leaves and purple-blue lobed flowers carried in whorls around the stem. Can be used as ornamental hedge, or plant in grey border.

I

Iberis sempervirens A hardy perennial sub-shrub with good dark green foliage and heads of dead white flowers in May and June. 'Little Gem' is a dwarf but spreading cultivar.

ILEX For garden design the evergreen holly has many uses. Can be grown as upright columns or used for formal clipped hedges. Forms of *Ilex × altaclarensis* and *I. aquifolium* have almost toothless glossy leaves, some green and some with florid silver or gold variegation which maintains colour even in deep shade. *I. cornuta* and *I. crenata* are very slow growing and best for connoisseurs; and *I. perado* has flattened exotic leaves for position as a specimen in shrubbery.

IMPATIENS The half-hardy annuals are useful for quick and colourful summer effects in new empty gardens and for mixing in containers. Many bright new forms of *Impatiens holstii* grow to 9in (23cm) or more.

Indigofera gerardiana (now *I. leterantha*) A deciduous sub-shrub for a sunny border. Elegant grey-green pinnate leaves appear in May, or even as late as June, followed by rose-purple flowers from July to October (5ft: 1.5m). Good for late border near nerines. Plant spring bulbs around base as growth starts so late.

IPOMOEA The morning glories are grown as climbing annuals. They have heart-shaped green leaves and blue-mauve to purple flowers. Full sun and shelter.

179 *Ilex × altaclarensis* 'Lawsoniana' has green leaves with central yellow splashes. The leaves become almost spineless as the plant develops. (PB).

IRIS A huge genus varying from the useful German flag iris with lovely coloured flowers and sword-shaped leaves to small bulbous species for choice positions. The former are grown from rhizomes and need full sun. Innumerable garden varieties are available. *Iris pallida* has forms with pale blue flowers and silver or gold variegated leaves, very useful for full sun. *I. pumila* is a dwarf species for restricted space. The Japanese *I. kaempferi* and *I. laviegata* need a moist site, the latter has attractive variegated leaves. For a hot bed with very poor soil plant the Algerian iris, *I. unguicularis,* which will flower all winter with soft lavender flowers above strap-shaped leaves.

180 *left* *Ilex aquifolium* 'Ferox', the hedgehog holly, makes a stiff prickly hedge, almost impenetrable to animals and children. (PB).
181 *below* *Iris laevigata.* (PB).

Isatis tinctoria The common dyer's weed or woad plant. Biennial with glaucous rosette of leaves and erect racemes of clustered pale yellow flowers. Will seed readily in cracks. Delicate.

Itea ilicifolia Thrives in sun or half-shade and can be trained against a wall. Evergreen glossy holly-like leaves and splendid pale yellow catkin flowers in late summer make this shrub very attractive and desirable. Underplant with astrantias, shining bergenias or with grey foliage plants.

J

JASMINUM The evergreen shrub *Jasminum humile revolutum* is hardy and can be grown free-standing in a shrub border. Carries bright yellow flowers in summer. *J. officinale* is a deciduous climbing plant for a warm sunny wall or trellis with very sweetly scented flowers. Good variegated forms are attractive and rather less vigorous. *J. × stephanense* is a most delightful climber with fragrant pink flowers. All jasmines do well in pots.

JUNIPERUS The juniper has several prostrate forms as well as upright columnar forms which do not grow too vast. Aromatic foliage varies from green to yellow, grey and steel blue, but in general the plain green colours are quietest in a restricted space.

K

Kalmia latifolia A rhododendron-like evergreen shrub for acid soils, revelling in heat and moisture. Has saucer-shaped bright pink flowers in clusters in June. Can be grown successfully in pots in specially prepared lime-free soil.

Kerria japonica 'Variegata' A low-suckering form of the single-flowered deciduous kerria with attractive pale leaf variegation and pale yellow flowers. Grows to 2ft (60cm).

182 The single form of *Kerria japonica*. (HS).

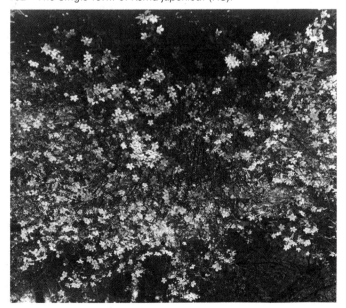

Kirengeshoma palmata Japanese perennial growing to 3ft (1m) with arching dark stalks and yellow bell flowers in September. Needs moisture and prefers acid soil, in sun or shade.

Koelreutria paniculata Deciduous small tree with pinnate leaves, pink on opening turning yellow in autumn. Bears yellow flower panicles in August, then bladder-like fruits. Must have sun to thrive and flower, but makes a splendid crown in any case.

Kolkwitzia amabilis 'Pink Cloud' is the best form of the deciduous beauty bush. Dense twiggy medium shrub for full sun. Drooping branches are covered in bell-shaped pink flowers in May and June. Prune after flowering. Associates with alchemilla and pale yellow *Hemerocallis flava*.

183 *Kolkwitzia amabilis* 'Pink Cloud'. (PB).

L

LABURNUM Small to medium deciduous trees which thrive under almost any conditions. Bright yellow flowers in May. The Scotch laburnum *L. alpinum* makes a better tree than the common *L. anagyroides* and flowers two weeks earlier. Can be trained for arbours.

Lamium galeobdolon 'Variegatum' is a very vigorous dead nettle for groundcover in shade. Not altogether suitable for smaller gardens but could be useful for dry shady corner. *L. maculatum* has marbled greeny-grey and white leaves and dull mauve flowers, but its pink and white forms are attractive and less invasive. All can be grown effectively as flat cover inside box-edged beds. *L.m.* 'Beacon Silver' has silvery-grey leaves and is excellent dwarf cover for shade.

LATHYRUS Perennial sweet pea very useful for odd rough corners. Can be trained up sticks, over stumps or down banks. The white flowered form is more attractive than *L. latifolius* itself which has muddy mauve-pink flowers. The perennial *L. vernus* (9in : 23cm) has pleasant purple and blue flowers in spring.

Laurus nobilis, the bay laurel, is an evergreen pyramidal shrub with culinary aromatic foliage. Can be clipped

into shapes but also makes a useful hedge in warm gardens. Very attractive grown in pots but must have regular feeding and soil changes.

LAVANDULA Indispensable aromatic shrub for full sun. *Lavandula angustifolia* 'Hidcote' has grey leaves and dark flower heads, making a low (2ft: 30cm) hedge. *L. angustifolia* 'Loddon Pink' has unusual pale pink flowers and the form 'Nana Alba' is dwarf with white flowers. A very tender lavender, *L. lantana*, has white woolly leaves (semi-evergreen) and bright violet flowers. *L. stoechas*, the French lavender, has very aromatic leaves and strange terminal flower heads of dark blue. All need cutting back after flowering. Keep the heads to make lavender bags.

Lavatera bicolor Half-hardy shrubby mallow for warm gardens or for pots. Has attractive pale and dark mauve flowers. *L. trimestris* (2ft: 60cm) is an annual for borders or tubs, with lovely white and rose flowering forms.

LEPTOSPERMUM A genus of slightly tender evergreen shrubs for coastal or sheltered gardens. The most attractive ones have grey leaves and white flowers. *Leptospermum lanigerum* has very silvery foliage (6ft: 2m) and white flowers, and *L. grandiflorum* is similar with flowers 3in (7.5cm) across. Lovely in sunny borders and with other grey-leaved plants or with *Acanthus mollis*.

LIGUSTRUM The common privet is despised because it is often seen at a disadvantage battling with poor conditions and neglect, but it is in any case inferior to *Ligustrum ovalifolium*, especially the golden and silver forms. Better still as a free-standing shrub or small tree is *L. lucidum*, an evergreen with dark leaves and panicles of white flowers in August.

LILIUM A marvellous genus requiring sharp drainage and cool root run. Most prefer acid soil although the madonna lily, *Lilium candidum*, thrives in alkaline conditions. For the small garden lilies are probably best grown in pots which can be sunk in beds or moved

184 *left* Lamium galeobdolon is useful for groundcover in deep shade. (HS).

185 *above* Ligustrum lucidum, one of the best small trees for town gardens. (HS).

about as the flowers appear. Most are expensive but worthwhile for their exotic scent and beauty. It is probably best to have lilies in flower and full fragrance at the time of year you are most in your garden, rather than try to cover the whole flowering season from June to September. Use a good soil mixture such as John Innes No 2 and stick for simplicity to stem-rooters which are easiest in pots. 'Cinnabar', 'Destiny' and 'Enchantment' are all mid-century hybrids with upright flowers, maroon-red, soft yellow and nasturtium-red respectively. By the end of July, *L. auratum platyphyllum* is in flower – white large petals with distinctive golden rays – and different forms will continue until September. The scented Turk's caps, *L. speciosum* (and forms), with large pink-white bowl-shaped flowers are half-hardy and should be kept in a cold greenhouse during the worst of winter. They need acid soil. Others, of course, like *martagon* and *regale,* will often thrive and even increase given a good loam and shade for roots but their unpredictability makes pot culture a better bet.

Limonium latifolium, sea lavender, forms a perennial rosette of downy green leaves with wiry branching stems holding panicles of tiny lavender-blue flowers from July until September (24in: 60cm).

Liquidambar styraciflua, sweet gum, is a deciduous tree, eventually tall but growing slowly, and handsome when young. The fresh green leaves are like those of a maple (but alternate not opposite). Often grown for autumn tints but individual trees vary in this respect and can be disappointing. They like good loam.

Liriope muscari are useful evergreen groundcover plants for sun or shade. Broad grassy leaves and mauve-lilac flower spikes of 12in (30cm). A slightly tender variegated form is very attractive in full sun.

186 *Liriope muscari* is a useful carpeter. Its variegated form is prettier but not so hardy. (HS).

Lithospermum diffusum Semi-evergreen low groundcover for sunny rockeries. Needs acid soil but likes good drainage. *L. diffusum* 'Grace Ward' has large bright blue flowers. Excellent for falling over edges and low walls.

LOBELIA The blue bedding *Lobelia erinus* is useful for odd sunny corners or for mixed planting in pots. True perennial lobelias include *L. cardinalis* with bronze foliage and scarlet-lipped flowers, prefering moist soil. Plant in drifts for vivid impact (3ft: 1m). A little tender.

Lomatia myricoides Small (6ft: 2m) spreading evergreen shrub thriving in warm gardens, in sun or shade. White flowers are very fragrant. Should be seen more often, especially when underplanted with variegated hostas, variegated pachysandra or with thick planting of *Brunnera macrophylla* or omphaloides. Needs an acid soil and a warm garden.

LONICERA For the smaller garden choose honeysuckle carefully to get flower and scent. The rampant *Lonicera japonica* 'Halliana' is very fragrant, flowering over a long period in summer, and with the evergreen *L. japonica* 'Aureorecticulata' is most useful for covering and screening. The latter, which can be grown to climb in shade or as a mound in a border or down over a low

wall, has a network of golden variegated leaves. *L. × brownii* 'Fuchsoides' is the scarlet trumpet climbing honeysuckle, up to 10ft (3m). *L. nitida* 'Baggesens Gold' is an excellent foliage evergreen shrub for a dry bed in shade.

LUNARIA Honesty is still a favourite old-fashioned biennial which gives an air of maturity to a garden. A white-flowered form and one with variegated leaves come true from seed and are worth searching for.

187 *above*   *Lunaria rediviva*, a perennial honesty, in flower. (PB).
188 *below*   *Lunaria annua* with its winter seedpods. (PB).

LYCHNIS The best forms in restricted space are the campions with silver leaves, and *L.* 'Flos Jovis', which has both crimson and white flowered forms, rapidly spreading to make attractive clumps.

Lysimachia nummularia, creeping Jenny, is a vigorous trailing perennial evergreen with golden leaves on almost prostrate stems. Bears single yellow cup-shaped flowers. Prefers moist soil but adaptable to sun or shade. Avoid *L. punctata* which is dull and invasive.

M

Macleaya cordata A very invasive herbaceous perennial. Can be restrained from root suckering by planting in narrow beds. Lovely deeply lobed bronze-grey leaves and pink-white plumes. Height 5ft (1.5m).

189 *Magnolia kobus.* (HS).

MAGNOLIA Aristocratic plants, most of them needing more space than the smaller garden allows. Some take twenty years to flower, and frost can spoil the bloom of those which flower in early spring. Nevertheless, if

190 A close-up of the flower of *Magnolia stellata.* (PB).

space can be found it is hard to resist at least one. *Magnolia kobus* makes a modest specimen tree, with small white flowers profusely borne. *M. stellata* is probably a variety of it and makes a round bush with starry flowers. A cultivar, *M.* × *loebneri* 'Leonard Messel', is excellent with pink flowers and modest habit. *M.* × *soulangiana* is common and can be pruned to spread against a south-facing wall, flowers white inside, stained purple outside. *M. sieboldii* is shrubby and produces flowers a few at a time from May to August. *M. grandiflora*, the magnificent evergreen, gets very large but can be trained against a wall, although take care as its strong root system undermines foundations.

MAHONIA Another splendid evergreen genus with many excellent plants to choose from. Has sculptural leaves and deliciously scented lily-of-the-valley flowers. *M.* 'Buckland' is a shade-tolerant prolific winter-flowering hybrid, better than 'Charity' but similar. *M. aquifolium*, a small suckering shrub, can act as groundcover in shade, with polished green-bronze leaves and yellow flowers in dense clusters in March and April. *M. nervosa* is a dwarf suckering species with lustrous leaves, flowering in May and June. *M. trifoliata* 'Glauca' is an exotic grey-leaved Mexican mahonia, not very hardy but ideal for an important site against warm wall.

MALUS A large group of ornamental trees flowering in May. Hedges of espalier-shaped apple or pear trees make good divisions in small gardens as well as in old-fashioned kitchen gardens, and are both useful and attractive. *Malus floribunda*, one of the finest species, makes a small tree with very profuse pink to rose flowers, and a broad crown. *M. toringoides* and *M. tschonoski* have good incised foliage which colours well in autumn.

191 *Mandevilla splendens* is a handsome white-flowered climber for sheltered gardens. (HS).

Malva moschata Drought-resistant perennial useful for flowering in late summer and seeding freely *in situ*. Can be grown as an annual in smaller garden leaving space for early spring bulbs before planting out. Deeply cut green leaves and white or rose-pink flowers (2ft: 60cm).

Mandevilla suaveolens Sun-loving tender deciduous climber, spectacular for warm gardens, or can be grown as an annual. White fragrant flowers and slender heart-shaped leaves.

Matthiola bicornis, night-scented stock, is a bushy annual with long narrow grey-green leaves, mainly grown for strongly fragrant flowers which open at night during July and August.

MECONOPSIS The Himalayan poppies are most beautiful, needing woodland conditions and rich damp acid soil. *Meconopsis grandis* is one of the best, growing to 5ft (1.5m) with bright blue flowers, 4in (10cm) across, above dissected hairy leaves. The much smaller Welsh poppy *M. Cambrica* can invade the garden, seeding wildly, but has rich green ferny foliage and delightful yellow or orange flowers. All are perennials.

192 *Meconopsis betonicifolia*, the Himalayan poppy, grows taller than *M. grandis*. (HS).

Melianthus major Sub-shrub with noble grey-green divided pinnate leaves. Hardy but dies down in winter (except in almost frost-free gardens). Bracken fronds can be used for protection. Needs full sun and looks particularly good surrounded by annuals such as *Cleome spinosa* and *Echium* 'Blue Bedder' or by permanent grey foliage planting.

Melissa officinalis, lemon balm, has hairy aromatic leaves with delicious lemon scent when crushed in the hand. The golden form 'Aurea' is attractive with speckled variegated leaves. Do not allow to seed as it rapidly makes clumps.

MENTHA Mint is normally grown for culinary purposes but the apple mint, *Mentha rotundifolia,* has a decorative variegated form with leaves heavily splashed with

white. Rather invasive and untidy, but thrives in part shade. *M. longifolia* has lovely grey-green leaves and is useful as a spreading perennial in a foliage border. The smaller *M. × gentilis* (18in:45cm) also has a variegated form and makes an edging plant in full sun. *M. requienii* is a prostrate carpeting species with a strong peppermint aroma. It loves to spread in shade.

Milium effusum 'Aureum', Bowles' golden grass, has bright yellow leaves, is low-growing (15in:38cm) in shade and very useful for brightening a dark corner.

Miscanthus sinensis 'Zebrinus' is the most decorative form of this large ornamental grass. It is a perennial, dying down in winter, but in small gardens treat as bamboo for decorative effect. Yellow cross-banding on elegant arching green leaves. Can reach 6ft (2m). Very striking in pots.

Monarda didyma is a perennial which hates drought but needs sun. Makes a dense clump of dark leaves with a strong pleasant fragrance. Height 2ft (60cm) with flowers in whorls. The old cultivar 'Cambridge Scarlet' is still the best.

193 *Monarda didyma* 'Croftway pink', an improved form of bergamot. (PB).

Morina longifolia A very elegant thistle-like perennial with rosette of rich green leaves. Hooded tubular flowers in pink and white (3ft: 1m). Fairly hardy but dislikes wet soil in winter. Very worthwhile.

Morus nigra A tree of character with an air of the Old World from which it came five hundred years ago. Slowly maturing to 20ft (6m), wider than it is high, unless pruned every year to single stem. Handsome leaves. Fruit is like loganberry. Plant in grass.

Myrrhis odorata Sweet Cicely. Fragrant flower with delicate cow-parsley head and ferny leaves. Height 2ft (60cm). For sun or shade.

MYRTUS The common myrtle, *Myrtus communis*, is an aromatic-leaved evergreen shrub, hardy against a warm

194 *Myrrhis odorata*. (PB).

wall. Excellent for town gardens and for containers. Usually grows to 6ft (2m). White flowers in July are followed by purplish berries. *M. communis* 'Tarentina' has smaller hard leaves and is hardier than the type. Both have forms with variegated leaves. Try to grow near doors or windows as they look very attractive with stone or brick work.

N

Nandina domestica, the Chinese sacred bamboo, is a charming evergreen shrub with pale pinkish pinnate leaves, assuming bronze tints in autumn. White terminal flowers in summer, thriving in sun or half shade. Needs rich feeding. Height 4ft (1.2m). A new form, *N. domestica* 'Pygmaea', has dwarf habit and 'Nana Purpurea' has leaves distinctly tinged purple in summer.

NARCISSUS The Lent lilies, *Narcissus pseudonarcissus,* thrive in native meadows, and also look beautiful when naturalized. In a small space you may want to make a choice from the little *N. bulbocodium* or *N. cyclamineus* species, which are very early flowering, 6in (15cm) high, and need a special spot in a trough or bed. Most of the large flowered hybrids are suitable for grass, but in restricted space it may be best to put them in pots which are later used for summer annuals. I love some of the pure white forms.

NEPETA Catmint. The well known *Nepeta × faassenii* has grey-green leaves and bears sprays of lavender blooms for many summer weeks. If cut down in July will flower again in late summer. A perennial but very suitable for edging and making inner divisions in garden. Plant with pale pink roses and especially the hybrid musk 'Penelope'. Grow under espalier apple or pear trees. *N. hederacea,* sometimes called ground ivy or *Glechoma hederacea,* has an elegant variegated form useful in pots. A very low-sprawling perennial.

Nerine bowdenii Bulbous sun lover for well-drained soil. Leaves appear in spring and pink lily-like flowers in September and October. An alternative to amaryllis for smaller gardens. Flowers are long lasting in water.

Nerium oleander Tender evergreen for pots or for warm town garden. Mid-green narrow leaves and attractive pink or white flowers. A variegated form has striking foliage. If grown in a container, water copiously.

Nicotiana affinis The scented tobacco plants are indispensable for their evening fragrance, and are best grown as annuals (although they often survive a mild winter). The form 'Limelight' has lovely lime-green flowers but no scent. Very suitable for pots, quickly filling up space with fresh green foliage.

Nothofagus cliffortioides is one of the smaller of the Southern beeches. An evergreen with small hard crinkled leaves, it is a very fast-growing and useful tree because it casts little shade and looks nice all year. Prefers acid soil. Most nothofagus grow too large but space might be found for *N. fusca,* which has brown coppery leaf colour and flaking bark.

NYMPHAEA The hardy water lilies which flower over a long period in summer have elegant sweetly scented blooms. There is a large number of species and garden forms but choose the smaller plants. Be prepared to thin out frequently as all charm is lost if the water surface becomes completely obscured by the floating leaves.

195 *Nymphaea odorata* 'Sulphurea grandiflora' has heavily fragrant large yellow flowers. (PB).

O

Ocimum basilicum, the sweet basil for salads and cooking, is an annual with soft green aromatic leaves. A decorative purple form exists.

Oenothera missouriensis A useful evening primrose, almost prostrate in habit with green leaves and large yellow flowers. Trails over edges and low walls.

OLEARIA The daisy bushes are evergreen shrubs of variable hardiness. All have attractive foliage and mainly white clusters of flowers. For a small space choose *Olearia phlogopappa* (3ft: 1m) with grey oval leaves, and white, blue or pink daisies in May. Fairly hardy. *O. × haastii* is perhaps the hardiest, with hard oval leaves and white flowers in July and August. Very

196 *Oenothera missouriensis*, a prostrate evening primrose with large flowers. (HS).

197 *Ornithogalum nutans*, a native wild flower, look lovely in grass in light shade. (PB).

useful for hedging in coastal gardens or in sheltered town gardens, tolerant of pollution. *O. macrodonta* is a large plant but could be an important specimen in free-standing position. Height 9ft (3m). Very beautiful holly-like grey spiny leaves and fragrant white flowers in June. Can be grown in shade but flowers less freely. *O. mollis* has wavy-edged silver leaves and makes a rounder shrub up to 3ft (1m). A useful foliage shrub as it keeps its silver appearance even in winter. White flowers in May. *O. cheesemanii*, a hardy long-flowering species, makes a good small shrub for semi-shade. It has green leaves with buff undersides. Underplant with *Euphorbia robbiae* or *E. cyparisus*.

Omphalodes cappadocica and *O. verna* are spring-flowering perennials with bright blue flowers over green leaves, rapidly forming clumpy groundcover. The latter flowers first, starting in March. Suitable for edge of woodland or front of beds, a prettier and more controllable forget-me-not.

ONOPORDON Giant grey-leaved thistle up to 6ft (2m) in height and very decorative. Full sun and will seed freely unless prevented. Glows silver in evening light. *Onopordon arabicum*, a hardy biennial, is one of the best.

Ophiopogon planiscarpa 'Nigrescens' Small almost black-leaved grassy plant, very exotic looking. Needs planting in clumps of at least five in front of border (6in:15cm).

ORIGANUM Marjoram. An aromatic herb which is beautiful and ornamental as well as useful. Full sun but not fussy about soil. *Origanum vulgare* 'Aureum' has bright foliage in spring and makes a decorative mound. For rockery conditions the tiny *O. rotundifolia* is attractive with curious hop-like bracts of creamy-yellow growing to 4in (10cm). *O. laevigatum* has green leaves and purple flowers in summer (12in:30cm).

Ornithogalum nutans Hardy bulb for naturalizing. Strange pale green and white flowers above strap leaves (18in:45cm). Very attractive.

OSMANTHUS Evergreen shrubs. *Osmanthus delavayi* has small dark leaves and white tubular very fragrant

flowers in April. Will flower even in shade, like *Choisya ternata*. *O. heterophyllus* makes an excellent hedge and has several good leaf forms. Useful architectural shrub suitable for framing doorways and for growing formally in pots. Can be cut hard to keep in moderate size.

198 *Osmunda regalis*. (HS).

Osmunda regalis, the royal fern, has pea-green fronds and is good for waterside planting. Prefers acid soil but will succeed in any good mulch of peat or leaf mould.

Osteospernum barberiae (syn. *Dimorphotheca barberiae*) and its form 'Compacta' are the hardiest of these Cape marigolds. Sun-loving purple-pink daisy flowers are borne above long downy green leaves through summer. Good in full sun. Less hardy but perhaps more attractive is *O. ecklonis*, which is bushy with erect stems bearing pale blue-white flowers. Take cuttings in autumn. Very suitable for pots as drought resistant.

Othonnopsis cheiriifolia Paddle-shaped blue-grey leaves carry large orange-yellow daisy flowers in summer. Full sun and good drainage will make this a hardy perennial, but it will not tolerate water around its roots.

Oxalis adenophylla (3in:7.5cm) Rosette of crinkled grey leaves with long cup-shaped flowers of satin-pink from May to July. Sun and good drainage.

Ozothamnus rosmarinifolius Medium-sized evergreen shrub with grey-green linear leaves. The new form 'Silver Jubilee' has very silver foliage so use it if obtainable. Flowers open from dense pink buds to corymbs of white daisies. *O. ledifolius* is a small aromatic shrub with golden leaves, suitable in restricted space.

P

Pachysandra terminalis Useful low-growing evergreen shrub with toothed deep green leaves. Best in acid soil and shade. A good variegated form contrasts well with glossy green foliage of *Fatsia japonica* or golden-leaved elder bushes.

199 *Pachysandra terminalis* in flower. A most useful evergreen for groundcover. (HS).

PAEONIA The paeony is a decorative genus with beautiful flowers and good foliage. Among the herbaceous species are the old-fashioned *Paeonia officinalis*, which flowers in May with single or double flowers from rich dark red to pale pink and white. The double forms are best for picking. *P. lactiflora* hybrids have many gorgeous June flowerers. Taller growing, they usually need some support as flower heads are very heavy. The early species, *P. mlokosewitschii*, has glaucous green leaves and pale yellow flowers. *P. potaninii* is a suckering shrub with deeply fretted leaves and maroon flowers. Do not disturb any of these herbaceous paeonies and feed richly. Do not plant deeply. The Moutan tree paeony, *P. suffruticosa*, has many beautiful forms. Plant where eastern early morning sun cannot reach buds. Very elegant foliage and flowers. Low-growing perennials such as *Campanula portenschlagiana* look attractive planted below.

Papaver orientale The oriental poppy has many good forms with coarse hairy leaves and usually scarlet or pink flowers with a purple-black blotch in centre. The opium poppy, *P. somniferum*, has smooth pale-green leaves and seeds freely. Many good forms with pink and red flower colours. Very hardy and nice to have in drifts or in odd corners. Seedlings are easily pulled out if not wanted.

Parahebe catarractae Semi-hardy dwarf shrub or sub-shrub making a lovely mound 9in (23cm) high with white to rose-purple hebe-like flowers. Very useful in pots or raised beds. Perhaps hardier than thought as seems to shoot readily from the base after cold winter.

PARTHENOCISSUS Type of vine especially useful for twining over pergola or trellis in shady backyards. Clings by leaf tendrils or adhesive pads but needs some supporting frame to start it off. *P. henryana* has bronze leaves with silver veins and is effective in deep shade. *P. quinquefolia*, the true Virginia creeper, clambers up high walls. Five-lobed leaves turn bright orange and red in autumn. *P. tricuspidata* 'Veitchii' is a form of the Boston ivy, with scarlet and crimson autumn colour and blue fruits.

Passiflora caerulea, the passion flower, is a suckering evergreen climber, needing hot sun for flower and fruit. The white form 'Constance Elliot' is beautiful and hardier than the type. Twines to 20ft (6m).

PELARGONIUM Mainly tender sub-shrubs for pots or summer bedding, some with deliciously aromatic foliage. The common zonal pelargoniums are usually referred to as geraniums but must not be confused with that genus of hardy cranesbills. *P. crispum* 'Variegatum' grows to 2ft (60cm) and has fragrant balm-scented leaves. Pink flowers from May to October. *P. graveolens* has deeply lobed toothed aromatic leaves and grows to 3ft (1m) with 1in (2.5cm) pink flowers. *P. peltatum*, the ivy-leaved geranium, has trailing stems and is very suitable for falling over edges of window-boxes or tubs. Fleshy green leaves and carmine-pink flowers. The zonal pelargoniums are hybrids and there are many good forms which flower freely all summer. Plant in ordinary well-drained soil, take cuttings in autumn and overwinter in frost-free glass house or on windowsill. Otherwise treat as annuals and replace each spring.

200 *Pelargonium* 'King of Denmark'. This zonal pelargonium needs full sun for a good display. (HS).

201 *Pelargonium* 'Harry Hieover', another zonal with very pretty leaves. (HS).

Peltiphyllum peltatum 'Nana' is a dwarf form of this perennial, which has umbrella-shaped leaves appearing in June after flowers are over. Flowers are tiny stars held in wide head. Plant in moist soil.

Penstemon hartwegii 'Garnet' has clear red tubular flowers and narrow green leaves. Treat as sub-shrub and cut back dead stalks in spring, as far as new growth. *P. campanulatus* 'Evelyn' is a bushy plant with tubular rose-pink flowers all summer (18in:45cm). Very decorative and delightful plants, probably not hardy in cold counties but cuttings are easily rooted.

202 *Pernettya mucronata*. (HS).

Pernettya mucronata Hardy evergreen, definitely for acid soils and thriving under woodland canopy. Best massed together for full effects of attractive bunches of white and pink berries. Makes a weed-proof groundcover, seldom above 2ft (60cm).

Perovskia atriplicifolia Sub-shrub which suckers when suited in dry sunny situation. Aromatic grey foliage and bright lavender-blue flowers up to 4ft (1.3m). Splendid in a foliage border or with another suckering shrub such as *Romneya trichocalyx* and makes a useful late summer flowerer.

PETUNIA Drought-resistant summer bedding annual for sunny bed, window-boxes or containers. Particularly good for roof gardens as it loves plenty of light. Many good garden forms with colourful double and single flowers from white to pink or dark purple. Best in groups of a single colour.

PHILADELPHUS Large genus of deciduous shrubs, some too large and vigorous for the smaller garden, but wonderfully fragrant in mid-summer. Prune after flowering. *Philadelphus* 'Belle Etoile' makes a compact bush up to 6ft (2m) with white flowers flushed purple at centre. *P. coronarius* 'Aureus' has golden foliage and prefers shade. *P.* 'Manteau d'Hermine' is a charming dwarf (3ft:1m) with double creamy-white flowers. *P. microphyllus,* a small-leaved twiggy bush, has intensely fragrant flowers. Underplant with spring-flowering bulbs, hostas, hellebores, etc.

203 *Philadelphus coronarius* 'Aureus', the golden-leaved philadelphus. (HS).

Philesia magellanica Small evergreen shrub for acid soil. Tender but will thrive in warm garden and in pots. Needs adequate watering. Bell-like rose flowers above rigid glossy leaves.

PHILLYREA Evergreen shrubs or small trees which can be clipped to form elegant domes or hedges. *P. angustifolia* is a compact bush with shining glossy narrow leaves. *P. decora,* a dome-shaped bush of up to 6ft (2m), but usually less, and wider than it is high, has large leathery glossy leaves and inconspicuous but fragrant white flowers in spring. *P. latifolia* makes an attractive small tree, very useful with shining leaves that flutter in the wind. Unfortunately slow growing, but lovely to have if you find it already in your garden.

PHLOMIS Medium-sized evergreen shrubs with hairy woolly grey leaves for sun. They look lovely associated with other grey foliage plants or with brightly coloured flowers. Best known is *Phlomis fruticosa* which may be the hardiest and has whorls of pale yellow flowers. *P. chrysophylla* is more attractive with rounded lime-green-grey leaves and paler primrose blooms. *P. italica* has longer thin leaves, very white and hairy, and pale lilac flowers, a very choice plant. All are inclined to get leggy and can be severely pruned each spring.

PHLOX Genus including alpine perennials, annuals and herbaceous border plants. The small *Phlox amoena* 'Variegata' grows to 9in (23cm) and garden forms of *P. subulata* and *P. douglasii*, which are even smaller, make attractive spreading plants in gravel or raised beds. The herbaceous *P. paniculata* is very vigorous in semi-shade but needs plenty of feeding and dividing every few years. The form 'Norah Leigh' has ivory-variegated leaves and responds to care and encouragement.

PHORMIUM New Zealand evergreen with long sword-like leaves. The best small species, *Phormium cookianum* (syn. *colensoi*), has many exciting leaf colours from plain green, striped cream and white and bronze-pink. Useful architectural plant for gateways or corners and for contrast with softer foliage. Any good soil will do. The variegated forms are tender in a winter such as that of 1978-9.

Phuopsis stylosa Most useful small edging plant, loving sun and with tiny pink flowers above narrow grey-green foliage (12in: 30cm). Spreads rapidly. Not seen often enough and ideal for the smaller garden. Use it instead of the larger catmint.

Phygelius aequalis is the best form of this slightly tender suckering shrub. Usually dies down in winter, but you can treat like penstemons, cutting back to new healthy growth. Flowers through long summer season, soft rosy-red blooms on long 3ft (1m) stems. A better plant than the commoner *P. capensis*.

Physocarpus opulifolius 'Luteus' A deciduous shrub (5ft: 1.5m) thriving in sun or shade and keeping its glowing golden leaf colour all through the summer.

204 *Pieris formosa* 'Forrestii', a decorative evergreen shrub for acid soil. (HS).

PIERIS Fine acid-loving evergreen genus of shrubs with brilliant red young foliage in spring and lily-of-the-valley flowers (sometimes spoiled by frosts). *Pieris formosa* 'Wakehurst' grows rather large but could be an important feature plant on a west-facing wall. *P. japonica* and varieties are all hardy. *P. taiwanensis* is medium-sized with reliable white flowers in March. Grow in acid soil in containers if in alkaline garden. Treat as camellias.

Pileostegia viburnoides Height 15ft (5m). Evergreen shrub which climbs by aerial roots in sun or dense shade. Slow to establish but worthwhile. Use instead of *Hydrangea petiolaris* for a change. Leathery narrow leaves and panicles of creamy white in late summer.

205 *Pileostegia viburnoides* can climb or make a wide bush. (PB).

Pittosporum tenuifolium A foliage evergreen which makes a regular conical shape against a wall. Can also be a delightful tall hedge in sheltered area. Wavy-edged undulating leaves and black twiggy stems, chocolate-brown scented flowers. Various coloured leaf forms are valuable. Among the best is *P. tenuifolium* 'Garnetii' which has attractive variegation spotted pink, and forms a dense bush. *P. tobira*, the Japanese pittosporum, is tender with fragrant white flowers in spring. Survives in London gardens or can be pot grown if given some protection in winter.

Polygonatum × *hybridum*, the beloved Solomon's seal, is ideal for shade with long arching stems bearing green delicate leaves and green-white bells in spring (3ft: 1m). Hostas, ferns and spring-flowering omphalodes look lovely in association.

POLYGONUM The perennial knotweeds tend to ramp but they are invaluable carpeters with long flowering periods. *Polygonum bistorta* (3ft: 1m) has light green leaves and pink flowers in May and June. *P. affine* 'Darjeeling Red' bears low spikes of red over excellent green foliage. *P. campanulatum* flowers late and is valuable for that reason. Thrives in shade.

POPULUS Most poplars are unsuitable for a small garden because their roots make the soil shrink and may

206 *Polygonum campanulatum* flowers for a long period in late summer. (PB).

seedpods and arching brown stems are attractive in winter. Forms of *P. fruticosa* are 'Katherine Dykes' with primrose flowers, 'Elizabeth' with canary-yellow flowers making a domed bush to 3ft (1m), and 'Mandschurica' with white flowers and silvery foliage. The herbaceous potentillas are useful too. A good one is *P. nepalensis* 'Miss Willmott' with cherry-red flowers (24in: 60cm).

PRIMULA A very large genus from which we will mention only a few of those dwarf species generally grown as hardy perennials. The genus includes the primrose and cowslip. All primulas look best planted in drifts of one colour. *P. juliae* (syn. 'Garryarde') is small (3in: 7.5cm) and produces wine-red flowers above dark leaves. 'Guinevere' is a pink form. *P. sieboldii* (9in: 23cm) has tufted hairy leaves and rose-pink flowers.

PRUNUS A very large group of spring-flowering trees and shrubs, mostly beautiful in flower, some among the finest of all. Includes plums, almonds, peaches, apricots, cherries and cherry laurel. Generally not interesting in leaf and the season of blossom is short. *P. conradinaea* makes a neat small tree and white flowers appear in March. *P. subhirtella* 'Autumnalis' flowers intermittently from November, often with a great

damage wall foundations. *Populus lasiocarpa* could be a specimen tree and looks superb with its huge heart-shaped leaves on a red stalk. Grows slowly.

POTENTILLA The shrubby deciduous cinquefoils are indispensable for smaller gardens. Use for hedges, for groups in borders or as individual specimens. Plant in sun or shade, in dry soil or moist, or hanging over low walls. Most flower almost all summer, and brown

207 *Potentilla fruticosa* 'Katherine Dykes' flowers from spring to autumn. (PB).

208 *Prunus laurocerasus* 'Otto Luyken' has beautiful glossy leaves and flowers freely. (HS).

display in February. Pink flowered. *P. sargentii* is a shapely tree with good brown bark, single pink flowers and wonderful leaf colour in late September. *P. serrula* has no beauty of flower but its dark brown shining bark is striking at all times. *P. lusitanicus* 'Variegatus' is a splendid evergreen foliage shrub with delightful variegated leaves; the type grows too large for the smaller garden. Forms of the cherry laurel *P. laurocerasus* 'Otto Luyken' and 'Zabeliana' are small, the latter with branches growing horizontal, but both with glossy leaves and thriving in shade.

Pulmonaria angustifolia A species of lungwort with narrow dark green leaves and sky-blue flowers on 10in (25cm) stalks. It and other pulmonarias make ideal groundcover for moist soils in shade, many with mottled variegated leaves. They rapidly form strong clumps.

Punica granatum, the pomegranate, needs a warm wall and full sun in order to flower and fruit. Pruning hard and tying back will help. Bronze shining leaves and bright orange-scented flowers. Usually grows to 6ft (2m) but a dwarf form 'Nana' is attractive for a narrow bed where space is limited.

PYRACANTHA Firethorns are excellent large evergreens for north and east-facing walls. Can be trained very formally on horizontal wires. Hawthorn-like spring flowers give white frothy effect and are followed by red or orange berries. One of the best, *Pyracantha coccinea* 'Lalandei', grows to 12ft (4m). Very hardy and wind-resistant. Can be used for wind protection on exposed balconies and rooftops.

PYRUS The old perry pears are still seen in the lanes of Worcestershire and make graceful trees with tessellated bark. Garden forms have something of the same quality, even when pruned to pyramid, bush or espalier shape. *Pyrus salicifolia* 'Pendula' is now quite common as a small weeping tree and has very attractive grey leaves.

R

Ranunculus aconitifolius Height 2ft (60cm). The double form of this plant, the fair maids of France, is rare and worthwhile. Deeply cut dark green leaves and dense double buttons of pure white. For moist soil and partial shade.

Raphiolepis umbellata Slow-growing evergreen shrub with rounded leathery leaves. Terminal clusters of scented white flowers are borne in June. Height 3ft (1m). Needs sun and rich soil.

Rhamnus alaterna 'Argenteovariegata' Excellent evergreen foliage plant for sun or shade. Normally grows to 12ft (4m) against a wall where it is most striking. Bulky dense appearance with attractive cream and green leaves. There are several variable forms about under same name.

Rhazya orientalis (18in: 45cm) Blue-flowering perennial with wiry stems and willow-like leaves (18in: 45cm). Well-drained soil and sun. Looks effective under roses and in massed clumps with herbaceous geraniums.

Rheum palmatum Ornamental rhubarb of up to 6ft (2m) with large decorative leaves. The form *R. palmatum* 'Atrosanguiniem' has vivid red leaves and cerise panicles of fluffy flowers. Needs moist soil. Takes the place of the giant gunnera where space is limited.

RHODODENDRON Difficult to make a decision. Plants in this genus range from large 60ft (18m) bushes to

209 *Rhododendron yakushimamum.* No illustration can do justice to the handsome silvery leaves which are brown-felted beneath. (HS).
210 *Rhododendron williamsianum.* (HS).

creeping shrubs. Almost all are acid-loving. Most of them also belong aesthetically to the large woodland natural garden and look absurdly out of place in the smaller town or suburban garden. Even in a country garden where the right conditions exist I cannot feel that rhododendrons fit into a mixed planting area. They seem most appropriate where they can be grown in glades away from the main garden area. However, tender species such as *R.* 'Fragrantissimum' are ideal for the sheltered town garden (and of course for pots with suitable soil mix). For foliage alone the relatively small *R. yakushimamum* (3ft: 1m) is valuable; it also has bell-shaped May flowers, pink in bud fading to white. *R. scintilans* has distinctive almost blue flowers (2ft: 60cm). *R.* 'Sappho' is white and grows to 6ft (2m). *R.* 'Crest', an Exbury hybrid, has primrose-yellow bell-shaped flowers in May. *R. williamsianum* has attractive leaves and early flowers, red in bud fading to soft pink. Height 4-6ft (1.3-2m). A little subject to frost damage so needs shelter.

RHUS Best known is *Rhus typhina*, the stag's horn sumach, which forms a gaunt bush with reddish young stems and large pinnate leaves which colour in autumn. The form 'Lacinata' has dissected foliage. Tolerant of town conditions but needs rich soil. Much more distinguished but not easy to obtain are *Rhus potaninii* and *R. verniciflua*, which make handsome small trees.

RIBES I am not fond of the fruiting currants although I recognize their garden value as early spring flowerers. The most interesting is the tender *R. speciosum* which requires the shelter of a warm wall and bears fuchsia-like red flowers from April to June. Needs training and pruning.

ROBINIA The false acacias are very suitable in the smaller garden, and even *Robinia pseudoacacia* itself does not seem too large as it has light delicate foliage casting little shade. Its form 'Frisia' is very beautiful with pale golden pinnate leaves. The gold colour is maintained all summer. *R. hispida,* the rose acacia, can be tied back against a wall as well as grown as a specimen in grass, and flowers best if given this additional warmth. *R. kelseyii* also has rose flowers and makes a graceful standard tree.

RODGERSIA A wonderful genus of excellent foliage and flowering perennials for moist soil. *Rodgersia pinnata* has burnished pinnate leaves with cream feathery flowers of up to 3ft (1m) and the form 'Superba'-has pink flowers. *R. podophylla* is very rampant, less so if given a dry situation. Lobed leaves, bronze when unfurling in spring, green later. Pale buff flowers in June and July.

211   *Rodgersia pinnata.* with its burnished rough leaves. (HS).

212   *Romneya trichocalyx.* The flowers are a pure white. (HS).

Romneya trichocalyx Ardent suckering sun lover. Sub-shrub usually requiring cutting down to ground level in spring. Beautiful divided grey foliage bearing huge heads of white papery flowers, yellow centred, in summer. Grows from 3ft to 6ft (1-2m). Propagate by root cuttings in winter.

ROSA Roses are apparently indispensable in British gardens. They need good soil and generally resent anything more than the lightest shade. Indeed they become ugly without adequate sunlight, with heads drawn upwards and bare wood bases. In a small space, too, it is difficult to use plants such as bush roses which need severe pruning annually and thus look misshapen much of the year. Modest-sized species and shrub roses make elegant shapes with arching branches, delicate foliage and sweetly scented flowers, and fit easily and aesthetically into mixed planting schemes. My preference is for roses with pale colours. Try not to hit the highlights with vivid vermilion and scarlet tones. Buttercup yellow looks nice in spring, such as *R. ecae* and *R.* 'Canarybird' with green fern-like leaves. In June *R. rubrifolia* is outstanding with soft green-grey leaves with a purple sheen intensified by plum-coloured stems. The small pink flowers are freely borne and followed by red-brown hips, lovely with grey or variegated leaved plants. The modern 'Nozomi' will trail over a low wall and has numerous white star flowers. *R. mutabilis* has single flowers from flame to buff-yellow to pink and flowers continuously from June onwards, happy in a bed or against a wall. The pink form of the prickly *R. paulii,* 'Max Graf' and 'Raubritter', all have pink flowers and are admirable trailing and carpeting plants, not too vigorous. The first two have pink single flowers and 'Raubritter' shell-pink and double. 'Cecile Brunner' is wiry with small pink flowers,

213   *Rosa* 'Max Graf', an ideal groundcover rose with glossy leaves and clear pink flowers. (HS).

admirable as a bush or in its climbing form.

For climbing roses see page 126. The season opens with the scented Banksian which has fresh pale green leaves, small primrose flowers, and loves a warm wall. In June 'Madame Grégoire Staechelin' with rich double pale pink heavy heads (flowering once only), 'The New Dawn' and the old rose 'Gloire de Dijon' are admirable.

'Golden Showers' has yellow flowers with dark glossy leaves, 'Aloha' double pink very fragrant flowers, 'Bantry Bay' semi-double pale pink, and 'Lady Hillingdon' coppery foliage and pale buff flowers. None is too large, but 'Lady Hillingdon' needs a warm wall. In part shade plant 'Mermaid', 'Félicité et Perpétue' and 'Alberic Barbier', the last-named has yellow pointed buds opening to pink over glossy healthy foliage.

For hedges (see page 120) there is a choice of rugosas: 'Blanc double de Courbet', 'Frau Dagmar Hastrup', pale single pink with large red fruit, 'Roseraie de l'Hay' double wine-red and large, and 'Alba' a rounded shape with white flowers and orange fruits. The hybrid musks include 'Ballerina' with small pink flower heads, 'Buff

214 *below* *Rosmarinus officinalis.* (HS).
215 *bottom* *Ruta graveolens* needs to be pruned after flowering and in the spring. (PB).

Beauty', 'Penelope' and 'Prosperity' with small semi-double scented white flowers (there is a pink form). All can make free-standing or tightly cut hedges. The gallicas, such as the striped 'Rosa Mundi' and 'Tuscany', with dark velvet maroon flowers, can be cut to keep in moderate size. 'Celeste', an alba rose with grey leaves, makes a pretty pink-flowered lax hedge. 'Iceberg' has white double flowers and 'Chinatown' yellow, both are strong repeat flowerers.

'Natalie Nypels' has rose-pink fragrant flowers continuous from June to late summer. 'The Fairy' has soft pink globular blooms held in large sprays, and grows to 2ft (60cm). 'Little White Pet', resembling a miniature 'Félicité et Perpétue', makes a charming 2ft (60cm) mound, lovely as a low hedge around paving.

On the whole, roses are greedy feeders. You need to keep the foliage healthy by mulching heavily in spring. They can be interplanted with attractive evergreen shrubs and herbaceous plants and look particularly well with the grey leaves of senecios, lavender and rue. They can also be underplanted with the less rampant geraniums, violas, dicentras, etc. A front edging of bergenias sets off rose flowers very well. Most need careful pruning to encourage new free-flowering growth. All the smaller roses mentioned can be grown successfully in pots. Deep narrow troughs are suitable – 18in (45cm) is the minimum depth – using a rich loam and feeding through the summer.

ROSMARINUS No garden can be without this aromatic evergreen. It is essential for cooking too. Needs full sun and regular pruning. Grey-green thin leaves and blue flowers. Will grow to 4ft (1.3m). *Rosmarinus officinalis* 'Fastigiatus', also known as Jessop's Upright, can be grown against a warm wall. A tender pink rosemary makes a prostrate mat in warm gardens.

RUDBECKIA There are many forms of this late-flowering perennial, known as black-eyed Susan on account of the conspicuous black cone in the middle of the yellow flower. Choose one with appropriate height, *Rudbeckia deamii* is 3ft (1m) and *R. newmanii* 2ft (60cm).

216 *Rudbeckia speciosa* 'Goldsturm' gives colour in October. (PB).

Ruta graveolens, rue, a small evergreen with blue-grey fern-like leaves useful in a foliage or herb bed and for flavouring salads. Height 2ft (60cm). Stiff terminal clusters of sulphur flowers in June or July. A variegated form is quite hardy. Requires full sun, good drainage and regular pruning to prevent legginess.

S

SALIX Quite a few willows are suitable for the smaller garden. The grey-leaved *Salix helvetica* and *S. lanata* do not grow above 3ft (1m) and make very elegant grey mounds in summer, the latter with yellow spring catkins. The almost prostrate *S. repens* is useful for damp soil. The larger *S. magnifica* has leaves like a magnolia and will grow to 15ft (4.5m) in a protected site with plenty of moisture. *S. fargesii* has burnished stems in winter, and can be cut down each spring. *S. caprea* 'Pendula', the Kilmarnock willow, makes a neat weeping shape, restrained and formal for restricted space.

217 *Salix lanata* has very furry grey leaves and upright catkins in spring. (HS).

SALVIA Unfortunately most people think first of the garish bedding salvia, but many good shrubby, herbaceous and annual species exist which are valuable in any garden. *Salvia microphylla* 'Grahamii', a tender evergreen (but will shoot from base after hard winter), flowers all summer with small red flowers above fresh green leaves. *S. officinalis,* the evergreen cooking sage, has good leaf forms including those with purple and variegated foliage. They make delightful mounds and are useful for warm borders. *S. ambigens* (syn. *guaranitica*) is an herbaceous perennial with bright blue dark flowers and soft heart-shaped leaves, a little tender. The hardier *S. involucrata* 'Bethelli' has heart-shaped green-bronze leaves with conspicuous veining and magenta-crimson flowers continuous from mid-summer. *S. patens* has bright blue flowers, and a pale blue form is even more attractive. Both should be grown from seed as annuals, and are suitable for pots in full sun. *S. uliginosa* suckers in a warm moist site and carries pale bright blue flowers well into the autumn.

Sambucus racemosa 'Plumosa Aurea' is the best of the elders for the smaller garden with very elegant golden fretted foliage, thriving in shade and needing regular

pruning. Lights up a dark corner all summer. Underplant with evergreen perennials such as periwinkle (*Vinca minor*).

SANTOLINA The cotton lavenders are aromatic evergreen shrubs for full sun, all needing regular cutting after the last spring frosts. *Santolina neapolitana* has grey feathery foliage and yellow flowers in summer. The form 'Sulphurea' has a prettier more subtle colour. *S. virens* has finely divided thread-like green leaves. Tender in exposed gardens but makes neat hedges if kept regularly trimmed.

218 *Santolina neapolitana* loves to sprawl over warm pavement. It also makes an attractive low hedge. Prune in spring. (PB).

Saponaria officinalis, the soapwort, has campion-like double pink flowers and spreads vigorously. The lather from the leaves is used for removing dirt and grease from certain materials. The small *S.* × 'Bressingham' (2in: 5cm) is a hardy perennial for rockery sites, making low hummocks of green with rich pink flowers in May and June.

SARCOCOCCA *Sarcococca ruscifolia* is a winter-flowering small evergreen shrub for shade. Carries very sweet-smelling tiny flowers above glossy green leaves, followed by dark red berries. *S. humilis* suckers and makes a low clump 1ft (30cm) high, but wide spreading, and has black fruit.

SAXIFRAGA London pride is a well-known edging plant. *Saxifraga umbrosa* is pretty and there is a more unusual variegated form. *S. stolonifera* (9in: 23cm) is a creeping species with red stems and silvery veined leaves for full shade. One of the best saxifrages for a cool position is *S. fortunei* (12in: 30cm). Its deep green leaves (deciduous) carry airy sprays of small white flowers. Red reverse to leaf and bronzed upper surface in form 'Rubra'.

Schizandra grandiflora Deciduous twining shrub for walls, fences and trellis. Deep crimson pendulous flowers, followed by scarlet berries on female plants. Prefers acid soil and part shade.

Schizophragma hydrangeoides Self-clinging climber for north walls. Rather similar to *Hydrangea petiolaris* but later flowering and pale yellow rather than white.

220 *Schizophragma hydrangeoides* is a slow-growing climber for a shady wall. (PB).

219 *Schizophragma hydrangeoides*, a close-up of the inflorescence. (HS).

Schizostylis coccinea, the Kaffir lily, is very useful, flowering in late September. 'Mrs. Hegarty' has clear pink flowers, and 'Viscountess Byng' a paler pink above flat sword-like leaves (2ft: 60cm).

SCILLA The little spring-flowering scilla, *S. sibirica*, is bright blue and spreads rapidly, each bulb producing three or four stems even in the first season and seeding to form large clumps. An invaluable plant for grass and shade. *S. peruviana* has large bulbs and dense blue heads composed of perhaps a hundred star flowers. May and June flowering. All scillas look breathtakingly beautiful under or near white flowering shrubs. Each year they surprise one by their vivid colouring.

SEDUM Stonecrop. Thriving in full sun and practically no soil. Try to establish it on walls and in paving cracks. The larger herbaceous sedums, such as *S. telephium* and its form 'Atropurpureum', are lovely in autumn, their flat heads often covered in butterflies. *S.* 'Autumn Joy' grows to 2ft (60cm) and quickly makes a spreading clump. Rich pink flower heads in September. The smaller border species make lovely tufted foliage plants. *S.* × 'Ruby Glow' (10in: 25cm) is excellent in full sun, with glaucous leaves.

Selinum tenuifolium is an ornamental graceful cow parsley with finely cut green leaves and white flat flower heads. Sun and warm garden. A refined version of sweet Cicely (*Myrrhis odorata*).

221 *Selinum tenuifolium* looks graceful in a sheltered garden. (HS).

SENECIO Large genus from which we might choose some evergreen shrubs for their attractive grey foliage *Senecio monroi* (4ft: 1.3m) has wavy-edged leaves and makes a compact tidy hedge in warm counties. *S. compactus* is a dwarf form of the popular *S.* 'Sunshine' – very useful for pots and odd corners, drought resistant

222 *Senecio leucostachys*, a most desirable feathery plant for warm gardens. (PB).

and needing full sun. *S. leuchostachys* has lax silvery-white deeply divided leaves and is tender, but if grown against a wall likes to twine among other shrubs. Similar to *Artemisia arborescens*. Cuttings easily struck.

Silybum marianum A biennial for full sun with glossy marbled white-green leaves (3ft: 1m). Very decorative and seeds abundantly. Grow in odd corners.

223 *Silybum marianum* can be allowed to self-seed. (PB).

Sisyrinchium striatum (12in: 30cm) has linear sword-shaped leaves and pale straw-coloured flowers. Seeds freely in paving. A variegated form is very desirable but a little tender. Others have pale blue flowers, and there are now good hybrids.

SKIMMIA These evergreen shrubs prefer deep acid soil and shade. Low height (2ft: 60cm). Mainly grown for crop of attractive red berries. Both sexes necessary.

Smilacina racemosa (3ft: 1m) An attractive perennial with arching stalks carrying light green leaves above which the tightly packed fluffy creamy flower heads look elegant. Shade and neutral soil. Lovely in spring.

Solanum crispum A spectacular hardy semi-evergreen climber. Its potato flowers of rich blue are especially fine in the form 'Glasnevin'. The white-flowered *S. jasminoides* is tender but very beautiful in warm gardens.

224 The *Sorbus vilmorinii* hybrid has very decorative berries. (HS).

Sophora tetraptera is an evergreen small tree with pinnate leaves and tubular yellow flowers in spring. Needs a warm wall. *S. microphylla* is very similar but has smaller and more numerous leaflets. *S. macrophylla* often behaves like a sub-shrub in a hard winter but shoots freely from the ground and bears the largest flowers.

SORBUS Small trees, mostly very decorative. Two main groups, *aria* with simple leaves as in the native whitebeam, and *aucuparia*, the rowan or mountain ash. Of the whitebeams, *Sorbus cuspidata* and *S. mitchellii* are the best, with rounded leaves green-grey above and white below, bearing fruits like crab apples. Of the rowans, *S. cashmeriana*, with large compound leaves and

225 *Sorbus vilmorinii*. The leaves alone make this tree worth growing. (HS).

white berries, is outstanding. *S. vilmorinii* is even more graceful but must be pruned to keep a single stem.

Spartina pectinata 'Aurea-marginata' has graceful ribbon-like foliage, striped with yellow. A perennial invasive grass for damp soil (5ft:1.5m).

Spartium junceum, the Spanish broom, grows tall but can be cut to keep moderate size. Excellent for sandy alkaline soil. Carries fragrant yellow pea flowers.

Spiraea × arguta, the bridal wreath, is a deciduous shrub which can be severely pruned after flowering. Pure white flowers are carried along branches in April and May. *S. bumalda* 'Gold Flame' is smaller with pale gold leaves, pink-tinged in spring. Semi-shade.

Stachys lanata The popular perennial with hairy silver-grey evergreen leaves. Useful for the front of sunny borders. Spreads rapidly. The form 'Silver Carpet' has no flower heads and you are thus spared the arduous work of cutting down the dull mauve spikes of the type.

Stauntonia hexaphylla Grows to 30ft (10m). Elegant twining evergreen with smooth green leaves in leaflets and scented white flowers in spring. Prefers neutral to acid soil and loves warmth.

Stipa gigantea Clumps of rushy foliage with 6ft (2m) stems bearing enormous heads of golden oats. Looks magnificent. Can be grown in container.

Stranvaesia davidiana An evergreen shrub which can be trained quite easily to form a single stem to make a tree. Never exceeds 15ft (5m). Carries a shapely crown of shining leaves, many of which turn red in autumn. The white flowers are small but numerous, followed by berries of pillar-box red.

Symphoricarpus orbiculatus 'Variegatus' The most interesting form of the deciduous coral berry, a suckering medium-sized shrub for shade with irregularly variegated leaves. Spreads rapidly and thrives in poor conditions.

Syringa microphylla Most lilacs are too large for the smaller garden but this pretty low-growing shrub (6ft:2m) with panicles of scented dark rose flowers is suitable. Repeat-flowers in autumn. Sun or part shade.

T

Tanacetum haradjanii (6in:15cm) Silver leaves deeply dissected in filigree pattern. Looks attractive growing over border edges and rims of pots. Dislikes wet in winter and loves full sun. Grow it with small phlox and campanulas.

Taxus baccata is the common yew for hedges or topiary, but *T. baccata* 'Adpressa' makes a small evergreen tree with a dense spreading habit. *T. baccata* 'Fastigiata', the Irish yew, has a useful columnar or pyramidal habit with funereal dark leaves. A golden form is striking.

Teucrium fruticans Shrubby evergreen germander with pale grey leaves and pale blue flowers lasting over a

226 *Spartium junceum*. (HS).

227 *Stipa gigantea* has a very graceful habit and flower head. (HS).

long season, especially if given a warm sheltered site. *T. chamaedrys* is an aromatic sub-shrub spreading underground. Can be cut into small neat hedging for inner divisions in the garden. Dark toothed leaves and rose-pink flowers.

THALICTRUM Hardy herbaceous perennials. *Thalictrum aquilegifolium* has fluffy heads of mauve above grey-blue pinnate leaves (2 – 3ft: 60 – 90cm). *T. dipterocarpum* is taller with mid-green leaves and mauve or white flowers. *T. flavum* is even taller at over 5ft (1.5m) with grey leaves and yellow flowers.

Thuja occidentalis has a form 'Rheingold' which is a small evergreen gold conifer very useful for neat hedges, turning bronze in winter.

THYMUS Aromatic dwarf evergreens for full sun and dry places. *Thymus × citriodorus* 'Aureus' (12in: 30cm) has lemon-scented small leaves. There is a charming variegated form called 'Silver Queen'.

Tiarella cordifolia A low-growing evergreen perennial for shade under trees or deciduous shrubs. Pale green maple-shaped leaves beneath erect spikes of creamy feathers in May and June. Rapid colonizer, but not a strangler of other plants. *T. collina* has pinkish flowers.

228 *Tiarella cordifolia* has fluffy flowers and good foliage. (PB).
229 *below Thalictrum aquilegifolium* is a very pretty hardy perennial for growing in clumps in sun. (PB).

Trachelospermum asiaticum Evergreen climbing shrub with small oval glossy leaves and inconspicuous creamy-white flowers, strongly scented. Full sun and warm garden. *T. jasminoides* is slightly less hardy, but with stronger fragrance from larger flowers.

TRADESCANTIA Old-fashioned attractive border perennial of which *Tradescantia × andersonii* (2ft: 60cm), a hybrid spiderwort, has particularly good flowers of dark purple, pink and white. They all form dense clumps of rush-like green leaves and have charming three-petalled blooms.

TULIP Almost impossible to advise in this huge genus. Among the small species suitable for a choice position is *Tulipa clusiana* with grey-green leaves, white flushed red flowers (9in: 23cm). *T. fosteriana* has grey-green leaves and scarlet flowers (12in: 30cm). *T. greigii* has attractive veined foliage, marbled in brown and bronze, and orange-scarlet flowers. *T. kaufmanniana,* the waterlily tulip, has petals opening into star formation above grey leaves, and white flowers flushed red and yellow (10in: 25cm). Other larger species and garden hybrids are a matter of personal choice.

V

Verbascum bombyciferum (4ft: 1.2m) Biennial rosette of grey hairy leaves with yellow spikes in June and July. Will seed freely *in situ*. V. 'Golden Bush' (2ft: 60cm) has a bushy branching habit and long-lasting flowers. Plant in clumps with small hebes.

VERBENA Mostly used as annual summer bedding plants but *Verbena bonariensis* makes a very attractive perennial for border or container. Blue flowers on long stalks, continuous flowering from June to October. Grow from seed. Even better, but rarer, is *V. corymbosa* which bears its flat heads on short stalks and suckers freely. Most of the annual verbenas are hybrids.

Vestia lycioides is a small evergreen suckering shrub with tubular pale flowers very profusely borne. Can be badly hit by low temperatures but shoots again from the base. *Chiastophyllum oppositifolium* makes a pretty complementary groundcover under it.

VIBURNUM A genus of many outstanding shrubs, both evergreen and deciduous. *Viburnum davidii* is a wide-spreading shade-loving evergreen with leathery leaves and dull white flower heads followed by exciting turquoise fruits (plant both sexes for pollinating). A good suppressor of weeds. *V. tinus* (laurustinus) and its variegated form flower in the winter and the latter has red stems and pale leaves splashed cream. More tender than the type and best against a wall. If space is sufficient no shrub can compete in beauty with *V. plicatum* 'Mariesii', which has horizontal tabulated branches, deciduous, but covered in spring in white lacy flowers. At least a 10ft (3m) spread and eventually as high. Can be cut back and I have seen it trained against a wall. *V. henryi* is of medium size, evergreen with stiff branches carrying white panicles, followed by red fruit which later turns black. Attractive elliptical glossy leaves.

230 *Viburnum tinus* is one of the best winter-flowering shrubs and prefers shade. (HS).

231 *Vestia lycioides* is very free flowering. (PB).

VINCA Three species of these small mat-forming shrubs are worth growing in restricted space. *V. difformis*, more or less herbaceous in habit, is excellent with pale blue flowers produced in autumn and winter. *V. minor* is invasive but the pale variegated form with white flowers is less so, and thrives anywhere, sun or shade. A double purple-flowered form is also useful. The variegated form of *V. major* can be grown in pots very effectively and although quite tall is not difficult to control.

VIOLA Hybrid pansies and true viola species offer a large range. *Viola labradorica* 'Purpurea', a most delightful self-seeder with small mauve flowers over dark purple leaves, quickly establishes itself in cracks in walls and stonework. *V. cornuta* has rich green leaves for groundcover under shrub roses or any deciduous shrubs in sun, and blue or white flowers. *V. septentrionalis* has rhizomes just below the soil surface and quantities of pure white flowers in spring (6in:15cm).

Vitis vinifera, the grape vine, has many decorative forms which produce fruit in a hot summer. Grown over a pergola, the form *V. vinifera* 'Purpurea' looks pretty with grey-purple leaves. The vigorous *V. coignetiae* (60ft:18m) is hardly suitable for a small garden but could be grown along a boundary fence, or up an old tree. Leaves are very large and colour bright red and crimson in autumn.

W

Weigela florida 'Variegata' A deciduous shrub, invaluable for plant association, with pink flowers and fresh green leaves edged with cream. Can be pruned to almost any size and is lovely with evergreen shrubs and with foliage plants which cover the ground. It flowers in May and June. Prefers sun but thrives in town gardens in half-shade. It is also a good shrub for containers.

WISTERIA The best wisteria when space is limited is the Japanese *Wisteria floribunda* 'Macrobotrys' with long dangling racemes of lilac-purple and forms with rose, violet-blue and double violet-blue flowers. The white *Wisteria sinensis* is ethereal and very beautiful, particularly if grown as a standard or over an arbour or pergola.

Y

Yucca filamentosa has greyish-green leaves with thread-like hairs on margins. There is a fine variegated form. The foliage is less hard and less pointed than other species. An architectural plant growing to 2ft (60cm). Evergreen.

Z

Zantedeschia aethiopica is a form of arum lily. Deciduous with shining green leaves and flowers with white spathes. It likes full sun and moist soil. Suitable for natural clumps round informal pond, or in beds at edge of geometric pool (18in:45cm).

232 *top* *Zantedeschia aethiopica*, the hardy arum lily. (PB).

233 *above* *Zauschneria californica* has scarlet flowers and silvery leaves. (PB).

Zauschneria californica for full sun in well-drained bed. Tender sub-shrub with trumpet-shaped scarlet flowers above grey-green leaves in August (12in:30cm).

Plants for Special Purposes

Small trees
Climbers
Wall plants
Architectural foliage
Grey-leaved plants
Gold and silver variegated leaves
Golden foliage
Purple and bronze leaves
Fragrant foliage
Fragrant flowers
Hedging plants
Low groundcover
Low plants for front of borders
Plants for shade
Plants for damp places
Plants for containers
Plants for warm sheltered gardens

SMALL TREES
Abies koreana
Acer
Alnus
Aralia
Betula
Caragana
Carpinus
Catalpa
Cercidiphyllum
Cercis
Chamaecyparis
Cornus
Cotinus
Crataegus
Cryptomeria japonica 'Elegans'
Cupressus
Eucalyptus
Ginkgo
Gleditsia
Ilex
Koelreuteria
Laburnum
Liquidambar
Magnolia
Malus
Nothofagus
Populus
Prunus
Pyrus

Rhus
Robinia
Salix
Sophora
Sorbus
Stranvaesia

CLIMBERS
Actinidia
Akebia
Ampelopsis
Campsis
Celastrus
Clematis
Cobaea
Eccremocarpus
Hedera
Humulus
Hydrangea
Itea
Jasminum
Lonicera
Mandevilla suaveolens
Parthenocissus
Pileostegia
Rosa
Schisandra
Schizophragma
Solanum
Stauntonia
Trachelospermum
Wisteria
Vitis

WALL PLANTS
Acacia
Abutilon
Artemisia arborescens
Buddleia auriculata
Buddleia crispa
Carpenteria
Ceanothus
Coronilla
Cestrum
Chaenomeles
Crinodendron
Cytisus battandieri
Desmodium praestans
Escallonia
Eupatorium ligustrinum
Fremontodendron
Ficus carica

Garrya
Laurus nobilis
Lavatera bicolor
Lippia citriodora
Magnolia
Myrtus
Punica
Pyracantha
Senecio leucostachys
Sophora
Stranvaesia
Teucrium fruticans
Viburnum tinus 'Variegatus'

ARCHITECTURAL FOLIAGE
Acanthus
Alchemilla
Angelica
Aralia
Arundinaria
Bergenia
Carex
Cordyline australis
Cynara
Dicentra
Eryngium
Eucalyptus
Euphorbia
Fatsia
Ferula
Festuca
Hedera
Helictotrichon
Heracleum
Hosta
Humulus
Iris
Macleaya
Melianthus
Miscanthus
Morina
Nandina
Onopordon
Osmunda
Othonnopsis
Paconia
Phormium
Rheum
Robinia
Rodgersia
Silybum
Stipa

GREY-LEAVED PLANTS
Abies koreana
Acaena 'Blue Haze'
Achillea taygetea
Artemisia (all)
Atriplex halimus
Anaphalis triplinervis
Anthemis cupiana
Ballota pseudodictamnus
Buddleia crispa
Cassinia leptophylla
Cerastium tomentosum
Cistus (some)
Coronilla glauca
Cynara cardunculus
Cytisus battandieri
Desmodium praestans
Dianthus (most)
Dicentra (most)
Dorycnium hirsutum
Elaeagnus angustifolia
Elaeagnus commutata
Elaeagnus macrophylla
Eriophyllum lanatum
Eryngium (most)
Eucalyptus (most)
Euphorbia (many)
Festuca glauca
Geranium renardii
Glaucium (most)
Hebe albicans
Hebe pinguifolia 'Pagei'
Helianthemum (some)
Helichrysum (most)
Helictotrichon sempervirens
Hippophae rhamnoides
Hosta sieboldiana
Juniperus (some)
Lavandula (all)
Leptospermum (many)
Melianthus major
Olearia (most)
Onopordon arabicum
Othonnopsis cheirifolia
Perovskia atriplicifolia
Phlomis (most)
Romneya trichocalyx
Ruta graveolens
Salix helvetica
Salix lanata
Santolina (most)
Senecio compactus

Senecio leucostachys
Senecio monroi
Stachys lanata
Tanacetum haradjanii
Teucrium fruticans
Thymus (some)
Verbascum bombyciferum

GOLD AND SILVER VARIEGATED
LEAVES
Ajuga reptans 'Burgundy
    Glow'
Ajuga reptans 'Variegata'
Aralia elata 'Aureovariegata'
    and 'Variegata'
Carex morrowii 'Variegata aurea'
Cornus alba 'Elegantissima'
Cornus alba 'Spaethii'
Coronilla glauca 'Variegata'
Cyclamen (most)
Daphne odora
    'Aureo-marginata'
Euonymus fortunei radicans
Euonymus japonica (various)
Fragaria vesca 'Variegata'
Fuchsia magellanica 'Veriscolor'
Fuchsia 'Sharpitor'
Hakonechloa macra 'Albo-aurea'
Hebe andersonii 'Variegata'
Hedera (many)
Holcus mollis 'Variegatus'
Hosta (many)
Hypericum moserianum
    'Tricolor'
Ilex (many)
Kerria japonica 'Variegata'
Lamium (many)
Ligustrum ovalifolium
    'Argenteum' and 'Aureum'
Iris laevigata
Iris pallida (gold and silver
    forms)
Liriope muscari 'Variegata'
Lunaria (variegated form)
Miscanthus sinensis
    'Zebrinuus'
Myrtus communis 'Tarentina'
    (variegated form)
Myrtus communis 'Variegatus'
Pachysandra terminalis
    'Variegata'
Parthenocissus henryana
Pelargonium (many)
Phormium cookianum (many)
Pittosporum tenuifolium (many)
Rhamnus alaterna
    'Argenteovariegata'
Salvia officinalis 'Icterina'
Salvia o. 'Tricolor'
Saxifraga umbrosa 'Variegata'
Saxifraga stolonifera (marbled)
Sedum (various)
Silybum marianum
Sisyrinchium striatum
    'Variegatum'
Spartina pectinata
    'Aureo-marginata'
Symphoricarpus orbiculatus
    'Variegatus'

Thymus 'Silver Queen'
Vinca minor (various)
Vinca major 'Variegata'
Viburnum tinus 'Variegatum'
Weigela florida 'Variegata'

GOLDEN FOLIAGE
Acer japonicum 'Aureum'
Carex riparia 'Aurea'
Cassinia fulvida
Catalpa bignonioides 'Aurea'
Chrysanthemum parthenium
    'Aureum'
Gleditsia triacanthos 'Sunburst'
Humulus lupulus 'Aureus'
Lonicera nitida 'Baggesens
    Gold'
Lonicera japonica
    'Aureorecticulata'
Lysimachia nummularia
Milium effusum 'Aureum'
Origanum vulgare 'Aureum'
Philadelphus coronarius
    'Aureum'
Physocarpus opulifolius 'Luteus'
Robinia pseudoacacia 'Frisia'
Sambucus racemosa 'Plumosa
    aurea'
Spiraea bumalda 'Gold Flame'
Thuja occidentalis 'Rheingold'
Thymus citriodorus 'Aureus'

PURPLE AND BRONZE LEAVES
Ajuga reptans 'Purpurea'
Astilbe (various)
Berberis thunbergii 'Rose Glow'
Bergenia 'Abendglut'
Cotinus coggygria 'Foliis
    Purpureis'
Lobelia cardinalis
Nandina domestica
Ocium basilicum
Ophiopogon planiscarpa
    'Nigrescens'
Phormium cookianum (purple
    seedlings)
Pittosporum tenuifolium
    'Purpureum'
Rheum palmatum
    'Atrosanguinem'
Rodgersia (some)
Saxifrage fortunei 'Rubrum'
Sedum (some)
Vitis vinifera 'Purpurea'

FRAGRANT FOLIAGE
Angelica
Anthemis cupaniana
Artemisia
Buxus
Helichrysum
Hyssopus
Laurus nobilis
Lavandula
Lippia
Lovage
Melissa
Mentha
Myrtus

Nepeta
Ocimum basilicum
Origanum
Pelargonium
Perovskia
Philadelphus
Rosmarinus
Ruta
Santolina
Salvia
Teucrium
Thymus

FRAGRANT FLOWERS
Abelia
Acacia
Asperula
Azara
Buddleia
Ceanothus
Choisya
Clematis armandii
Clematis flammula
Clerodendron
Coronilla
Corylopsis
Cytisus
Daphne
Dianthus
Dictamnus
Drimys
Elaeagnus
Erica
Escallonia
Eucryphia
Gaultheria
Geranium
Gypsophila
Hamamelis
Heliotropium
Hemerocallis
Hesperis
Hoheria
Jasminum
Lavandula
Ligustrum
Lilium
Lonicera
Magnolia
Mahonia
Matthiola bicornis
Monarda
Myrrhis odorata
Narcissus
Nicotiana
Nymphaea
Osmanthus
Pelargonium
Philadelphus
Polygonatum
Rhododendron
Romneya
Rosa
Sarcococca
Syringa
Trachelospermum
Viburnum
Viola
Wisteria

HEDGING PLANTS
Acer campestre
Apple espalier (Prunus)
Arundinaria
Aucuba
Berberis
Bupleurum fruticosum
Buxus
Carpinus
Chaemycyparis
Choisya
Cotoneaster
Crataegus
Cupressocyparis leylandii
Escallonia
Elaeagnus
Euonymus
Fagus sylvatica
Fuchsia
Griselinia
Hebe
Hippophae
Hypericum
Hyssopus
Ilex
Juniperus
Kerria japonica 'Variegata'
Laurus nobilis
Lavandula
Ligustrum
Lonicera
Mahonia
Myrtus
Olearia
Osmanthus
Pear espalier (Pyrus)
Phillyrea
Pittosporum
Pyracantha
Quercus ilex
Rosa
Rosmarinus
Ruta
Santolina
Senecio
Skimmia
Symphoricarpus
Tamarix
Taxus baccata
Teucrium chamaedrys
Thuya

LOW GROUNDCOVER
Acanthus
Ajuga
Alchemilla
Arundinaria pumila
Arundinaria pygmaea
Asperula
Bergenia
Brunnera
Chiastophyllum
Cotoneaster (some)
Cyclamen
Danae racemosa
Dicentra
Erica (some)
Euonymus fortunei
Euphorbia (some)

185

Festuca glauca
Geranium
Hedera
Helleborus
Hosta
Hydrangea petiolaris
Hypericum
Juniperus (some)
Lamium
Liriope
Lonicera (some)
Lysimachia nummularia
Mahonia (some)
Omphalodes
Pachysandra
Polygonum (some)
Prunus (some)
Pulmonaria
Rosa (some)
Sarcococca
Saxifraga
Stachys lanata
Tiarella
Viburnum davidii
Vinca
Viola
Zauschneria californica

LOW PLANTS FOR FRONT OF
  BORDER
Acaena
Agapanthus
Ageratum
Ajuga
Alchemilla conjuncta
Alyssum
Anaphalis
Arabis
Armeria
Artemisia (some)
Bergenia
Campanula (some)
Cardamine
Cerastium tomentosum
Chiastophyllum
Convolvulus
Dianthus
Eriophyllum lanatum
Euphorbia (some)
Festuca glauca
Gazania
Gentiana
Hebe (some)
Helianthemum
Helichrysum
Hypericum moserianum
  'Tricolor'
Hypericum olympicum
Impatiens
Lamium
Liriope
Lysimachia nummularia
Omphalodes
Othonnopsis
Parahebe
Phlox (some)
Polygonum (some)
Potentilla (some)
Primula

Saponaria canadensis
Saxifraga
Sedum
Sisyrinchium
Teucrium chamaedrys
Tiarella
Tulip (small species)
Viola
Zauschneria californica

PLANTS FOR SHADE
Alchemilla
Anemone hupehensis
Arenaria
Arundinaria
Asperula
Astilbe
Aucuba
Bergenia
Brunnera
Buxus
Camellia
Cardamine
Chaenomeles
Chiastophyllum
Choisya
Cotoneaster (some)
Cyclamen
Danae racemosa
Daphne (some)
Dicentra
Digitalis
Elaeagnus
Epimedium (some)
Eranthis hyemalis
Erica (some)
Eucryphia
Euphorbia (some)
Fatshedera
Fatsia
Ficus pumila
Fragaria vesca 'Variegata'
Galanthus
Garrya elliptica
Gaultheria
Geranium
Griselinia
Hakonechloa
Hedera (most)
Helleborus
Helxine
Hemerocallis
Heuchera
Houttuynia
Humulus
Hydrangea
Hypericum (some)
Ilex
Lamium
Ligustrum
Lilium
Liriope
Lonicera (some)
Lysimachia nummularia
Mahonia (some)
Meconopsis
Omphalodes
Osmanthus
Pachysandra

Parthenocissus
Pernettya
Pileostegia
Polygonatum
Polygonum
Pulmonaria
Rhododendron
Rodgersia
Sambucus
Sarcococca
Saxifraga (some)
Schizophragma
Skimmia
Smilacina
Spiraea
Symphoricarpus
Tiarella
Viburnum (some)
Vinca
Viola (some)

PLANT FOR DAMP PLACES
Alnus
Aponogeton (water)
Arundinaria
Astilbe
Carex
Cautleya
Cornus
Cyperus
Gaultheria
Gentiana (some)
Hosta
Houttuynia
Iris (some)
Kirengeshoma
Lobelia cardinalis
Miscanthus
Nymphaea (water)
Osmunda regalis
Peltiphyllum
Physocarpus
Polygonum (some)
Populus
Primula
Ranunculus aconitifolius
Rodgersia
Salix
Salvia uliginosa
Sambucus
Schizostylis
Symphoricarpus
Zantedeschia

PLANTS FOR CONTAINERS
a) Permanent
Abutilon
Acacia
Acanthus
Acer (some)
Agapanthus
Ampelopsis
Arundinaria
Aucuba
Azara
Buddleia
Buxus
Camellia
Campanula

Ceratostigma
Chamaecyparis
Cheiranthus
Choisya
Clematis
Convolvulus
Cordyline
Coronilla
Cotinus
Cotoneaster
Danae
Daphne
Dorycnium
Enkianthus
Escallonia
Eucryphia
Fatshedera
Fatsia
Felicia
Ficus
Francoa sonchifolia
Fritillaria
Fuchsia
Gleditsia
Hebe
Hedera
Helichrysum (some)
Helictotrichon sempervirens
Hosta
Humulus
Hydrangea
Hypericum
Ilex
Jasminum
Kalmia
Laurus nobilis
Ligustrum
Lillium
Lippia
Lonicera (some)
Mahonia (some)
Melianthus
Myrtus
Nandina
Narcissus
Nerium
Origanum
Osteospernum
Othonnopsis
Parahebe
Parthenocissus
Pelargonium
Philesia
Phormium
Pieris
Pittosporum
Prunus (some)
Pyracantha
Rhododendron
Rosa
Rosmarinus
Ruta
Salvia
Sarcococca
Senecio
Solanum
Stipa gigantea
Teucrium fruticans
Trachelospermum

Tulip
Vinca major 'Variegata'
Yucca
Zantedeschia

b) For summer containers
(treat as annuals)
Ageratum
Cobaea
Eccremocarpus
Echium
Fuchsia
Gazania
Helichrysum (some)
Heliotropium
Impatiens
Ipomaea
Lilium
Lobelia
Mandevilla
Nicotiana
Osteospernum
Pelargonium
Petunia
Verbena

PLANTS FOR WARM SHELTERED
    GARDENS
Acacia
Argemone
Artemisia (some)
Buddleia auriculata
Buddleia crispa
Celmisia
Cheiranthus
Cistus (some)
Cobaea
Coronilla glauca 'Variegata'
Cordyline
Crinodendron
Desmodium praestans
Dorycnium
Eccremocarpus
Escallonia bifida
Eupatorium ligustrinum
Euphorbia mellifera
Fabiana
Felicia
Ficus pumila
Francoa
Fremontodendron

Fuchsia (some)
Gazania
Grevillia rosmarinifolia
Griselinia
Hebe (some)
Helichrysum (some)
Jasminum (some)
Kalmia
Lavatera bicolor
Leptospernum
Lilium (some)
Liriope muscari 'Variegatum'
Lobelia cardinalis
Lomatia
Mahonia trifoliata 'Glauca'
Mandevilla suaveolens
Melianthus major
Nandina domestica (and forms)
Nerium oleander
Nothofagus cliffortioides
Olearia (some)
Othonnopsis
Ozothamnus
Parahebe
Penstemon

Phlomis (some)
Phormium (those with
    coloured leaves)
Phygelius aequalis
Punica
Raphiolepis umbellata
Rhododendron (some)
Ribes speciosum
Rosmarinus officinalis 'Roseus'
Salvia (some)
Santolina
Senecio
Solanum jasminoides
Sophora
Stauntonia hexaphylla
Tanacetum haradjanii
Teucrium
Trachelospermum
Verbena
Vestia lycioides
Yucca
Zantedeschia
Zauschneria

Selected Nurseries

David Austin *Roses*
Bowling Green Lane, Albrighton, Staffs
Bees Ltd
Sealand, Chester
Walter Blom & Sons *Bulbs*
Leavesden, Watford, Herts
Bressingham Gardens *Herbaceous*
Diss, Norfolk
Broadleigh Gardens *Bulbs*
Barr House, Bishop's Hull, Taunton, Somerset
Thomas Carlile Ltd
Loddon Nurseries, Carlile's Corner, Twyford, Berks
Beth Chatto *Unusual Plants*
White Barn House, Elmstead Market, Colchester, Essex
Clifton Nurseries
Clifton Villas, Warwich Avenue, London W9
Great Dixter Nurseries (Christopher Lloyd)
Northiam, Rye, Sussex
Hillier's Ltd
Ampfield House, Nr Romsey, Hants
W. E. Th. Ingwersen Ltd *Alpines*
Birch Farm Nursery, Gravetye, East Grinstead, Sussex
Margery Fish Nursery *Small herbaceous*
East Lambrook, South Petherton, Somerset
John Mattock Ltd
Nuneham Courtney, Oxford
Notcutts Nurseries Ltd
Woodbridge, Suffolk
Perryhill Nurseries
Hartfield, Sussex

Ramparts Nurseries *Grey foliage plants and Pinks*
Bakers Lane, Colchester, Essex
G. Reuthe Ltd
Jackass Lane, Keston, Kent
Southcombe Nurseries
Widecombe in the Moor, Newton Abbot, Devon
Southdown Nurseries
Redruth, Cornwall
Treasures Ltd
Tenbury Wells, Worcs.

For Uncommon Plants

County Park Nursery
Essex Gardens, Hornchurch, Essex
Jack Drake
Inshriach Nursery, Aviemore, Inverness
Peter Foley
Holden Clough Nursery, Bolton-by-Bowland,
Clitheroe, Lancs
Old Court Nurseries Ltd (Paul Picton)
Colwall, Malvern, Worcs
J. and E. Parker-Jervis
Martens Hall Farm, Longworth, Abingdon, Oxon
Keith Steadman
Wickwar, Glos
Stone House Cottage Nursery *Tender Shrubs and Climbers*
Stone, Kidderminster, Worcs

A Note on Weedkillers

Weedkillers, used sensibly, are invaluable in any garden, both for initial clearance of the tough perennial and persistent weeds, and for normal maintenance. The best and most economical method of applying suitable herbicides is with a pressure sprayer, with a liquid capacity of one or two gallons (4½ or 9 litres). By adjusting the fine spray nozzle you can 'spot' kill individual weeds.

These herbicides are divided broadly into three types:—

1 Foliage-applied contact herbicides, such as a paraquat/diquat mixture – normally available as Weedol – which are effective only through the leaves with which they come in contact. The leaves are scorched and the plant dies, but the herbicide has little effect on the root system, and none at all on soil. These contact mixtures can also be used selectively on lawns as they do not damage grass. There are a number of proprietary brands from which to choose.

2 Foliage-applied herbicides which act through the leaves and penetrate effectively to the roots. This takes about three weeks and the plants become visibly twisted before dying. Glyphosate, which is marketed as Murphy's Tumbleweed, is safe and effective, and, like Weedol above, is inactivated by the soil so can be used even where there are roots of desirable plants nearby (e.g. ornamentals or vegetables). Various selective weedkillers of this type also exist, usually marketed as 2, 4-D or 2, 4, 5-T. Planting and sowing can take place after their use as soon as the weeds have died.

3 Soil-applied residual herbicides which actually kill plants already growing and sterilize the soil for a period, preventing germination of annual seedlings. For most gardens, it will not be necessary to apply heavy doses of these long-lasting herbicides (such as sodium chlorate and ammonium sulpamate) but a short-term one such as simazine – marketed as Weedex – controls seed germination for a few months and is invaluable in rose or shrub beds where there are no herbaceous plants. It can be used for paths if a heavier dose is applied. If there are persistent deep-rooted weeds in the paths, simazine can have paraquat/diquat added for greater contact effect.

Simazine plus a 2, 4-D mixture (available as Herbon Blue) will be effective with nettles, brambles and bindweed provided that repeated applications are made over a period.

Another useful herbicide, available in granules, is Casoron G which is easy to scatter, but follow the instructions carefully. It contains dichlobenil, which will kill tap-rooted weeds and prevent weed seed germination. It is safe to use on established rose beds, etc., but not where there has been new planting. Other selective pre-emergent herbicides are safe to use with most herbaceous plants and, of course, vegetables. They contain the less persistent propachlor or a propham/chlorpropham (marketed as Herbon Orange or Herbon Garden Herbicide). There is also an excellent booklet called *Chemical Weed Control in Your Garden*, available from Grower Books London, 49 Doughty St, London WC1N 2LP, which goes into the whole question more thoroughly.

The main pests in a flower garden are aphids and caterpillars and outbreaks of these can be controlled by spraying, either with a direct contact insecticide – which kills the insect or leaves a deposit on the plant which the insect then eats; or by a systemic insecticide which is absorbed into the sap of the plant, later killing insects which attack and suck. Caterpillars are best controlled by the former and aphids by the latter. In a small area, especially in an enclosed airless town garden, it may well be best to spray regularly with a mixture which effectively deals with both problems and prevents an outbreak and breeding. There are many proprietary brands available.

The main fungal diseases are mildew, black spot, rust and botrytis and in a small area it is worth spraying before you notice any symptoms because once disease is definitely present treatment must be continued at regular weekly intervals through at least one growing season. Many gardeners prefer to spray regularly, as clearly effective prevention is best. Above all, remember that vigorous, healthy plants are less susceptible to all diseases.

GLOSSARY

ALTERNATE
Occurring first on one side and then on the other , here applied to leaves on a stem

ANNUALS
Plants that germinate from seed, flower, die and reproduce seed all in one season. Can be hardy, half-hardy or tender. Some plants would in natural conditions live longer, but are treated as annuals for gardening purposes

BIENNIALS
Plants that germinate from seed in one year and bloom and die in the following season

BRACT
A modified leaf, often green, at the base of a flower stalk or behind a flower head

CALCIFUGE
Disliking lime

COLONIZE
To establish naturally – a plant forming a collection or group of itself

COLUMNAR
Tall, cylindrical or tapering

COMPOUND
Composed of two or more similar parts

CORYMB
A flat-topped or dome-shaped flower head

CULTIVAR
Garden variety, a form normally originating in cultivation and not given a Latin name.

DISSECTED
Divided into many narrow segments

DECIDUOUS
Plants with seasonal leaf fall

EXOTIC
A non-indigenous plant, generally looking unnatural

FASTIGIATE
Of upright narrow habit, occupying little space

FORM
Used here to describe a variety, sub-species or cultivar

FROND
The whole leaf of a fern

GENUS
(plural genera) A group of species of common structural habit. In designating a plant the name of the *genus* is placed first

GLAUCOUS
Covered with a bloom, bluish-grey

HABIT
Manner of growth

HERBACEOUS
Non-woody stemmed plants dying down to ground-level in the winter, but sometimes retaining evergreen frost-proof leaves

HEADS
Collection of flowers at the end of a stem

HYBRID
A plant resulting from a cross between different species

MICROCLIMATE
Special conditions – differing from the prevailing climate – which exist in a garden or part of a garden

NATURALIZING
Growing plants under near natural conditions so that they maintain themselves.

OPPOSITE
Used for leaves situated in pairs on either side of the stem

PANICLE
A branched inflorescence, with the youngest flowers on top

PERENNIALS
Plants living for several years

PINNATE
Feather-like arrangement of leaflets on either side of a central stalk

PLEACH
To interlace branches to form a screen

PROSTRATE
Used to describe plants that tend to grow flat on the ground

RACEME
An elongated inflorescence with stalked flowers

RAIN SHADOW
Area where rain does not penetrate, for example under dense canopy of trees or foliage or at the base of a wall

RECURRENT
Appearing or coming again, used particularly of rose flowers

REPEAT FLOWERING
Usually means a second complete but less vigorous show of flowers in the same summer season

RHIZOME
An underground stem

ROSETTE
In an herbaceous plant a bunch of leaves, almost flat on the ground, from the centre of which the stem rises

SELF-CLINGING
Using adhesive pads to cling to a surface, not needing a frame to climb on

SEMI-EVERGREEN
A tree or shrub fully evergreen in its native habitat but which drops leaves during periods of extreme temperature

SPATHE
The large bract surrounding the flower, as in arum lilies

SPECIES
The type plant inside a genus which will breed true to seed. The name of the species – usually taken from a Latin word – in designating a plant is placed second and has a small initial letter

SUB-SHRUB
A woody plant of which the stems will probably fail to produce new leaf growth in the spring, but new growth will commence from the base

SUCKER
An underground stem which produces a new shoot. When the plant is a graft these stems are from the stock plant and must be cut away

BIBLIOGRAPHY

Bean, W. J., *Trees and Shrubs Hardy in the British Isles*, Vols 1, 2 and 3, John Murray 1970-6

Brookes, John, *Room Outside*, Thames and Hudson 1969
Brookes, John, *The Small Garden*, Marshall Cavendish 1977

Chatto, Beth, *The Dry Garden*, Dent 1978

Crowe, Sylvia, *Garden Design*, Country Life 1958

Ellacombe, Canon, *In a Gloucestershire Garden*, Edward Arnold 1895

Fish, Margery, *A Flower for Everyday*, David and Charles 1965

Gibson, Michael, *The Book of the Rose*, Macdonald 1980

Godfrey, Walter, *Gardens in the Making*, Batsford 1914

Hillier's *Manual of Trees and Shrubs*, 4th edn, David and Charles 1977

Hobhouse, Penelope, *The Country Gardener*, Phaidon 1976

Jekyll, Gertrude, *Wood and Garden*, Longman Green 1899

Jekyll, Gertrude, *Wall and Water*, Country Life 1901

Jekyll, Gertrude, *Colour Schemes in the Flower Garden*, 3rd edn, Country Life 1914

Jellicoe, S. and G., *Modern Private Gardens*, Abeland-Schuman 1968

Jellicoe, S. and G., *Water*, Black 1971

Johnson, Hugh, *The Principles of Gardening*, Mitchell Beazley 1979

Kemp, E., *How to Lay out a Garden*, Bradbury & Evans 1858

Loudon, John Claudius, *The Suburban Gardener and Villa Companion*, 1838

Lucas-Phillips, C. E., *The New Small Garden*, Collins 1979

Page, Russell, *The Education of a Gardener*, Collins 1971

Readers Digest *Encyclopaedia of Garden Plants and Flowers*, 2nd edn, 1978

The R.H.S. *Dictionary of Gardening*, 2nd edn, Clarendon 1956

Stevens, David (ed), *Planning a garden*, Orbis 1979

Taylor, George, *The Little Garden*, Collins 1948

Thomas, Graham Stuart, *Perennial Garden Plants*, Dent 1976

Thomas, Graham Stuart, *Plants for Groundcover*, Dent 1970

Wood, Dennis, *Practical Garden Design*, Dent 1976

INDEX

References in *italic* refer to the illustrations. The alphabetical 'Select List of Plants' pp 146–83 is not included in the index

Abelia × *grandiflora*, 134
Abutilon spp, 108; *A. vitifolium*, 102, 131; *78*
acacias, 110; *19*
Acanthus spp, 134; *30*, *134*; *A. mollis*, 94, 141
Acer griseum, 108; *A. palmatum* 'Dissectum', 141
acid soils, 45-8
aconites, 93
Actinidia chinensis, 126; *A. kolomikta*, 126
ageratums, 143
Alchemilla spp, 102, 134; *A. mollis*, 94, 141; *32*, *97*, *147*
Alisma plantago, 90
alkaline soils, 45-8
almonds, 108
alyssum, 143
Ampelopsis brevipendunculata, 125; *A.b.* 'elegans', 125
anaphilis, *8*, *32*
anchusa, *97*
Anemone spp, 93, 141; *A. blanda*, 116
Angelica archangelica, *44*
annuals, 23, 143
Anthemis nobilis, *71*
apples, 57, 108, 120; *20*
Aralia elata, 141
arbutus, 108, 110
archangelica, 94, 134, 143; *44*
Artemisia spp, 121, 134, 141, 143; *A. absinthium* 'Lambrook Silver', 134; *A. arborescens*, 131
artichokes, 134
ash, 108
atriplex, *116*
aucubas, 134, 141
Auratum lilies, *67*
azaleas, 45, 140

backyards, 86-7
Ballota pseudodictamnus, 134
bamboos, -141; *20*, *84*
banks, 73, 80
bay tree, 102, 133, 141
beech, 110, 116, 120
begonias, 143
Berberis spp, 114, 115, 120; *B. darwinii*, 120; *B.* × *stenophylla*, 120
bergenias, 121, 134, 143; *27*, *29*, *39*, *85*

Betula jacquemontii, 108
birches, 107, 108
Boston ivy, 124
box, 94, 114, 116, 141
brooms, 143
Brunnera macrophylla, *21*
Buddleia alternifolia, 130; *B. auriculata*, 130; *B. crispa*, 130
Bupleurum fructicosum, 134; *150*

camellias, 38, 45, 102, 108, 131, 141; *45*, *85*
campanulas, 103, 141
catalpas, 108
catmint, 121, 141
Ceanothus spp, *129*; *C.* 'Cascade', 131; *C. papillosus roweanus*, 131; *C. thyrsiflorus*, *30*
Celastrus orbiculatus, 125
Cerastium tormentosum, 103
Cercidiphyllum japonicum, 108; *105*
cestrums, 131
Chaenomeles speciosa, 130
Chamaecyparis lawsoniana 'Ellwoodii', 133; *C.l.* 'Kilmacurragh', 133
cherry laurel, 133
Chinese gooseberry, 126
Choisya ternata, 134, 141; *30*
cistuses, 143
clay soils, 26, 50-2
Clematis spp, 28, 125, 141, 143; *100*, *122*; *C. armandii*, *127*
Clerodendron trichotomum, 110
climbers, 60, 122-8, 143
Cobaea scandens, 126, 143
compost, 54, 70, 80
conifers, 94, 102, 107, 108, 130, 133-4, 141
containers, 53, 102, 135-43
Convolvulus cneorum, *75*, *151*
Cornus alba, 108; *C.a.* 'Elegantissima', *97*; *92*; *C. controversa*, 108
Coronilla glauca, 131; *153*
Cotinus coggyria, 143
Cotoneaster spp, 80, 117-20, 130, 143; *24*, *53*, *122*; *C. horizontalis*, *27*, *97*
cottage gardens, 11-12
country gardens, 21-2, 58-9
crab apple, 110
Crataegus monogyna, 120
creeping jenny, *82*

Crinodendron hookerianum, 131
Cupressocyparis leylandii, 116
curry plant, *70*
Curse of Corsica, 103
curved features, making, 60
cyclamen, 93, 116
Cytisus battandieri, 131

delphiniums, 29
design principles, 55-68
Dianthus spp, 143
Dicentra formosa, *154*
dogwoods, 101, 108
Doryncium hirsutum, *67*
drainage, 26, 50, 53
Drimys winteri, 131

Eccremocarpus scaber, 126, 143
Elaeagnus spp, 108, 117-20, 141; *27*, *132*; *E. pungens* 'Maculata', *94*
elder, 108
Enkianthus spp, 140, 141
epimediums, 80, 117
Ericaceae, 45
eryngiums, 94, 102, 134; *32*
escallonias, 121
espaliered fruit trees, 57, 120
eucalyptus, 108
Eucryphia spp, 45, 102, 108, 110, 131; *155*; *E. milliganii*, 131; *E.* × *nymansensis* 'Nymansay', 131
Eunymus fortunei, 134; *E.f. radicans*, *100*; *E. japonicus*, 134
Euphorbia spp, 102, 134; *E. characais*, *27*; *E. griffithi* 'Fireglow', *155*; *E. robbiae*, 134

Fatsia japonica, 102, 141; *85*, *104*, *128*, *134*
ferns, *97*
fertilizers, 54, 137-8
Ficus carica, 130; *F. pumila*, 126
firethorns, 130
formal gardens, 16-17
foxgloves, *80*, *100*
Fremontodendron californicum, 131
fritillaries, 141
front gardens, 22-4, 62-3
frosts, 33
fuchsias, 141; *138*

Garrya elliptica, 108, 130
gazanias, 143
Geranium spp, 80, 116, 143; *100*, *134*; *G. renardi*, *158*; *G. sylvaticum*, *67*

Gingko biloba, 108
grass, 79-80
grasses, 80, 141
grey-leaved plants, 94, 114
griselinias, 121
ground cover, 80-4
Gymnocladus dioicus, 108

hawthorn, 120
heaths, 45
Hebe spp, 102, 121, 134, 143; *66*; *H. andersoni* 'Variegata', *158*; *H. salicifolia*, *71*
Hedera 'Angularis Aurea', *18*; *H. canariensis*, 124; *H. colchica*, 124; *38*; *H. helix*, 124; *38*; *H.h.* 'Goldheart', *122*
hedges, 57, 111-21
helianthemums, 134
Helichrysum spp, 143; *H. angustifolium*, *70*; *H. petiolatum*, *139*
heliotrope, 143
Heliotropium peruvianum, 143
hellebores, 102
Helxine soleirolii, 103; *36*
Heracleum mantegazzianum, 94
herbs, 70, 143
Hoheria spp, 131-3; *H. sexstylosa*, 131
hollies, 107-8, 114, 116, 117, 133
honeysuckles, 114, 126; *19*, *84*, *100*
hornbeam, 108, 114, 120
Hosta spp, 94, 101, 134, 143; *27*, *45*, *48*, *80*, *81*, *94*; *H. sieboldiana*, *92*, *158*
Humulus lupulus 'Aureus', 126, 143; *128*
hyacinths, 141
Hydrangea spp, 130, 141, 143; *24*, *80*; *H. petiolaris*, 124, 141; *27*; *H. quercifolia*, 130
hypericums, 102

Idesia polycarpa, 108
Ilex × *altaclarensis*, 108, 133; *I.* × *a.* 'Lawsonian', *137*; *I. aquifolium*, 107-8, 117, 133; *I. a.* 'Ferox', *162*
Ipomea hederacea, 143
Iris spp, 94, 102, 134, 141; *22*, *32*, *76*, *97*; *I. laevigata*, *162*; *I. pallida*, *82*
Itea ilicifolia, 130
ivies, 23, 80, 101, 114, 117, 124, 141, 143; *24*, *27*, *29*, *36*, *38*, *54*, *65*, *67*, *122*, *139*